THEOCRACY:
Can Democracy Survive
Fundamentalism?

THEOCRACY:
Can Democracy Survive Fundamentalism?

—

Resolving the Conflict between
Fundamentalism and Pluralism

P. J. Tierney

iUniverse, Inc.
Bloomington

Theocracy: Can Democracy Survive Fundamentalism?
Resolving the Conflict between Fundamentalism and Pluralism

iUniverse books may be ordered through booksellers or by contacting:

iUniverse
1663 Liberty Drive
Bloomington, IN 47403
www.iuniverse.com
1-800-Authors (1-800-288-4677)

ISBN: 978-1-4759-2927-0 (sc)
ISBN: 978-1-4759-2929-4 (hc)
ISBN: 978-1-4759-2928-7 (e)

Printed in the United States of America

iUniverse rev. date: 07/16/2012

Dedication

I dedicate this book to my children Brendan, Jessica, Andrew, and Rachel; to my son-in-law, Russell; and to my granddaughter, Tierney, in the sincere hope that they will enjoy the full freedoms of democracy and personal faith that I have been privileged to enjoy throughout my lifetime.

Contents

Preface

Democracy in the United States is in jeopardy. It is threatened by fundamentalism. Corrective measures are called for. This book offers an analysis of fundamentalism and proposals to remedy the problems it presents to democratic society.

Raised strictly Roman Catholic in the 1950s, as a child I was instructed to obey God as the church explained God's will. Priests and nuns taught us that we should always obey God in every aspect of our lives. They emphasized that church tradition was the only reliable way to know God. Following God's will as the church taught it was the highest good and our basic duty as Catholics.

During adolescence, I personally accepted Jesus Christ as my Savior and Lord. As an evangelical/charismatic Christian educated at various evangelical institutions of higher learning, I was taught that the Bible was the only, infallible Word of God. It reveals God's perfect will and instructs us how to live our lives in virtually every situation. Following its teachings was what it meant to follow Jesus. Obeying scripture's teachings was the highest good and our duty as Christians.

I have served as a Christian minister for more than thirty-seven years. During that time I have been privileged to oversee more than half a dozen churches in as many states. I have worked with Christians of all stripes in the Northeast, the Mid-Atlantic, the South, and the West Coast. I have also assisted churches in Canada, Great Britain, Costa Rica, and the Dominican Republic. I have collaborated intimately with those who primarily identify themselves by their denominational affiliation as well as with those who call themselves traditional, liberal, evangelical, charismatic, Catholic, or fundamentalist Christians.

I have been a Christian believer for the better part of sixty years and a lifelong citizen of a democracy. I come to this task, therefore, wearing two hats, as a Christian and as an American. Over the decades I have found that there have been tensions between the two of one sort or another. And I have had many occasions to wrestle with the apparent discrepancies or conflicts between them. Tension is part of life.

During that time, I have come to conclude that Christian fundamentalists have found it increasingly difficult to collaborate with their fellow citizens in American democratic society. Christian fundamentalists have certain prime directives. Their core commitment to those prime directives limits their ability to participate in the democratic process in good faith. Fundamentalists are taught above all else to obey their prime directives.

As I listened to the morning news one day, I heard one reporter say that Pakistan has a problem. She said most Pakistanis believe that Islamic law should take precedence over all other laws. They believe that Islamic law should be the basis of all laws.

The reader may conclude that Islamic fundamentalism is one thing but that Christian fundamentalism is not nearly as extreme. And yet, Christian fundamentalists have also demonstrated growing intolerance for other perspectives. Increasingly, too, many have actively sought to extend the explicit principles of their faith into the political arena. Intentionally or not, they have been groping for an integrated political philosophy, one that weds their faith, their values, and their goals for social change with practical political methodologies to implement them.

In principle, or at least according to their publicity, Christian fundamentalists have no intention to lessen democratic ideals or practices in the United States. They simply want to replace some of the current values of the country with their values. They want to adapt the legal methods for implementing those values so as to make the system more malleable to their efforts. They claim not to want to change democracy, simply the system by which laws are enacted and values are inculcated. A critical mass of Christian fundamentalists hopes to take dominion over American democracy, not to do away with it. And yet, that clearly violates the vision that originally created the United States and its system of government.

This book has several intentions. It intends to define fundamentalism, particularly Christian fundamentalism. It differentiates it from traditional Christian renditions. It seeks to explain its root causes, goals, and express strategies. It describes its political evolution. It identifies its departures from previous Christian efforts to influence society and government. It examines its efforts and their underlying motivations through several lenses, including history, psychology, political theory, ethics, logic, current events, and the Bible itself. Based upon those disciplines, it seeks to identify some of the excesses of the contemporary Christian fundamentalist approach. It seeks to offer other options for people of faith. It does not attempt to curtail the involvement of fundamentalists in the American democratic process, but to redirect it. It also offers practical suggestions for coping with the inroads of fundamentalism so as to strength democracy within pluralistic American society.

My goals are fivefold. The first is to support democracy within pluralistic societies under circumstances in which critical masses of ideologically single-minded citizens seem motivated to get their way over others at the cost of democracy itself. The second is to strengthen democracy in pluralistic society by suggesting ways for the citizens of the United States to avoid extremism and the internal conflicts that it generates. The third is to help moderate the fundamentalist tendency to employ power politics and to demonize others, or vice versa. The fourth is to try to help protect Christ's reputation so that he is not regarded by those who have adverse reactions to Christian fundamentalists as a mere tool of power mongers. And the fifth is to suggest alternative meanings to the plight of humanity at this particular point in history.

P. J. Tierney
Spring 2012

Acknowledgments

Among my various shortcomings, there are two that screamed out for help in this endeavor. My small motor skills are limited. And I seem to have a blind spot to specific details.

I am virtually blind to typographical and grammatical errors. I can stare at a sentence, at length, without noticing errors in it. But Judith L. Taylor has all the necessary grammatical talents that are needed to supplement what I lack. I relied on her at one of the parishes I served and have turned to her for help in this project too. I am indebted to her devoted and skillful work in reviewing this book for publication. Thanks, Judy!

I am also artistically challenged. I desperately needed help with the cover design. When I described the theme of this book to my elder son, Brendan, he set to work on it. He listened to what I had to say and used his talents to graphically represent the book's theme. Unlike his father, Brendan is an artist. I couldn't possibly have done it without his artistic abilities. I deeply appreciate Brendan Tierney for creating the cover artwork. Thanks, Brendan!

Introduction

My fourth-grade teacher at St. Angela's School was Sister Mary Joseph. It was the autumn of that year, and the pupils in my class were very excited. It wasn't our subjects or catechism memorization that engaged us. It was the upcoming presidential election. John F. Kennedy was running against some other guy to become president of the United States. Sister Mary Joseph held a mock election. The outcome was unanimous. Kennedy received thirty votes from the thirty students in the class. It wasn't that we knew him personally, though we were Bostonians too. It wasn't that we shared his political positions. We wouldn't have known a political position from a yoga position back then. They were both equally alien to us.

We unanimously elected Kennedy and cheered in class when he was actually elected, simply because he was Catholic. He was one of us. Incidentally, Sister Mary Joseph encouraged us, or else we wouldn't have been aware that Kennedy was running for president or that he was Catholic. We were strongly influenced by authority figures and by the notion that a person in such an august position was like us.

Back then, the adults around the dinner table in my home sometimes discussed politics. I was stunned to learn that many Americans hadn't wanted Kennedy to be elected. I learned that they had precisely the same reason for their aversion to Kennedy that inspired the students in my class to vote for him. He was a Catholic. I never entered into those adult political conversations, but I was shocked by the revelation.

And so I spoke up and asked, "Why wouldn't people want a Catholic to be president of the United States?" Someone replied, "They're afraid that the pope will control the country and make everyone do what the Catholic Church teaches." *What's wrong with that?* I wondered. I had been insulated by my subcultural bubble.

Back then there were certain unwritten rules. There were two among the rest. You never talk about religion or politics in public. It only creates arguments and hard feelings. And you never let your religion dictate your political decision making. It might divide the country unnecessarily. People did the latter, of course, but they were never obvious or outspoken about it.

Things were different back then. Most Americans were practicing Christians. Nevertheless, their doctrines and codes of conduct rarely seemed to inform or even relate to political issues. President Kennedy could never be accused of promoting the Catholic Church in America, let alone Catholic beliefs and values or a Catholic code of conduct. He and most everyone else compartmentalized their faith from public life. Likewise, Catholics didn't vote for Kennedy because he would promote their shared faith. Instead, it was because they saw him as one of them, and because they thought that he would promote their socioeconomic interests. They compartmentalized their faith. Some might say that they were cultural Catholics more than ideological ones.

These days, both of those unwritten rules are violated all the time. In fact, those rules don't seem to exist anymore. It seems to have become a virtue among some to build politics around religious convictions. Things have changed. Nowadays, a smaller percentage of Americans are actually practicing Christians. And yet, a far larger proportion of those who do practice the Christians faith are fundamentalists. They are very fervent about their faith. They actively resist compartmentalizing their faith. They criticize cultural Christians and consider them not to be Christians at all. They are far more dedicated to configuring everything around their faith and the values that their faith emphasizes. That has come to include politics.

Christian fundamentalists have certain prime directives. Their core commitment to these prime directives limits their ability to participate in the democratic process in good faith. The main driver of their stance as citizens of American democratic society is that commitment. First and foremost, they are citizens of the kingdom of God. That determines their positions as citizens of the United States.

Many nations do not permit their citizens to share dual citizenship with other nations. That restriction is based on the reasonable concern that their allegiance to another government might compromise the best interests of the nation. They have potentially conflicted interests as citizens.

Fundamentalists have prime directives and core allegiances that limit their ability to participate in democratic societies without making every effort to extend those convictions to others. That predisposition tends to be uncompromising, ever expanding, and relentless. It creates a conflict of interests. Fundamentalists do not see it as a conflict of interests. They firmly believe that any nation would be best served by following their beliefs and values. But it does create a conflict of interests from the vantage point of other citizens of pluralistic democracies who may embrace different perspectives.

By definition, not everyone in a pluralistic democracy shares the same beliefs, values, or code of conduct. Democracy in a pluralistic society has certain primary goals. One of those goals is to safeguard the rights of citizens to hold their own beliefs, values, and codes of conduct without having those of others imposed upon them. Some citizens may not want fundamentalist values, let alone doctrines, to be imposed on all citizens. There are many Christian fundamentalists who hope to do just that. It constitutes a conflict of interests. And that conflict of interests is equivalent to dual citizenship insofar as it is single-minded and uncompromising.

Some might ask how it could possibly be in anything but the best interests of a democratic nation to be infused with the core values of the Christian faith. It is simply because people, even people of shared Christian faith, often disagree about them. Profound disagreement over core convictions can divide the citizens of a democracy to such an extent that the unity of a nation can be undermined. When unity is undermined, especially at the level of vision for a nation, that nation can become severely weakened. And when citizens of divergent political visions treat one another as enemies, the integrity of democracy itself can be threatened by the polarization. It is that threat that has inspired the writing of this book.

Chapter 1

—

Blind Faith

Fundamentalists Resist Other Perspectives

The young man passed a hitchhiker as he drove along the freeway. She was an attractive young woman with long blonde hair, wearing cutoff jeans on that warm summer day. The driver was married, but she caught his eye anyway. He drove on for several miles and simply couldn't get her out of his thoughts. His mind seemed captivated by her image.

His imagination ran wild as he drove. *What would it be like if I turned around and picked her up? Would she find me attractive too? What if she did? Could I pull off the highway, lean over, and ...? Stop it!* he thought. He tried to think of something else. He turned on the radio. She wouldn't get out of his mind. He prayed for God's help. He kept thinking about her, though. He prayed some more and sang a hymn. His thoughts became more risqué. Then he thought about what the Bible said. Suddenly he knew what he had to do.

He turned off the highway at the next exit, pulled over to the side of the road, and stopped the car. Taking the key from the ignition, he went back and opened the trunk. He knew that it was there somewhere.

Frantically fumbling through the rubble, he finally laid his hand on it. Gripping the screwdriver in his hand, he returned to the driver's seat and closed the door. He looked down at the tool in his hand. He prayed. And then he took it and plunged it into his right eye. Without hesitation, he did the same to his left.

The young driver blinded himself. After all, the Bible said it, and he believed it. That's all there was to it. Jesus is reported to have said, "If your right eye causes you to stumble, gouge it out and throw it away. It is better for you to lose one part of your body than for your whole body to be thrown into hell" (Matthew 5:21).

That young man was deeply troubled. Whatever profound psychological disturbances might have suspended his personal defense mechanisms from self-inflicted harm, they also caused him to follow his misguided beliefs without hesitation and without compromise. He didn't consider the long-term consequences to himself or the collateral damage to others, no matter how negative they might be. He simply wanted to be faithful, no matter what.

Belief, strong personal faith, is one of the most powerful forces at work in the human mind. It can shape virtually everything about the way people see things. It informs worldview and perspective. It guides, even drives, people's actions. It has the power for incomparable good and for just as much destruction, whether in personal conduct or in the conduct of international relations.

Faith can be used or misused, and the difference is often one of discernment and outcome. Frequently, it can be seen only in hindsight. Blind faith is so convinced of its own indisputable veracity that it can be unhesitant, uncompromising, and unrelenting. It is frequently closed to other perspectives. Fundamentalist faith of whatever persuasion tends to be blind faith.

The recently published *God's Century: Resurgent Religion and Global Politics* reports that contrary to earlier predictions, there has been a dramatic, worldwide increase in religious affiliation and political activity during the past several decades. Allow me to summarize several of their main points in my own words. The authors indicate that during the first half of the twentieth century the intellectual, scientific, and political elite, including some religious leaders, anticipated the inevitable decline of religion around the world, both in membership and influence. They point out that, in fact, the opposite has taken place. They note that many religions have swelled in numbers and political influence during the past several decades. In some cases the increase has been dramatic.[i]

God's Century observes that some religious adherents have become radicalized during this same period of time. As I understand their analysis the authors contend that political disenfranchisement largely has been responsible for the radicalization of various religious groups and their increasingly aggressive tactics. They note that essentially secular governments had largely excluded religious groups from meaningful participation in national policy discussions. They argue that suppressing religious groups and excluding them from political decision-making have fueled religious radicalization. Among their other practical recommendations the authors conclude that including religious groups in the processes of political decision making will decrease religious radicalism and violence.[ii]

In my opinion the authors of that otherwise extremely insightful and well researched book exhibit something of a naïve attitude in one respect. To be provocative, their naïveté is equivalent to Neville Chamberlain's attitude toward the rise of National Socialism in Germany during the 1930s. More serious consideration must be paid to the fact that much of the rise of religious affiliation during the past four decades has actually been a rise in adherence to religious fundamentalism. Fundamentalism has spread most extensively in the three Abrahamic religions of Judaism, Christianity, and Islam.

Religious fundamentalism has changed during the past generation. It has become intensely focused on making comprehensive root changes to the societies within which its adherents live. It has a different mind-set, a different set of strategies and goals than the more subtle force

3

for good that traditional religious expressions have often been at other times in history. While the inclusion of fundamentalists in the political processes of democracy may well reduce the incidents of violence, it will not lessen their radicalism.

The fact is that during the past forty years the various renditions of fundamentalism have been far more active and effective in propagating their faith than traditional mainstream religions have. This has been particularly true of Islamic, Christian, and Jewish fundamentalism. Furthermore, fundamentalist groups of various religious orientations have proven themselves not content merely to be invited to the table of political policy discussions.

Fundamentalists have become far more uncompromising in their convictions and far more comprehensive in their goals to change their respective societies. They are convinced that their principles are the only absolutely true ones for everyone and in every situation. They have increasingly demonstrated that they are not satisfied to play a part in political policy discussions. They seem convinced that their way is the only way to accomplish God's purposes and to promote the best for their particular countries.

Fundamentalist faith is often blind faith. It is so completely convinced that its way is the only true and valid way that it is closed to other points of view. Increasingly, fundamentalists have striven to impose control over others within their respective societies, rather than simply seeking to protect and exercise their personal religious freedoms. They seem blind to the long-term, collateral damage that their authoritarianism may cause a nation, especially if that nation is a democracy.

A serious question facing modern democracies all over the world is this: How will democracies cope with and maintain their integrity under the increasing influence of growing numbers of fundamentalist citizens? Democracy is not naturally well suited to accommodate fundamentalism, and fundamentalism is not naturally well suited to tolerate pluralism within a democracy.

Chapter 2

—

Not Lawless, Just Legalistic

Basic Strengths and Weaknesses of Fundamentalism

I do not mean to suggest that fundamentalists in general or Christian fundamentalists in particular are lawless folks. Ordinarily, the converse is true. They are not usually given to criminal behavior. Fundamentalists are taught to be righteous.

Fundamentalists have often been among the most scrupulous, law-abiding citizens. Fundamentalists will pay most taxes most of the time. Fundamentalists will often vote and may even become politically active. Fundamentalists will far more often than not obey the laws of the road and are extremely loath to commit crimes. In that sense, fundamentalists are sterling citizens—scrupulous, moral, and upright. Fundamentalists are taught to obey the law.

What I am saying is that the primary commitments of fundamentalists often put them at odds with the values of others and tend to subvert the practical requirements of compromise in an effective pluralistic democracy. There is a conflict between fundamentalists' commitment to obey their understanding of God's will on the one hand, and to participate in facilitating the practicalities of diversity within pluralistic democracy on the other hand.

Let me share a tangentially related case in point. I served as senior pastor of a very large and affluent mainline denominational church in the heart of the South. It had thousands of active members. Though I was known to have had a background in Catholicism, as well as evangelicalism and Neo-Pentecostalism, I was also known to be a moderate cleric. I was committed to the diversity of the church and to empowering each of the variously oriented groups within the congregation. I believed that it would make the church stronger for each person and group to be able to follow their God-given passions and persuasions. My goal within that church was to create a larger tent to include everyone.

That church had a history of passively suppressing its evangelical and charismatic parishioners, some of whom evidenced a fundamentalist mind-set. I treated those segments of the congregation with greater equanimity than they had previously enjoyed. I encouraged them to exercise their spiritual passions as much as anyone else. They were given permission to invite magnetic speakers, even fiery speakers, to inspire their faith and to uplift the church. Consequently, their fervor grew, and so did their numbers, to a lesser extent.

As ardor and numbers grew, so did their frustration with the fact that everyone did not share their way of knowing God and of expressing that knowledge. Their frustration gave way to complaint. They complained among themselves. They complained to outside fundamentalist luminaries, including ones who had spoken at the church. Some of those luminaries reinforced their frustrations, often soliciting private financial support for their own ministries in faraway places, as it happened. Their advice was simple, that a church cannot please God and truly follow God's ways or receive God's full blessing if it includes Christians of varying perspectives in its leadership. If a church wanted to benefit from God's blessings, they said, its leadership must be single-minded in belief.

Consequently, those passionate fundamentalist parishioners started to use political means to seek the goal of taking greater control over the lay leadership of the church. They had a strategy. Five new members were elected to the governing board each year. Each year they recruited two or three like-minded candidates to stand for election. Although in the minority, every fundamentalist was urged vote only for those like-minded candidates and for no one else. They cast only two or three votes instead of five, and only for those of shared faith. Their plan was that, eventually, the majority of the governing board would think and vote the same way, God's way. Over time, the board could change the basic requirements for future candidates by instituting particular doctrinal affirmations of faith. Soon the entire board would share one point of view. From that position, they could govern the church. Anyone who did not share the same perspective would have a choice. They could conform or leave. Other perspectives would be passively suppressed, as they had been for many years, but God's purposes would be served.

That is only one instance of the way in which a critical mass of fundamentalists can attempt to take control of a democratic community. It is done with the sincerest conviction that God's purposes will be accomplished. By definition, they believe that it will be better for the community. Fundamentalists tend to regard the disenfranchisement of those with different views from their own as a necessary step in the achievement of the goal of instituting God's will. That can play itself out in churches, schools, town committees, and state legislatures, or on a national level. The ends justify the means. They tend to regard those who differ from them as enemies to be overcome, rather than compatriots with different points of view. And they may rationalize questionable tactics by quoting Jesus, who said, "Therefore be as shrewd as snakes and as innocent as doves" (Matthew 10:16b). And yet, they will ignore that Jesus clearly taught: "You have heard that it was said, 'Love your neighbor and hate your enemy.' But I tell you, love your enemies and pray for those who persecute you, that you may be children of your Father in heaven" (Matthew 5:43). "But to you who are listening I say: Love your enemies, do good to those who hate you" (Luke 6:27). And again, "Whoever is not against us is for us" (Mark 9:40).

What begins for fundamentalists as a movement to promote their rights to practice their faith can easily end in restricting other people's rights. Fundamentalists will use democracy, appropriately enough, to achieve justice for their own freedom of religion. But since embedded within their faith is the conviction that theirs is the only ultimate truth, fundamentalists will then use those same democratic processes to disenfranchise others or to extend control over them in order to accommodate their religious sensibilities. They blur their understanding of God's purposes with their own sensibilities. Fundamentalists will frequently make every effort to impose their values on others in order to achieve what they consider to be optimum religious freedom. And that freedom of religion expands to include the accommodation of their particular religious sensibilities. This is what I mean when I claim that fundamentalists are compromised in their ability to participate in pluralistic democratic societies in good faith.

Chapter 3

—

Fundamentalism:
A Religion in Its Own Right

Fundamentalism as a Discreet Religion

One of the distinguishing characteristics of the current generation has been the rise of fundamentalism. Some have said that fundamentalism is a modern phenomenon. They claim that fundamentalism is little more than one hundred years old. But that refers to a narrow definition of the term. Whether a modern phenomenon or not, in fact, history may be on the threshold of an *Era of Fundamentalism.*

Notice that I have referred to the rise of fundamentalism and an era of fundamentalism rather than fundamentalist Islam, fundamentalist Christianity, or fundamentalist Judaism, etc. That is because I have come to notice that similar dynamics exist among the various versions of fundamentalism. And those dynamics are at least as significant as particular doctrines in terms of their impact. Actions speak louder than words, as the adage states. Fundamentalist dynamics evidence deeper beliefs than those enshrined in doctrines.

A controversial study was conducted over an eight-year period, between 1987 and 1995. The "Fundamentalism Project," as it was called, was overseen by Martin Marty and Scott Appleby. It yielded a set of five volumes on modern fundamentalism and its effects. The results of the study were controversial on at least two levels. Some critics believe that it is inappropriate to use the term "fundamentalist" to include those who do not wish to be considered as such. Those who do consider themselves to be fundamentalists object to the idea of being categorized with fundamentalists of other religious traditions.

 Nevertheless, the study concluded that, regardless of specific religious affiliation, fundamentalists of various persuasions share several common characteristics. Among them are the following:

- Fundamentalists of different religious persuasions believe that men should lead and that women and children should follow their lead.
- The rules of a fundamentalist religion are complex and rigid and must be followed.
- Fundamentalists of various persuasions do not accept pluralism. They believe that their rules apply to everyone everywhere.
- Fundamentalists clearly differentiate between insiders and outsiders. Insiders are those who follow the prescribed faith system, and everyone else is seen as an outsider. Insiders are nurtured whereas outsiders are distrusted or even fought.
- Fundamentalists long for an idealized past, when they believe that their religion was pure and as God intended.[iii]

As I have already mentioned, some argue that it is intellectually inappropriate to identify anyone as fundamentalist or to classify any segment of a society with fundamentalism that does not claim to be. But that is inordinately self-selective and subjective. Some would prefer to use the term in its historical sense. But that is far too limited. Restricting the use of the term "fundamentalism" to its historic identification is very exclusive indeed. It would rule out its application to any contemporary Muslim groups, for example.

The term "fundamentalism" originally referred to a movement among some American Protestants. That movement originated in the 1880s, though the term itself was coined in 1922. Fundamentalism in that sense was a movement that came into being in reaction to a modernist drift in biblical studies and theology. That drift was led by intellectuals and clergy in several mainline Protestant denominations.

Some Protestant schools of theology became enamored of the idea that religious studies should adopt a more modern, scientific approach. Several of them were attached to prominent universities, such as Princeton. Influenced by then cutting-edge currents in academia, professors and their divinity students set to work applying what they considered to be more credible scientific tools to their disciplines. They began to employ archeology, literary criticism, and theories of religious evolution to biblical studies. Scholars completely reexamined the Bible through those new lenses.

Academics were guided by such then avant-garde theories as the "Graf-Wellhausen Hypothesis," for example. Independently, K. H. Graf and Julius Wellhausen developed a documentary hypothesis that the writings of the first five books of the Hebrew scriptures, the Torah or Pentateuch, were not actually authored by Moses. The theory proposed that the books of the Pentateuch were a compilation of four different traditions that were developed over hundreds of years.

Their hypothesis was based on an evolutionary assumption. Brain functions and human thoughts have evolved over time, in the same way that organisms have. And like biological evolution, the evolution of human thought has developed from simpler to the more complex constructs.

Graf and Wellhausen simply applied that premise to religious thought. On the basis of that theory, and removing divine revelation from the equation, biblical scholars concluded that the first five books of the Hebrew scriptures could not have been written as early as had been assumed and certainly not by a single author. Literature and concepts that had been attributed to Moses were simply too sophisticated for people in the second millennium BC. They noticed significant differences in vocabulary and literary style in different books. And so they determined that the Torah could not have been written by one person. Instead, they concluded that the contents of those five books must have been redacted over time and that several authors wrote them. Therefore, they were the result of deliberate human processes rather than spontaneous divine inspiration.

Such scholarly developments resulted in a thoroughgoing reconsideration of the Christian faith. It called into question the originality and authenticity of the teachings in the Bible. The credibility of miracles described in its writings was questioned as well. Biblical scholars like Rudolf Bultmann, in his *History of the Synoptic Tradition* (1921) and *The New Testament and Mythology* (1941), "demythologized" the entire New Testament. They considered miracles to have been metaphors or simple fabrications. They rejected the historical accuracy of many of the biblical stories and analyzed them as myths instead. The virgin birth of Jesus, his resurrection, and his divinity were regarded skeptically. It goes without saying that the authority of the Bible, let alone its infallibility, was clearly jeopardized. The Bible was in danger of being relegated to the position of just another collection of ancient writings, without divine inspiration or authority. That sent shock waves throughout the Christian community of the time.

Traditionalists were alarmed and energized. They envisioned that Christianity would fade into oblivion within only a few generations if modernism were not contradicted. Protestant traditionalists rallied to defend what they regarded as the "fundamentals" of the Christian faith. They proposed certain core doctrines that they considered to be fundamental. Those doctrines included the divine inspiration and infallibility of the Bible in matters of faith and practice, the divinity of Christ, his virgin birth, his bodily resurrection and return, and the conviction that Christ's death by criminal execution was provided by God as the only means for the forgiveness of human sins. In 1922 they began to call themselves fundamentalists.

Albeit original, that is a very specific, technical, and restrictive use of the term "fundamentalism." It is not sufficiently applicable to current circumstances in the world. Many Christians of various persuasions share those specific beliefs. These days, they are better termed "orthodox Christians," "traditional Christians." or "Bible-believing Christians."

I intend to be provocative at this point. I would argue that Christian fundamentalists in today's world are a different breed altogether. Most are not exclusively concerned with particular doctrinal matters pertaining to the Christian faith. Many have already affiliated themselves with faith communities of preferred theological choice in which there are no conflicts relative to the Bible, basic doctrine, and core standards of conduct. Furthermore, I would argue that the underlying dynamics of a religion are at least as definitive as the particular doctrines embraced by a religion. Jesus seemed to think so. He did not say that it would be by people's doctrines, values, standards, or political affiliations that his followers would be known. Instead, he explained that his followers would be known by the fruit (the dynamics and outcomes) of their actions and their attitudes. He rarely spoke of doctrinal matters but emphasized mind-set and behavior.

I would argue that religious fundamentalism is a discrete category of religion in and of itself. Whatever doctrinal differences that exist among the different expressions of modern fundamentalism pale by comparison to their similarities of mind-set, attitude, approach, and strategic behavior. Whatever the particular religious appellation, whether Christian, Muslim, Jewish, or other, fundamentalists share the same underlying mind-set. That shared mind-set has discernible characteristics. The following is a list of characteristics common to fundamentalists of various traditions:

13

- Fundamentalists of different persuasions share in common some of the same core doctrines and code of conduct, though they may express them somewhat differently.
- Fundamentalists share most of the same basic moral values.
- Fundamentalists believe that their conceptualization of God or Supreme Being is the one and only true one, exclusive of all others.
- Fundamentalists demonize different conceptualizations of God.
- Fundamentalists possess some body of authoritative literature.
- Fundamentalists believe that their sacred literature is solely inspired and infallible.
- Fundamentalists interpret their sacred literature literally.
- Fundamentalists believe that their inspired literature is meant to govern their lives and the lives of everyone else.
- Fundamentalists believe that other "facts" or "truths" should be subordinated to the truth of their sacred scriptures and tested by it, including scientific data.
- Fundamentalists believe that submitting to and obeying their understanding of the truth is of the greatest importance.
- Fundamentalists believe that they are accountable to their understanding of God for practicing their faith in the particular way they believe it must be practiced.
- Fundamentalists believe that promoting their faith and their way of practicing it is an essential element of their mission.
- Fundamentalists believe that it is valid to impose the values of their understanding of God's truth on others.
- Fundamentalists are resistant to compromise, because they regard discussion as a way to convince others of or convert others to the truth of what they believe.
- Fundamentalists regard those who disagree with them in public discourse on matters related to their faith and values as adversaries, or at the very least as benighted.

- Fundamentalists are prone to ascribe the motivation of their adversaries to the power of evil.
- Fundamentalists have come to regard political processes as means to the end of extending the influence of their values to others.
- Fundamentalists do not accept pluralism and tend to be intransigent and judgmental of those who disagree with them.

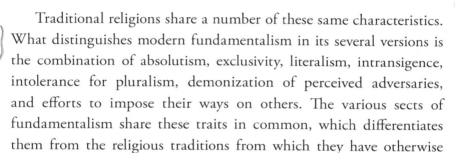

Traditional religions share a number of these same characteristics. What distinguishes modern fundamentalism in its several versions is the combination of absolutism, exclusivity, literalism, intransigence, intolerance for pluralism, demonization of perceived adversaries, and efforts to impose their ways on others. The various sects of fundamentalism share these traits in common, which differentiates them from the religious traditions from which they have otherwise originated.

Albeit significant, the differences between the various versions of fundamentalism are fewer. Fundamentalists of different religious traditions call the Supreme Being by different names, using different languages. They appeal to different collections of inspired literature, whether Torah, the Bible (including Old and New Testament writings), Quran, or others. They adhere to different rituals, practices, and customs.

Ponder for a moment the differences that exist between the various denominations of the same traditional religions. Catholic and Pentecostal Christians, Sunni and Shiite Muslims, Hasidic and Reformed Jews differ from each other as much as fundamentalists of different religious identifications do. And most fundamentalists normally reject those who do not share their approach to faith within their own identified religion even more stridently than they do adherents to other religions. After all, heretics are more dangerous than infidels. Infidels, by definition, are unbelievers and can be dismissed out of hand. But heretics within the same religion can undermine the exclusivity of the faith and its mission.

It has become increasingly evident to me that fundamentalism is actually a religion in its own right. Other identifying words used to describe fundamentalism define, for lack of a better term, denominations of fundamentalism. Fundamentalist mind-sets and dynamics are the common denominator. Fundamentalism is the religion. No matter how ardently adherents will protest to the contrary, the particular religious categories of fundamentalism are sects of fundamentalist religion.

Admittedly, not all fundamentalists are religious in the traditional sense at all. They may, in fact, incorporate atheism within their fundamental ideology. Whenever there is a body of formal principles that are literally interpreted and rigidly adhered to, fundamentalist dynamics have increasingly been prone to emerge. For many years Communists betrayed a fundamentalist mind-set. Ironically, some scientists have demonstrated several fundamentalist traits.

In the United States there are several examples of a drift toward nonreligious fundamentalism. One form of nonreligious fundamentalism is connected with the Constitution of the United States. The "Original Intent" movement now holds sway in some corners of American jurisprudence and in some legal institutions and law schools. That approach to the practice of law in the United States emphasizes the original intentions of framers of the Constitution. It accentuates the meaning of the concepts enshrined in the Constitution back to the eighteenth century or in the particular times when subsequent amendments were made to it. There seems to be increasing resistance to making allowances for social developments over the passage of time. Advocates of Original Intent treat the Constitution the way Christian fundamentalists approach biblical interpretation.

The general dynamics of fundamentalism also seem to manifest themselves in other fields. Economic theory has increasingly shown itself to be subject to that propensity. Whether Keynesian, "free market," communist, "trickle down," socialist, or others, increasingly, political and economic leaders seem to treat theories in the field of economics as matters of core doctrine. Regardless of changing circumstances, political, economic, and business leaders are more liable to embrace unproven economic theories as paradigms for general decision making. That constitutes faith. Insofar as that faith includes absolutism, exclusivity, literalism, intransigence, intolerance for pluralism of thought, and efforts to impose their ways on others, it is a form of fundamentalism.

Fundamentalists of whatever persuasion are so dedicated to their own beliefs and principles of practice that they will press those ideas to the detriment of practical democratic process within pluralistic societies. They are absolutely convinced that their beliefs are right for everyone all the time. Some of what I will be saying may be applicable to other expressions of fundamentalism. But since I am a Christian and an American, I will emphasize fundamentalism in my religious and political traditions. I will focus on Christian fundamentalism within American democratic society.

Chapter 4

—

Government and the Bible

Forms of Government Extant in the Bible

Christian fundamentalists have been groping for a political philosophy to wed their faith with democracy. And that is a formidable task because the Bible offers no political ideology consistent with democracy.

It is only natural that Christian fundamentalists try to find justification for virtually every action and guidance for virtually every enterprise within the Bible and/or Christian tradition. And this presents a significant problem for fundamentalists within pluralistic democracies. There is an inherent tension between fundamentalism and democracy in pluralistic societies such as the United States. For Christian fundamentalists, one of the core reasons for that tension is that there is no proposition in scripture, no direction in the Bible, and no precedent in Christian tradition for functioning as citizens within a democracy, particularly democracy within a pluralistic society.

The Bible and Christian tradition have nothing to say about democracy. Democracy is not a biblical concept. If anyone claims that

19

it is a traditional Christian ideal, let alone a biblical concept, he or she is misinformed or perhaps purposely misinforming others. When it comes to government, theocracy was the ideal set forth in the Bible. Short of that, monarchy was the ordinary form of government extant in biblical times and enshrined as normative within the Bible.

Why is it that the Bible has nothing to say about democracy? If democracy is a superior system of government, why would it not have been revealed as such in sacred scripture? Democracy was not mentioned in the Bible for the same reason that the existence of gravity, Earth's revolution around the sun, bacteria, viruses, black holes, electricity, penguins, nuclear energy, pandas, the Western Hemisphere, the North and South poles, and vitamins also were omitted. The people during the times of the biblical writings were unaware of it, or if they were, they rejected the idea out of hand. The biblical writings encompass an epoch during which the Jewish people were unfamiliar with democracy. As far as we know, in ancient times, democracy existed for a relatively short period of time, in particular in Greek city states, and only during what is known as the "intertestamental period." That interval, literally the period between the Old and New Testaments, was approximately a four-hundred-year period during which no biblical books, except for apocryphal literature, were written (350 BC to 50 AD).

More than that, the biblical conceptualization of humans would have discounted the desirability of democracy. According to the Bible, humans are like sheep. This perspective is consistently set forth in the biblical writings. Like sheep, humans wander, following our own immediate appetites. Like sheep, we are vulnerable. Like sheep, we tend to be clueless about danger until it is too late. Like sheep, we humans do what we want until we get into trouble, and then we cry out for help. Like sheep, humans are certainly not capable of independence and are not to be trusted with it. Humans need the oversight of shepherds to protect and lead them.

Consistent with that perspective, according to the Bible, we humans need strong leadership to keep us from going astray. When fledgling hints of democratic process incidentally seemed to crop up in biblical stories, they were associated with people's unfaithfulness, and the outcome was always negative. It is only logical that the Bible should assert that authoritative leadership is necessary. Interestingly, that has been the rationalization for despotism throughout the centuries.

The Bible refers to four forms of government. They were theocracy, tribal patriarchy, charismatic leadership, and monarchy. All four were authoritarian in nature. Ultimately, the Bible describes only one perfect form of government, and that is theocracy. Theocracy is that state of being to which we look forward in heaven.

Theocracy is that form of government, that way of organizing people, which is focused upon God's rule of human community. The Jewish historian Flavius Josephus wrote during the latter part of the first century AD. He was the first to coin the term. He defined theocracy as government in which God and His Law is determinative. Josephus wrote, "our legislator [Moses] ordained our government [Jewish] to be what might be termed theocracy, ascribing authority and power to God."[iv] More recently, Emanuel Gutman has written in his article "A Religion in Israeli Politics" that theocracy exists when the "origins of government and state power derive their legal authority from religion, and derive their legitimacy from a divine source."[v]

In Judeo-Christian tradition the more familiar term for theocracy is the *kingdom of God*, the rule of God, and his law. The idealized vision of the kingdom of God is largely found in the Hebrew prophetic writings and the New Testament's book of Revelation. Those writings emphasize the characteristics of God's kingdom, not its operation. Those qualities include images of harmony with God, perfect peace among God's people, complete provision of abundant resources, perfect justice, worship, satisfaction, and joy.

That vision, however, never includes a practical plan for *how* those conditions would be achieved, implemented, or administered in this world. In the Bible, the state of being in the kingdom of God seems to be accomplished miraculously by means of God's transformation of the human heart. Jesus never suggested that the kingdom of God or of heaven would actually be instituted politically. He said that the kingdom of God was to be found "within you" (Luke 17:21), as a state of personal being instead of a political state. Changes would materialize because people would want only to bask in God's love and do what God wants. In point of historical fact, the Bible never describes any time when such government or state actually existed. In the Bible, the kingdom of God as a state of collective being seems to be an apocalyptic vision of perfection after God completes his plans on earth.

Even if it were achievable, how could theocracy be implemented and administered? Well, absent God's immediate presence and concrete intervention in routine human affairs, it must take some form of human mediation of God's rule. By definition, without God's constant direct leadership, human intermediaries must represent God's will. That requires either some form of oracle, or in most fundamentalist groups, individuals who interpret, communicate, and administer God's revealed and unequivocal truth. In order to preserve objectivity, that unequivocal truth must be found in some form of sacred writing.

For Christian fundamentalists, that is where the Bible comes into play. To Christian (and Jewish) fundamentalists, the Bible is God's Word. It is God's will, written down. They firmly believe that God intends it to govern people's lives until God establishes his perfect rule.

The Bible chronicles several times during which attempts were made to establish God's sovereign rule within community. Key individuals led those efforts. Of course, Moses was the most notable. He was, after all, the one who delivered God's law to the Israelites, according to the Torah. Joshua tried to follow in his footsteps once they entered the Promised Land. Samuel also tried to lead the Israelites on those occasions when they were open to it. Hezekiah, Nehemiah, and Ezra made sincere efforts to focus people on God's sovereign leadership by calling the Israelites to renew their allegiance to God and to following God's law. Then, too, the apostolic community described in the book of Acts eagerly sought God's practical leadership in every aspect of their collective life.

All those efforts to establish human-mediated theocracy, while perhaps worthy, either failed to catch hold or to endure over time. There have been two simple reasons for the failures. First, in the course of human history, God seems never to have chosen to impose his rule by consistent practical intervention or direct leadership. And second, empirical data seems to indicate that God never made people to act as puppets, even when some of them actively sought his sovereignty. Therefore, theocracy never seemed practical. And so the biblical characters turned to other practical forms of government to organize themselves.

The Bible describes those other three forms of government. The Bible depicts instances or periods in which patriarchy, charismatic leadership, or monarchy existed. I hasten to add that those three forms of government never successfully accomplished the desired outcome of God's reign, at least not for very long. There may have been exemplary instances of each, but they never extended beyond a single generation. And those attempts were embodied in particular historical leaders, whether Abraham, Moses, or King David. Let's take a look at each of those forms of government.

The Bible does not actually describe any particular form of government before the time of Abraham, prior to 2,000 BC. Well, perhaps that's not precisely accurate. Of course, no one really knows when or if the story actually took place. But the first biblical story that implies some sort of organized community decision making and action taking is commonly referred to as the story of the Tower of Babel. It describes a community public works project, in which a city edifice was built in some collectively organized fashion.

Genesis 11:4 seems to suggest some rudimentary form of democratic process. It says, "Then they said, 'Come, let us build ourselves a city, with a tower that reaches to the heavens, so that we may make a name for ourselves; otherwise we will be scattered over the face of the whole earth'" While the story may intimate that the project was initiated by the community democratically, the manner in which it was organized and executed was not explained. However it happened, the project failed miserably. The tower collapsed, and the participants became seriously disunited. They couldn't even communicate with each other after the disaster because God suddenly caused them to speak different languages.

God was credited with the failure. In fact, the story clearly suggests that collective human organization threatened God's preeminent leadership position. The moral of the story is that humans cannot be trusted with the power that self-determination affords. If humans were to organize themselves effectively, they could threaten to dethrone God. That story was anything but an endorsement of democracy.

For lack of a better term, tribal patriarchy was the earliest way in which the most prominent biblical characters organized themselves. Like sheiks or petty kings, patriarchs were undisputed male tribal leaders. Abraham, the preeminent biblical patriarch, was regarded by his contemporaries as that kind of leader. Local kings seem to have treated him as an equal. The leaders of prosperous households, powerful families, tribes, and cities were treated with equivalent respect. Patriarchs unilaterally led the people within the communities under their authority.

There seem to have been at least three purposes for that primitive form of leadership. It prevented extended family/tribal divisions or free-for-all conflicts for leadership within a tribe. It also discouraged aggression by outside groups. And patriarchs controlled work and resource distribution within the community in order to stave off insufficient resources and competition for them. These three—avoidance of internal conflict, resistance to external aggression, and management of resources—seem to have been the most basic motivations for primitive government. Framed more positively, the three basic reasons for government were order, security, and resource distribution—organization, protection, and provision.

Those goals respond to the basic realities of human existence. Like all organisms, each human needs a secure environment within which to survive. Like all organisms, humans need sufficient basic resources to thrive. Like all organisms, each human needs defense from outside predators. And like all clustering organisms, there are those who are stronger and could maliciously dominate the others. Humans need safety from those who would oppress them within their groups.

Under this form of governance, the character of the patriarch made all the difference when it came to the quality of life of the members of the community. If the patriarch was strong, kind, and just, the quality of life of the members of the community would be safeguarded. If not, vulnerability, abuse, and oppression were commonplace.

The next form of government was similar but had a significantly different twist. It was charismatic leadership. Like patriarchy, charismatic leadership was unilaterally administered. And it had the same goals— organization or regulation, protection, and provision. But it was different in one respect. God chose the leader and inspired or empowered him to lead for the purpose of making people do what God wanted them to do. That, from a spiritual vantage point, is what charismatic meant. Derived from the Greek word for gifts, charisma did not refer to a magnetic personality but to a divinely gifted person.

Moses was the penultimate example of charismatic leadership. Moses spearheaded the liberation of the Hebrew people from an inhospitable environment with aggressive predators, slavery in Egypt. He led them to the place where God wanted them to live in safety. He instructed them on how God wanted them to live in the meantime and once they arrived at their destination.

Arguably, the Hebrew people seem to have been organized as a theocracy during that forty-year period of "wilderness wandering." According to the biblical writings, God freed the Hebrews from slavery in Egypt, directly punished the Egyptians for their predatory behavior, and provided the Hebrews with principles to live by, food to eat, water to drink, and the hope of a promised destination to reach. Nevertheless, according to the writings of the Torah, Moses served as God's surrogate. He was the charismatic leader of the Hebrew people during their forty-year trek to the Promised Land. In some respects Moses's relationship with the Hebrews was not unlike the pope as the Vicar of Christ for the Roman Catholic Church.

And yet, Moses could not perfectly mediate God's leadership. He was only human and imperfect, after all. He was often frustrated with the Hebrew people. He was occasionally even frustrated with God. Moses was frequently dispirited. At times Moses actually expressed death wishes. Moses so lacked trust in God and was so impatient at a place called Kadesh, that he disobeyed God's specific instructions.

Clearly, throughout their wanderings, the Hebrews neither lived in harmony with God nor with each other. Their community life demonstrated none of the characteristics symptomatic of God's rule. Moreover, such as it was, Moses's method of governance virtually depleted him. It did not last once the Hebrews entered the Promised Land. That method of governance could not survive beyond Moses's leadership. It fell apart, and gave way to a loose confederation of tribal patriarchies. No matter how much Moses may have pointed to the supremacy of God and his law as the basis of community governance, since it did not survive beyond his death, it was more an example of charismatic leadership than it was of theocracy.

As an aside, at this point I will shift from using the term Hebrews to Israelites. They were the same people. The term Hebrew referred to Abraham's home region of Hebron. Once they returned home, the Hebrews realized that Abraham had had other descendants in their homeland beside themselves. He had descendants through his first son, Ishmael, as well as through their ancestor Isaac. Isaac, in turn, had two sons as well. Isaac's first son was Esau. His second son was their ancestor Jacob, alias Israel. They identified themselves by their relationship to Israel and justified their claim to Abraham's land as Israel's descendents.

There were other examples of charismatic leadership among the Israelites. Joshua was one. The Israelite judges, like Samson or Gideon, were others. Then too, like Nehemiah, God gave certain other leaders specific missions as well. And yet even charismatic, divinely inspired leaders had their foibles and failures. As mentioned, Moses became frustrated with the people he led, impatient with God, often generally dispirited, even suicidal at times, and unfaithful. Joshua oversaw genocidal military tactics. Sampson was seduced by or seduced Bathsheba and lost his ability to lead. Self-interest ordinarily reared its ugly head. Sooner or later, humans have always proven themselves to be imperfect conduits for mediating God's perfect ways.

One other biblical leader warrants emphasis in passing. His name was Samuel. He was a charismatic leader. What made Samuel uncharacteristic was that he served three roles. He served God as a priest as well as a prophet. As a priest he interceded with God on behalf of the Israelites. As a prophet he communicated messages from God to the people. And from time to time, he served as something of a judge as well. On occasion he organized the Israelites to fight against aggression by neighboring tribes. He functioned as a prophet, as an official priest, and as a leader. Prophets, priests, and leaders normally served discreet roles.

Not only was Samuel an unusual example of charismatic leadership, but also he was a transitional one. The Israelites had a problem. Samuel was a charismatic leader. He was guided and gifted by the Spirit of the Lord, but he was growing frail with age. His demise was in sight. And yet, God had not identified another charismatic leader to replace him. Like many pastors' kids, Samuel's sons did not share their father's strong faith. They were corrupted by self-interest. That prompted the tribal leaders of Israel to schedule a summit meeting with Samuel. The subject of their concern was a delicate matter. They did not want to be taken advantage of by his sons once Samuel was gone. And so they petitioned Samuel to ordain a king for Israel, like the kings of neighboring peoples.

Samuel was crestfallen. A conversation ensued between Samuel and God. That conversation was revelatory when it came to God's apparent attitude toward government in general, and monarchy in particular. God's perspective is described in the eighth chapter of the first book of Samuel. This is what God told Samuel: "Listen to all that the people are saying to you; it is not you they have rejected, but they have rejected me as their king. As they have done from the day I brought them up out of Egypt until this day, forsaking me and serving other gods, so they are doing to you. Now listen to them; but warn them solemnly and let them know what the king who will reign over them will claim as his rights" (1 Samuel 8:7–9). That was the seminal moment of Israelite monarchy in the Bible and in later Christian tradition.

What did God have to say about monarchy? Paraphrasing Samuel's words, a monarch will draft your young men into his army to fight wars and to serve his own purposes. A monarch will tax you to pay his expenses. A monarch will enrich himself at your expense. A monarch will use his subjects as servants. And so if they were to choose monarchy, people would lose many of their tribal and familial freedoms. Obviously, monarchy was not an ideal form of government. But it was the normal one for that period. And it prevailed throughout the rest of the biblical times.

The Israelites chose monarchy over, excuse the expression, absentee theocracy. By absentee theocracy I mean God's rule without God's direct, consistent, and concrete leadership. Why did the Israelites reject theocracy? It was because absentee theocracy requires human mediation. Imperfect people are completely unable to mediate God's rule with any degree of consistency or accuracy. Samuel may have done a fair job at it for a while, but the Israelites knew that his sons would not.

According to the story, those ancient Israelites knew the shortcomings of theocracy all too well. They were accustomed to crises developing in human affairs, but God's intervention had been unpredictable. The people simply didn't want to continue to go from crisis to crisis, waiting for God to intervene whenever events got their worst. And so the patriarchs of the tribes of Israel, in the fashion of an oligarchy, voted for monarchy because it seemed more reliable in the face of potential dangers than charismatic leadership had been.

Monarchy is the form of government that prevailed during the remainder of the biblical times. It is mentioned in the Bible far more often than any other form of government. It persisted from the time of Samuel throughout the rest of the biblical writings. Monarchy was similar to tribal patriarchy but more far-reaching. Whether the title conferred upon the monarch was pharaoh, suzerain, king, or emperor, the idea was the same. Monarchy was a form of government in which a single individual unilaterally ruled the rest of the people within his jurisdiction, either by fiat or by the rule of law imposed by the monarch.

Frequently, monarchs were bestowed with divine, semidivine, or superhuman status by the communities they ruled. The pharaohs of Egypt and emperors of Rome were the most obvious cases of rulers who were attributed with divinity. Although they were never deified, even some of the kings of Israel were idealized. Some of them were regarded as possessing superhuman abilities that had been given to them by God. David had his heroic heart, his skills in battle, his physical beauty, his poetic gifts, and his musical talents. Solomon had his incomparable wisdom.

Such innate superiority served to invest the monarch with the idealized collective identity of the people he ruled. It kept his position somewhat safe from internal competition. It protected the system from chaos. And it engendered greater confidence among the populace in the face of threats by outside forces. After all, who wants to fight a superhero, let alone a god!

It was normal for monarchies to be stratified societies. Of course, the most powerful stratum of society was the royal family. The next most influential segment of society was often religious. It was composed of priests and prophets or soothsayers. They were often the monarch's most important advisors. The ruler also appointed official surrogates who were delegated with particular responsibilities for the realm. They were often awarded with positions of nobility. Another stratum consisted of wealthy and influential subjects, military leaders, and the like. Yet another, far larger layer was composed of peasants of various sorts. And still another was composed of an often vast slave class. The Bible consistently states that God is partial to the least privileged. God discouraged oppression of the poor and disadvantaged.

Once again, as in patriarchies, the general quality of life among the citizens of a monarchy was completely dependent upon the disposition or character of the monarch and his surrogates. In many ways David was a bridge between charismatic leadership and monarchy. He was inspired and empowered by God to overcome Goliath. And yet even King David, the epitome of the ideal king in most respects and prototype of the messianic king, was not without his flaws. Like Judge Samson before him, David had a weakness for the ladies. He also acted unjustly at times, most notably in the case of Uriah the Hittite, whom he ostensibly murdered.

The Bible instructs rulers to subject themselves to God. If a ruler feared God or was accountable to God, justice should follow. And if he did not, he would serve his own interests instead. If the ruler's surrogates were accountable to God, they would be faithful stewards, and if not, they would be corrupt. The general biblical attitude was that people were blessed when the king feared the Lord because justice would prevail. Hence, subjects prayed for their governing authorities in the hope that God would make the king just. Monarchy may not have been the most desirable form of government, but according to the biblical writings, it was most certainly normative.

As I have claimed, the Bible offers no specific guidance for the citizens of a democracy. Christian fundamentalists, especially of the Protestant persuasion, will always look to the Bible for direction and precedent. There they will find only intimations of theocracy and instances of tribal patriarchy, charismatic leadership, and monarchy. Those forms of government had three things in common. All of them were autocratic, authoritarian, and subject to the frailties of the leader.

Fundamentalists will yearn and work for God's more perfect leadership, for some degree of theocracy. But where will they look to find the right form of human mediation for God's leadership? They will look to the Bible, of course. There they will find authoritarian forms of government. Christian fundamentalists in the United States will reject monarchy out of hand. It contradicts American history and ethos. They will also reject tribal patriarchy because it is completely irrelevant to the ethnic melting pot of American society.

Instead, they will turn to charismatic leadership. They will work for some amalgamation of the electoral process and the appointment of charismatic political leaders of fundamentalist persuasion. They will do what they can to use democratic processes to install leaders acceptable to them. Their intent is to impose their godly values on society on their behalf. This they will seek to do in order to form a more perfect version of theocratic leadership, not to form a more perfect union in the nation.

Chapter 5

⁓

Leadership and Conformity in the Bible

What the Bible Says about Following Leaders

By and large, the people described in the Bible were conformists. They were often discontent and complaining conformists, but conformists nonetheless. Ideally, they obeyed. They submitted to the rules, regulations, and roles of their governing authorities. Abraham's family members followed his leadership as if it were God's. The Hebrews in Egypt submitted to the often severe rule of pharaoh's government. They had no choice. During the Exodus, the Hebrews obeyed Moses throughout their meandering, forty-year journey in the wilderness, albeit often with unrelenting complaint. They did so because they were afraid that God would abandon them if they did not. Likewise, they obeyed Joshua in order to remain within God's good graces.

Once ensconced within the Promised Land, dysfunction developed due to lack of centralized leadership, and the Israelites submitted themselves to various judges. As in the futuristic film about Judge Dredd, often the Hebrew judges were local peacekeepers and head-crackers who resolved disputes that arose among the peoples. As I've mentioned, God appointed and empowered them, and so the Israelites accepted their leadership. But the people wanted to have kings to rule over them. So God directed prophets or priests to ordain individuals to rule over the people as kings. The people obeyed, because kings had the divine right to rule over them and the power to back it up.

The faithful described in the Christian scriptures were also conformists. They obeyed. The apostles obeyed Jesus. The earliest Christians obeyed the apostles, who were akin to the charismatic leaders in the Hebrew scriptures. The apostles tried their best to obey God.

When they didn't know what else to do, the fledgling church followed the charismatic leadership of Peter. On one occasion (Acts 1:15–26) Peter decided that God wanted them to fill Judas's vacancy as an apostle. Consistent with the desire to obey God, Peter determined that they should seek God's theocratic intervention, God's direction. This is the process that Peter devised: Two longstanding disciples were put forward for the position of twelfth apostle. Everyone prayed for God's guidance of a lottery. The two drew lots to determine which one God wanted for the job. Rightly or wrongly, they neglected to add a straw for "none of the above." Later, it became apparent to some that God recruited someone else for the position. His name was Saul (Paul). The apostles sincerely wanted to submit to Jesus and to obey God. And yet, since humans are imperfect, no matter how faithful, righteous, and well-intentioned they might otherwise be, people always made mistakes.

The organization of the church in Jerusalem was disastrous. It perpetually teetered on the brink of destitution. That was largely due to the paradigm of community life that the apostles adopted. That way of community life was, for lack of a better term, essentially Christian communism. Each and every convert to faith in Jesus was required to give all his assets to the leadership of the church so that they could redistribute resources equitably, according to need. After all, that was the way Jesus did it during his three years of itinerant ministry. He and the disciples shared a common purse. And so the apostles conformed to that model. It was one thing for a handful of men to live from a common purse and to lodge at a disciple's house for the night or to sleep under the stars. But it was quite another matter for a community of thousands of disciples to live that way for very long.

There is a story in the fifth chapter of the book of Acts that underscored the imperative of that decision. Two new converts covertly withheld from the church the proceeds from the sale of a piece of property. They were struck dead for it. The point of that story was to suggest that communism was God's chosen way, but also that the apostles were God's intermediaries for governing the church.

The church firmly believed that they were obeying God and tried to implement a theocratic way of life. Alas, almost immediately issues of inequitable distribution arose within the community (Acts 6). Conflicts ensued. Reforms were implemented. But for the balance of its existence, the church in Jerusalem was dependent for its survival upon contributions from churches in other parts of the Roman Empire.

Those earliest Christians obeyed their understanding of what God wanted. They followed the leadership of the apostles. They conformed to their understanding of what God wanted for their community life. And they failed.

Though the apostles tried their hand at theocracy for a while, their efforts quickly reverted to charismatic leadership, bordering on monarchy. There was a conference in Jerusalem. It has been called the "First Church Council." It was the single most significant conference in the first three hundred years of the church's existence and arguably in the entire history of the Christian church. It convened to settle one issue, and the final decision on that issue was made by individual fiat.

A controversy threatened to tear the fledgling church apart. The disagreement focused upon one single concern, an absolutely essential one that would change the fabric of the Christian church forever. This was the question: Was it necessary for people to be Jewish in order to be legitimate followers of Christ and members of the church?

Those earliest Christians followed a process to arrive at a decision. The apostles listened to the debate over the question. Peter added his experience-based thoughts on the matter. They prayed for God's guidance. They reflected upon the Hebrew scriptures and prayed some more. Finally, James said this: "It is my judgment, therefore, that we should not make it difficult for the Gentiles who are turning to God" (Acts 15:19). One man made the final decision that it would not be necessary for Gentiles to become Jews before they could be saved and join the ranks of Jesus's followers. It was a landmark decision.

Designated human authority had already become definitive, and conformity w as essential. Submission to acknowledged human authority was necessary for submission to God's authority. Attempts at theocracy have always depended upon human mediation. Human mediation of God's will has always been authoritarian, and often misguided.

The earliest Christians also submitted to the established authorities of secular government. In fact, the New Testament provides only four guidelines for Christian citizens of a state. They should obey the governing authorities, who were pagans. They should pay their taxes. They should try to live exemplary, peaceable, and righteous lives. And they should pray for those in authority.

This is not to say that everyone in the Bible always conformed to authority. But nonconformity ordinarily came with very negative consequences. Abraham's wife, Sarah, persuaded him on matters pertaining to her stepson, Ishmael. This is what happened. Sarah was unable to become pregnant. Sarah had a maid. Her name was Hagar. Abraham and Hagar had relations. Hagar became pregnant, and from that time on rivalry intensified between Sarah and Hagar. Hagar gave birth to Abraham's first son. He was named Ishmael. Later Sarah conceived and gave birth to Isaac, Abraham's second son. As they grew, Isaac idolized his older brother. Presumably concerned that Ishmael would always predominate, Sarah insisted that Abraham disinherit and abandon Ishmael and his mother. Abraham appeased her and acquiesced. And it turned out badly for the family, dividing it forever. Nonconformity to tribal patriarchy had negative consequences.

Nonconformity to charismatic leadership also had negative consequences. The Hebrews took it upon themselves to make and worship a golden calf. It offended God, and turned out very badly for them. They were not permitted to enter the Promised Land, and wandered through the desert for an entire generation.

Nonconformity to the authority of kings had negative consequences as well. When David's son, Absalom, tried to usurp his father's throne it turned out very badly for him. He was killed.

Even resistance to pagan rulers had very negative consequences. When Israel resisted the Babylonian Empire, it turned out very badly for them. The Babylonians conquered the people of Israel and took them into captivity as a slave class in Babylon for just about seventy years (the Babylonian Captivity). Likewise, when the Jewish people tried to rebel against Roman rule, it turned out very badly for them. Roman troops occupied the nation. And when it happened again, the Romans eventually drove the Jewish people out of their homeland and distributed them throughout the empire (the Diaspora).

The moral of the biblical story is clear: do not disobey leaders, or it will turn out badly. God gave them their authority and power. Insofar as Christian fundamentalists look to the example of biblical characters for guidance, they will find examples of people conforming to authority. In that spirit, they will conform to the authority of charismatic leaders of perceived fundamentalist faith with less than usual reservation.

Chapter 6

⁓

Christendom: Government and Tradition

The Prescribed Form of Government in Christian Tradition

Naturally, during the fourth century AD when Christians gained sanctioned religious status within the Roman Empire, they even more completely supported monarchy. That support for monarchy soon became enshrined in Christian dogma. Eventually dubbed "the divine right of kings," the doctrine dictated that God gives kings the right to rule and to be obeyed.

That doctrine prevailed for more than twelve hundred years. The Christian church in the West officially sanctioned monarchy as the form of government ordained by God. The church taught that the best government anyone could ever hope for in this world was a faithful monarchy, one that feared God, served the Lord, and ruled justly.

The goal of the church remained constant. While they may not often have used the term theocracy, the church's intent was to promote God's rule in this world. The very term "Christendom" was a testament to that vision. It meant the kingdom of Christ or Christ's rule on earth. The "doctors" of the Christian faith believed that God's ordained vehicle for

Christ's reign on earth was mediated by faithful rulers. Monarchy was normative throughout the period we know as Christendom. With only a few exceptions the church actively honored and promoted monarchy from the time of the Emperor Constantine onward.

Monarchy took two forms. One was spiritual and the other was temporal. Like its Jewish antecedents, Christian doctrine always differentiated between the two. Theologically, in the western half of the Roman Empire, the church taught that the bishop of Rome was the sole vicar, the sovereign representative, of Christ in sacred matters. The pope ruled the church and its people on behalf of Christ as a spiritual monarch. Likewise, the church taught that the emperor, devout kings, and princes ruled the people on behalf of Christ in secular matters. In 800 AD, in order to reassert and underscore that principle, the pope authorized the coronation of Charlemagne as "Holy Roman emperor." His role was to administer the remnants of the former Roman Empire as Christ's kingdom on earth, Christendom.

Those theological constructs were not as firmly enshrined after the fall of the eastern half of the Roman Empire, however. It is not that leaders of the church in the East disagreed in principle with the goal of Christ's sovereign rule on earth, or that it should be mediated by human monarchs. They simply faced two practical impediments. The first was that they disagreed, in principle, with the preeminence of the bishop of Rome as the sovereign Vicar of Christ. They saw the patriarch of Constantinople and the bishops of other great metropolises as equally eminent and believed that ecumenical councils of bishops (oligarchy) should mediate Christ's rule in sacred matters. Second, the onslaught of Islam throughout eastern sections of the former Roman Empire eventually established Muslim potentates as rulers of the people in secular matters. Naturally, from their point of view, Muslims hostile to Christ could hardly mediate his rule on earth. Hence, in large sections of the former eastern half of the Roman Empire, the doctrine of the divine right of kings was emphasized far less. Their goal was to survive Islamic dominance rather than to rule the world on Christ's behalf.

In the West, the Roman Catholic Church accepted and supported the authority of the emperor and kings in every Christian country. The leaders of the Catholic Church, albeit frequently competing with kings for power and wealth, colluded with monarchs throughout the history of Western Europe. Popes recognized kings. Archbishops crowned them within the context of church ceremonies. Christian leaders legitimized monarchs. Monarchs, in turn, protected the privileged position of the church within their kingdoms. Christian leaders may have squabbled over taxes and the jurisdiction of secular courts in ecclesiastical matters, but they never questioned monarchy as divinely instituted.

The tremendous European upheaval at the confluence of the Renaissance and the Reformation affected virtually every aspect of life and social institution. Religion and government were profoundly affected. The Holy Roman Empire, or what was left of it, practically dissolved. Political lines were redrawn. Local rulers made decisions for their own reasons on whichever flavor of Christianity would prevail in their realms. The English monarch became the head and defender of the Church of England. The pope conferred upon the king of Spain the title, "Defender of the Faith." The rulers of the remnants of the Holy Roman Empire promoted Roman Catholicism. The rulers of the Scandinavian kingdoms established national churches with a bent toward Lutheran Protestantism. Naturally, so did most of the German principalities.

Protestant reformers upheld monarchy just as firmly as the Catholic hierarchy did. Martin Luther, for example, sanctioned the brutal suppression of populist movements. He justified the bloody defeat of the "Peasant's Revolt." European monarchs differed when it came to what version of Western Christianity they adopted, but those different versions of Christianity did not differ from one another when it came to belief in the absolute right of monarchs to rule. All versions of Christianity supported monarchy and its divine right to be sovereign.

As time passed, the European monarchies competed with each other for portions of a new economic frontier. Advances in nautical and military technology enabled the European monarchs to project their power to what had been remote parts of the globe. They found Africa, parts of Asia, and all of what is now called North and South America ripe for their dominance. What those monarchs wanted was more wealth and power. They wanted the natural resources extant within those locations. They wanted the added prosperity that trade in those new resources would bring to their kingdoms. They wanted the added military power that prosperity would buy. They wanted the prestige of additional lands to own and peoples to rule. They wanted to build empires for themselves.

As European monarchs scrambled to develop colonies in other continents, they took their versions of the Christian faith with them. Why? Well, it was partly to dignify their real motives for wealth and power. It was partly to extend their cultural influence. It was partly to win God's good favor for their exploits. And it was partly to satisfy whatever impulses they might have had to propagate their version of the Christian faith.

Whatever the reasons may have been, it created interesting bedfellows. Business adventurers, the military, royal officials, and Christian missionaries all ventured to capitalize on new prospects. In effect, missionaries provided thinly veiled disguises for the actions of venture capitalists and the military adventurers against indigenous populations. Missionaries entered those new colonies to serve the spiritual needs of the colonists and to convert the natives, or at least to deliver them from their benighted ways. They supported their monarchs, and their monarchs protected their missionary efforts, often with brutal military tactics. Many missionaries tolerated the enslavement of the indigenous peoples while trying to convert them. They tolerated the violent suppression of the indigenous populations' efforts at resistance and revolt. Christian leaders cooperated with their monarchs' colonial enterprises in order to gain permission to exercise their own religious efforts among indigenous peoples. Natives had a choice: subjugation or death.

The emphasis on the divine right of monarchs was not equally enthusiastic, of course. The more a monarch supported the efforts of church leaders to extend their version of Christian faith, the more ardently the faithful supported the monarch. The more a monarch promoted the church, the more the church regarded him as divinely inspired and worthy of allegiance. It was essentially a quid pro quo relationship.

As time passed, the European monarchies lost control over their colonies. Governments shifted, but all too often the power dynamics in those colonies did not. For example, former colonies in Latin America often fell under the control of military oligarchs and right-wing dictators. Common people suffered under equally ruthless oppression to what they had experienced under Spanish rule. Dictators tended to function as monarchs. They were consistently authoritarian and often replicated the brutality of Spanish military dominance. Autocrats bolstered the position of the small privileged elite within the countries they ruled. Plantation owners and other members of the elite, in turn, used their wealth to support the dictator in order to ensure the security of their own status.

The stance of the church did not change after colonies gained their independence from the European monarchies. The church normally refused to challenge Latin American dictators. With few exceptions the record of the church hierarchy's support of such authoritarian regimes was consistent with its support of monarchs. Catholic Church leaders largely supported Latin American dictators, or at least remained uncritical of them. That might have been a carryover from the idea of the divine right of monarchs. It might have been an application of the propensity of the faithful to conform to authority. It might have been a tacit support of the dictator's power in order to ensure the dictator's support of the church. In any case, church leaders contented themselves to treat common folks as sheep to be led and comforted without seeking to alleviate oppressive political conditions.

Leaders of the Catholic Church at the highest levels discouraged indigenous believers from resisting dictatorships. Some local ecclesiastical critics who did speak out were suppressed by the religious hierarchy. From the 1960s through the 1980s, certain Latin American clergy spoke out to promote social justice based in the teachings of Jesus. They advocated what has been called Liberation Theology. They had been radicalized by indignation over the injustices and oppression they witnessed. Among the teachings of liberation theologians was an implied justification of revolution. The Catholic hierarchy officially rejected those teachings. The church feared that Liberation Theology might be used by communist revolutionaries to advance their cause. The church totally rejected communism for its atheism and historic suppression of Christian expression. The pope silenced liberation theologians. They were specifically ordered to stop justifying resistance to oppression. Apparently church leaders were willing to sacrifice the economic and political freedom of common people for the sake of the church's freedom. And yet, it was the church's uncritical tolerance for economic inequity and social injustice in Latin America that had helped to create conditions that contributed to the rise of communist movements there. Many Christian leaders seem more comfortable with authoritarianism than with populist democratic movements. That is largely born of the authoritarianism that has been sanctioned in scripture and Christian tradition.

Chapter 7

⌒

Precedent? What Precedent?

No Authoritative Christian Basis for Democracy

The point of this general and admittedly cursory history of government in the Bible and Western church tradition is not to advocate monarchy or any other form of authoritarian government as opposed to democracy. My point is simply to indicate that Christian fundamentalists have no authoritative source of direction from the Bible, history, or Christian tradition to guide them in the exercise of their citizenship in pluralistic democracies. I have never heard fundamentalist leaders preach sermons or teach classes devoted to a theology of democracy, but they abound in kingdom theology. That is simply because no authoritative sources exist for a theology of democracy.

Fundamentalists need authoritative sources to guide their thoughts and actions. And so they will try to make them up as they go, and in such a way as to appear that they have a basis that has been inspired by God. They will look to the Bible and Christian tradition, even though they are devoid of specific guidance for citizens in a democracy. They may argue that St. Paul wrote at length about freedom. But the freedom of which he wrote was individual spiritual freedom. And that is a far cry from a blueprint for democracy as a system of government. They will try to reinterpret American history to justify biblical values. They will try to use democratic processes to institute policies, practices, and laws that replicate biblical laws in order to follow their understanding of God's ways.

Since the models of leadership in the Bible are all authoritarian and autocratic, they will tend to utilize democratic processes to impose their beliefs and values upon a pluralistic society in an authoritarian fashion. In order to rectify the inconsistency, they may try to create new political philosophies, composed of various strains, or simply justify authoritarianism by appealing to "tough" love as their rationale.

American Christian fundamentalists have few political alternatives. They abhor the very idea of monarchy. That is not so much because the Bible teaches it, but because they have been conditioned to do so by American history and ethos. And yet, especially under the burden of frustration, many crave faithful autocrats who will impose their values and beliefs on the rest of the citizenry of the nation. They crave a Moses or a Samuel, anointed and inspired by God, to lead America in the direction they believe it should go. And so they will invest inordinate trust in political leaders who seem to share their own beliefs. They will do so in the hope that those leaders will make the wider community godlier and more receptive to God's blessings.

A member of one of the churches I served was eager for me to impose what she thought should be more godly leadership. It was not that she doubted or disagreed with any elements of my faith. She and others were simply convinced that God wanted me to be more domineering in my leadership. They wanted me to enforce their convictions and to impose them on others. When I refused to do so, they decided to take up the slack by trying to do it themselves. They were frustrated by diversity in the church. And so, symbolic of their hopes, she gave me a sword. She intended the gift as a reminder of the authority I had. She also confided to me that God had told her to "lift me up." Before I left that church the woman asked me what I thought those words meant. I told her that I thought it simply meant that fundamentalists in the church would have done well to listen to me when I advised them to restrain their drive to control others. Fundamentalists are eager for charismatic leaders to exercise strong authority, but only when it serves their convictions. They tend to exclude themselves from its purview when designated authority involves the defense of diversity.

Whether they realize and acknowledge it or not, ultimately the logic of such efforts is to establish God's more perfect rule, to fashion the kingdom of God on earth, a theocratic community. But the efforts of fundamentalists always serve only their own particular vision of God's rule. Such efforts have always failed, precisely because they use increasingly authoritarian methods to impose their own subjective views as if they were absolutely and exclusively true. The inevitable outcome has always been some form of backlash to the authoritarianism and dogmatism of fundamentalism.

Chapter 8

~

Backlash

Attempts at Theocracy Have Always Failed

Perhaps it's the mountainous terrain and concentrations of people isolated from each other, the altitude, or the thinner oxygen levels. Whatever the causes, Switzerland has always been a bit different. Suffice it to say that democracy emerged in some Swiss cantons before it reached anywhere else in the modern world.

Geneva was one such region. It had been under the rule of the Duchy of Savoy. Yet in 1490, two years before Columbus's discovery of the New World, the citizens of Geneva elected its first Grand Council. It was initially composed of fifty members, later of two hundred, who were elected annually.

The Reformation swept into Switzerland in the sixteenth century. The city of Geneva became deeply divided between Catholic and Protestant factions. Deadly street fights broke out among citizens of different persuasions. Religious differences can incite ferocious violence, which is, of course, one of the reasons the founders of American democracy worked so hard to separate church and state. Within a single generation, a majority of Geneva's citizens had embraced Protestant ideals. The bishop of Geneva and many of the Catholic clergy were driven from the city and the surrounding canton.

Inspired by Reformation ideas and ideals and their newfound familiarity with the Bible, a critical mass of the citizens of Geneva heartily wanted to live a different way from the rest of the world. They wanted to reform their churches. They wanted to follow the teachings of the Bible. They wanted to be faithful to God. They wanted to live the way God wanted them to live. They wanted to be God's people. They wanted to experience God's kingdom on earth.

The elected leaders of the Council of Geneva set about that very quest. They were convinced that they needed to institute a practical system of laws, regulations, and methodologies to achieve their goals. And they were equally convinced that those laws should be founded upon biblical revelation.

They began by turning to one man to guide their efforts in reforming their churches. His name was Jean Calvin. He was a devout Protestant reformer, a lawyer, and a theologian. He was one of the greatest Protestant minds of his time and was widely respected in Protestant jurisdictions.

By 1536, Calvin had completed the first draft of what turned out to be his magnum opus, *The Institutes of the Christian Religion*. It was a vast and comprehensive catechism, which remains the standard of traditional Reformed doctrine to this day. It is an extensive code of doctrine, based in sacred scripture. It not only instituted a comprehensive theology but also envisioned the desirability of developing government in which God would be sovereign.

Catching wind of his reputation, in 1541 the city council invited Calvin to move to Geneva. It was their express purpose to employ his services to reform church governance there. After his arrival Calvin wrote *Ecclesiastical Ordinances*. It was a blueprint for how churches should function under the sovereign leadership of God—administered, of course, by church leaders. It called for the creation of "consistories," among other innovations. Consistories were essentially ecclesiastical courts. They enforced standards of orthodoxy and appropriate worship for a church, and the personal conduct of its members. Consistories were instituted to judge infractions in any of those matters.

A crucial change took place, however. Soon after the churches of Geneva adopted *Ecclesiastical Ordinances* and established consistories, Geneva's council decided to take on the role of meting out and executing the judgments made by church consistories. That decision removed the traditional boundary between church and state, and the two estates were effectively merged. As Emanuel Gutman postulated, the government of Geneva derived its legitimacy from God and its legal authority from religion. Calvin's *Institutes* and the *Ecclesiastical Ordinances* established the beliefs, rules, regulations, and laws for churches, but Geneva's decisions implemented them at a state level. The government regulated such personal behaviors as dancing and card playing. The government also regulated the beliefs and religious practices of the citizens of Geneva. In effect, what he and the Council of Geneva instituted was a theocracy, mediated by means of a form of representative democracy.

One incident dramatically illustrates the outcome. Michael Servetus was a widely criticized heretic. Servetus had the audacity to send Calvin a copy of the *Institutes*, in which he had written criticisms of Calvin's ideas. Servetus enclosed a note with the book, asking to visit Calvin to discuss their disagreements. Calvin was incensed. Not long after, Servetus had the bad sense to visit Geneva. He attended Calvin's church to hear one of his sermons. Calvin immediately asked the city council to arrest Servetus. He charged him with heresy, incorrect beliefs about baptism and the Trinity. The council eventually found Servetus guilty and sentenced him to death. He was burned at the stake with a copy of one of his own books chained to his leg. In the process, Calvin became a hero of faith, and his position was strengthened in Geneva. Theocracy can be brutal, and its leaders are not free from the drives of ego and personal retribution.

By 1585, Geneva had begun to turn away from its theocratic aspirations. The Geneva experiment failed in its efforts to institute God's kingdom within a political state. Problems developed almost immediately. Calvin himself was idealized and became too powerful. Calvin's work was exceedingly detailed and comprehensive. It was unwieldy. The elected civil leadership of Geneva became excessively scrupulous. Geneva became legalistic. Geneva became authoritarian. Government methodologies became oppressive. Geneva suppressed individual divergences from the norm. Some citizens oppressed other citizens on religious grounds but for personal gain or revenge. Gradually, the citizens became disillusioned with the injustices and intrusiveness of the system. Eventually, the citizens of Geneva changed their collective mind and rejected their theocratic system.

In many ways, Geneva was the seedbed of Calvinism. Ironically, over time, it became a center of humanism instead. It has become more synonymous with the humanist ideals embodied in such organizations as the League of Nations, the Geneva Conventions, the International Red Cross, and the United Nations rather than the Christian theocratic ideals enshrined in Calvin's vision of an ideal Christian state.

That dynamic is what I mean by backlash. Although it may be predictable in hindsight, backlash may be an example of the so-called law of unintended consequences. Backlash happens when the results of a course of action have been consistently disappointing or significantly hurtful to a critical mass of the people involved or to subsequent generations. The people directly involved feel disappointed, disillusioned, and disgruntled to such an extent that they not only reject the particular course of action, but also the convictions underlying it. They react by embracing different convictions and following different, often opposite, courses of action. History has demonstrated a number of examples of backlash in reaction to attempts to create theocracy.

The Geneva experiment was only one attempt to establish a localized political theocracy. There have been a number of attempts throughout history to create, or rather to cooperate with God in creating, God's kingdom on earth. Some of them have been apocalyptic in nature, like the Shakers, rooted in the ardent conviction that God would soon bring the world as we know it to an end. But other attempts have simply been grounded in the heartfelt human desire to please God, to follow his ways, and to receive God's more complete blessings, like the Puritans and Afrikaners. Perhaps not coincidentally, the Puritans and Afrikaners were influenced by Calvinism, as Geneva was.

The Reformation was a heady time in European history, and a turbulent one. It gave way to the violence of the Thirty Years' War (1618–48). That era of European warfare was a violent sorting out period. The war, or rather those serial conflicts, played out throughout much of Europe.

Those conflicts were fueled by two issues. Politically, the issue involved succession. It concerned who would succeed to the throne of the residue of the Holy Roman Empire. It involved regions strong enough to serve their own interests either by disconnecting from the empire or by remaining under its jurisdiction. But the underlying issue was religious. Battles ensued in various parts of Europe to sort out whether particular regions would remain under Catholic dominance or would exist as independent states. It determined which version of Christianity would be sanctioned in each state. Some principalities were sympathetic to Protestantism and others to Catholicism.

The Treaty of Westphalia temporarily drew political and religious boundaries on the European map. But conflicts continued until the Treaty of Munster in 1648. Even after that treaty was ratified, strife continued within various regions. It concerned which forms of Protestantism would be sanctioned within certain principalities. The question involved the degree to which other Protestant orientations were to be tolerated within jurisdictions in which one type predominated. In Scotland, for example, Calvinist Presbyterians felt compelled to drown Anabaptists in mock charade of their belief in adult baptism by immersion.

In Britain, naturally, the Anglican Church was the official version of Christianity sanctioned by the state. Beginning in the 1560s, one particularly fervent group of religious critics within the Anglican Church was the Puritans. They were inspired by biblical precepts, Calvinist teachings, and their radically scrupulous sensibilities. Puritans saw in the Church of England some of what they considered to be the very corruptions, theological heresies, and papist practices that had been rejected in Catholicism. While they remained Anglican because of their strong convictions about the unity of the church, the basis of their movement was summarized in the motto "Further Reform."

Puritans demanded further reform in the Church of England. They wanted to follow a purer way. They believed that God had called them to purity of faith, worship, morality, and lifestyle. As time passed some Puritans came to see their struggle in apocalyptic terms as contention against the Antichrist.

Not unexpectedly, their fervent criticisms were not well received by the authorities. They felt oppressed by the religious and political establishment due to its resistance to their demands. And so Puritans considered themselves victims of official persecution simply because their reforms were rebuffed and their sensibilities dismissed. They felt that they were not at liberty to exercise their faith as their consciences dictated.

People of ardent faith often feel persecuted for their convictions when they believe that their understanding of God's will is not sanctioned by established authorities. They tend to exaggerate the degree of persecution they suffer and how intolerable it is to them. They tend to demonize the authorities that impede their sense of mission. And those feelings fuel the extent of the actions they are willing to take to follow their convictions.

Reports of life in the Virginia and Plymouth colonies inspired one Puritan lawyer. John Winthrop and some of his brethren explored the feasibility of creating a new colony in New England. His vision was to establish a holy, Puritan commonwealth. Discretely, wealthy Puritans procured a majority share of a business called the New England Company. It is likely that King Charles was unaware that the principal motivation for the company's request for land was inspired more by the vision of establishing a Puritan community than achieving economic gain. The king granted the company a royal charter, which provided land for the company to found Massachusetts Bay Colony in and around what is now Boston.

In 1630, seven hundred Puritans sailed across the Atlantic Ocean in eleven ships to carve out a community in the wilderness of North America. En route, some members of the group became uncertain about their fate and dispirited. In response, Winthrop wrote and distributed a sermon called "A Model of Christian Charity." In it, he set forth a vision that he believed he had received from God. Winthrop understood the Puritans' "great migration" to the New World as divinely ordained. He persuaded them that God had predestined their enterprise. He revealed to them that God would establish them as a "Light on a Hill," one for the world to see and marvel. God had called them to be nothing less than a holy people and a perfect community under God's perfect rule. He envisioned that God would make them into a model Christian commonwealth. Though he did not use the words, it was his vision that the Puritans would be God's kingdom in a new world to begin to make the whole world new. His was an apocalyptic vision, one that was rooted in the notion that God soon would bring history to an end.

The Puritans looked for biblical precedence, of course. They compared themselves to the first people of God in the Bible. So, incidentally, did the Afrikaners of later history in South Africa. Like their Hebrew antecedents, the Puritans believed that their mission was to live as God's people, a uniquely pure and holy people. Like the Hebrews in Egypt, they experienced themselves as living in a hostile society, oppressed in England as fanatics. Like the Israelites, they believed that God was calling them out. Like them, they believed that God wanted them to become a free people, who could practice their convictions under God's rule without abuse. Like the Israelites, they stepped out in faith and faced potential death. They crossed a vast sea to reach their promised land, which they likened to the wilderness that the Hebrews traversed. And like the Children of Israel too, God preserved them. They survived, and that confirmed to them that they were, indeed, God's special people. They were convinced that God had a unique plan for them. Their mission was confirmed by their survival.

They entered their new world. And as they settled down, the Puritans implemented the strict precepts and regulations of their faith. They were so confident that they were called by God to be a light to the rest of the world that they named Boston's main hill "Beacon Hill" and erected a beacon on it. Predictably, after a while, far from experiencing God's unrelenting blessings, there were also hardships, illnesses, and want. They struggled to find meaning in whatever misfortunes they experienced. They came to conclude that since God was faithful and their mission was true, some evil among them must have caused God to withhold some of his blessings from them. Since Puritans were disposed to look for evil forces at work, they concluded either that the devil was oppressing them or that some evil practices must be blocking God's blessings or causing God's punishment.

Puritan leaders were theologically predisposed to think that the devil was attacking them. Preachers regularly warned their congregations that the devil was wandering the streets. They urged faithful Puritans to remain vigilant. Witchcraft was a particular concern.

That was the climate in Puritan villages and towns when three Salem girls began to evidence abnormal behavior. The girls identified witchcraft as the cause. And they accused a Caribbean household servant as the culprit. That was only the beginning. Witch hunt hysteria swept through the Massachusetts Bay Colony. The faithful hunted, prosecuted, and executed witchcraft suspects. That became the prescribed antidote to their afflictions and imperfections. Salem was the epicenter of the witch hunts. Neighbor accused neighbor as the hunt progressed. Often individuals accused others, inspired by calculated personal benefit or revenge. In any case, sincere Puritan spirituality had turned into hypervigilant self-scrutiny. They were compelled to look ever more scrupulously for evils to purge and personal practices to reform.

They had fallen prey to the pathology of Geneva. Their fervent efforts to establish God's kingdom on earth gave way to legalism and authoritarianism, severely enforced. And those efforts became increasingly scrupulous. Brutality ensued.

Fundamentalist efforts for ever-increasing perfection will often become hypervigilant because their faith needs to be relentless. Theocracy, after all, requires perfection, and there are always symptoms of imperfection. Therefore there are always needs for increased efforts at perfection. The intensity of efforts must increase simply to validate the mission and its goal. That is an inner flaw of fundamentalism. Like Geneva, the Puritan mission failed. They were only human, after all.

Once again, backlash ensued. Boston became the hub of the Enlightenment and of eighteenth-century humanism in America. It became the epicenter of deist religion. To this day, New Englanders are among the most resistant Americans to religious fervor. And the Commonwealth of Massachusetts is among the states most criticized for its humanist ideals. Its critics fail to recognize that the Commonwealth of Massachusetts is as liberal or as humanist as it is because of a process of cause and effect. And the original cause was the Puritanical effort to establish theocracy, which spawned backlash to its extreme efforts.

As we have seen, such efforts at theocracy must be mediated by humans, and humans have always been imperfect. Imperfect human intermediaries cannot implement perfection, least of all God's perfect will on earth. That is the fatal flaw in all efforts to institute God's kingdom on earth, no matter how well-intentioned or ardently devout those efforts might be. It may even be blasphemous to think that humans can attain God's perfect intentions. Such thoughts fall prey to the most deadly of sins, pride, which, as the Bible says, precedes a fall or failure and, I would add, backlash.

Of course, fundamentalists usually need to feel uniquely close to God and special to him. They often feel a fervent sense of calling to be a holy people, pure and distinctive. They are convinced that they have a mission to implement God's will. They believe that they have been called to further, if not to create, God's kingdom on earth. Though they may be aware of past failed attempts, they tend to exempt themselves from that likelihood, simply because they are so convinced that God is doing something special with them. But they can never escape the foibles of their own humanity and their imperfections. And so, such pursuits always fail. The people involved often feel frustrated and disillusioned with their failures. They harbor underlying fears that God isn't there, doesn't care, or finds them unworthy. That fear drives them to try to act even more rigorously. And the resulting level of control triggers opposing reactions. It inspires people in subsequent generations to reject the original mission and to follow an entirely different course. That is backlash.

Chapter 9

~

The Power of Eternal Insecurity

The Nature of Insecurity among Fundamentalists

"The Peace of the Lord be always with you." Christians have often said these words to each other, usually within the context of worship services. Christians also often pray for peace, whether for the peace of the world, in the lives of others, or for themselves. Likely, that is because peace is in such short supply in this world. But it is also because of the all-too-rare experience of peace within many Christians.

Many Christians lack contentment with themselves and with the state of their relationship or level of harmony with God. Over the years I have known and had the privilege of being in personal conversations with thousands of different Christian people, including more than a thousand Christian fundamentalists. One of the things that I can say to be true is that many share a lack of contentment, a lack of peace. Perhaps that is endemic to the human condition in general.

Many Christian fundamentalists experience that restlessness, specifically in relation to God. Most yearn to recapture that sense of palpable closeness with God that they experienced at a particular time in their lives—their conversion, their anointing with the Holy Spirit, or any moment of singular experiential closeness, when they felt God's undeniable presence. They will go from church to church, leader to leader, prayer meeting to prayer meeting, event to event, or activity to activity to try to experience, once again, that sense of personal closeness with God.

Forgive the overly personal observation of fundamentalist worship experiences. In many fundamentalist prayer meetings or worship services, particularly those of neo-Pentecostal or charismatic sorts, a pattern customarily unfolds. That pattern ordinarily begins with quiet prayer. Worshippers' eagerness, bordering on physical tension, can be palpable. Quiet prayer begins to give way to a low-level murmur of prayers among participants, sometimes in glossalalia (speaking in tongues). The murmurs of prayer slowly rise and gradually begin to crest into a crescendo. Individuals, aloud, speak their prayers or prophecies or words from God. Others offer approving utterances in response. The crescendo may rise and fade several times. And then there is quiet again, with expressions of gratitude to God.

The more emotions are keenly felt, the more genuine the worship and real presence of God is figured to be. The experience often includes a sense of individual fusion with God and the group, with a fugue sensation. But the most important point is that the participants feel greater confirmation of God's presence, of their faith, and of God's approval.

In the absence of such experiences, or others of equal significance, many will tend to blame themselves. They will identify their need for more—for more prayer, more Bible study, more righteousness, more service, more worship, more involvement in evangelism, more devotion, more sacrifice, more holiness, more fasting, or just more time with God. Some will blame their circumstances and try to find a more faithful, spiritually vibrant, or mission-oriented religious community or leader. Unreceptive to the idea that God never promised serial sensational experiences, many Christian fundamentalists will seek more and more, ever discontent with themselves and with the state of their ordinary relationship with God.

That lack of contentment gives rise to urges for greater commitment. Rarely satisfied with their own level of felt closeness to God and personal commitment, such Christian folks are vulnerable to extremist leadership. And that is especially true for Christian fundamentalists. The craving for more propels them into greater vigilance and greater personal efforts for perfection. And that, in turn, often leads them into ever more demanding efforts of mission to reform the world. That is what has fueled Christian fundamentalist efforts to find communities or missions in which they believe whatever impediments to their closeness to God will be removed.

It really comes down to an issue of trust. Can people be content to trust that God exists and that God loves them if they don't feel it? Absent those experiences and feelings, which confirm God's presence, power, and love, they will try to make efforts to take control in order to prove it to themselves. Some level of fear often drives those efforts. It is the lurking uncertainty that either God isn't there or doesn't care, or that God doesn't find them worthy. And those fears can be unnerving. Some folks will do almost anything to remedy them. Fear is a harsh taskmaster.

There is another fear as upsetting as the idea that God isn't there or doesn't care. It is the fear of eternity. Deeply embedded in the heart of virtually every Christian fundamentalist that I've had the pleasure to know is the desire to trust, love, obey, and please God. While in some instances that bedrock desire is grounded in the love of God, more often it has been grounded in certain insecurities in relation to God. That insecurity has to do with reservations over whether heaven will actually be their destiny.

There is an eternal insecurity within many Christian fundamentalists. By that I mean two things. Many Christian fundamentalists tend to be insecure about what will become of them in eternity. What's more, many Christian fundamentalists feel that insecurity throughout life.

Christian fundamentalists are literalistic in their approach to faith. Christian fundamentalists of a Protestant orientation understand the Bible as absolutely and literally true. Christian fundamentalists of a Catholic orientation understand Catholic doctrine as absolutely and literally true, and sometimes understand the Bible that way too.

I was in college. It was one of those rare occasions, for me at least, when I ate breakfast in the school cafeteria. I was sitting alone, engaged in an early morning trance. Suddenly, my trance was interrupted by one of my fellow students. He asked to join me as he sat down across the table. My only partly welcome breakfast companion watched me as I ate. I looked up and rudely stared back at him. He was an upperclassman and a Bible major. He overcame his reticence and launched into his concern. He asked, "How do you understand the unforgivable sin that Jesus mentioned?"

It was too early in the morning for such a question, I thought. So I replied with a question, in turn. "Why do you ask?" He answered at length, and very upset he was, too. The gist of his story was that he was up late into the night, trying to finish a term paper for one of his Bible courses, due that morning. He prayed for God's Spirit to guide him. But things had not gone well. In his frustration, he cussed at the Holy Spirit. And so he was dreadfully afraid that he had committed "blasphemy against the Holy Spirit" or the "unpardonable sin" mentioned in the Gospels of Matthew, Mark, and Luke. He was terrified that God would reject him for it and send him to hell.

My response seemed to relieve him. I said something like this, as I recall: "The work of the Holy Spirit is to enable people to believe in God, and to trust Jesus. Do you believe any less? The work of the Holy Spirit is to convict people of sin. Are you any less aware of your sins? The work of the Holy Spirit is to help people do better in the future. If you still believe in God and are keenly aware of the unworthiness of this particular act, and you are open to the Spirit's help to use this episode to improve you, then the Spirit is still with you, and, by definition, you haven't committed the unpardonable sin." While he seemed relieved, he still questioned his worthiness before God and his eternal destiny. But I finished breakfast.

The afterlife is graphically described both in the Bible and Catholic doctrine. Both sacred scripture and Catholic dogma describe two ultimate destinies. I say ultimate destinies because while Catholic doctrine includes a state of purgatory in the afterlife, it is inherently transitional and not ultimate. The two destinies are ordinarily referred to as heaven and hell.

With apologies to Dante, the Bible describes hell in far less detail than heaven. And yet, those few details are more graphic and have far more effect. Hell is simply described as a lake of fire in the book of Revelation. In the Gospels, Jesus described it as a slowly burning garbage dump, where its inhabitants remain perpetually deprived of resources, mere fodder for worms.

Heaven is described in detail in the book of Revelation. That imagery includes golden streets, pearly gates, alabaster walls with precious gems, and a great golden throne with the saints perpetually offering their adoration to God. For anyone, except perhaps the random gemologist, jeweler, or cat burglar, such a description of heaven is hardly intriguing. The only compelling feature, frankly, is the presence of God. Even the vision of constant worship must seem boring to most, however. The thought of a three-hour-long worship service is more than most can abide.

The image of flames, eternal deprivation, and gnawing worms, if worms can actually gnaw, far overshadows that description of heaven. And so, naturally enough, most people find themselves more compelled to avoid hell than to attain heaven, except insofar as they might meet loved ones there. Hell is a fearful image of loneliness and suffering.

I dare say that the fear of hell has driven more Christian decisions than the longing for heaven. Jonathan Edwards's now-famous sermon,

"Sinners in the Hands of an Angry God," was the catalyst of the first Great Awakening in America. His sermon featured the description of a spider daggling by its thread over a fire. That was Edwards's portrayal of the state of the sinner. It evoked profound anxiety in his listeners and prompted their desperate Christian commitment. Long before that, of course, many a fledgling medieval church revivalist received his greatest responses to the fear of hell or even purgatory rather than the promise of heaven. That unrivaled papal indulgence salesman, Johannes Tetzel, illustrated the point. He coined a jingle. It was this: "As soon as the coin in the coffer rings the soul from purgatory springs." He did not say, "... the soul to heaven springs."

Fear is a most powerful internal force, but the Bible is full of assurances to quell fear. The Bible says such things as this: "God is love" (1 John 4), "Perfect love drives out fear" (1 John 4:18), and "So do not fear, for I am with you; do not be dismayed, for I am your God. I will strengthen you and help you; I will uphold you with my righteous right hand" (Isaiah 41:10). The opposite of faith is not doubt but fear. And yet fear seems to motivate more fundamentalist behavior than faith or God's love.

How can I say that? It is because I have heard so many Christian fundamentalists talk about their fears. They seem to see threats all around. A number of fears come to mind. There is the fear that God may not be there or care. There is the fear of God's disapproval. There is the fear that loved ones will not be saved. Once there was the fear of the spread of communism because of its oppression of believers. Now there is the fear of the spread of Islam because of its oppression of Christians and those who do not believe in the Muslim image of God. There is still a fear of atheists taking over, of course, but atheists in the form of humanists and liberals rather than communists. There is the fear of secular sex education, the availability of birth control and abortion, because of the threat to moral standards. There is the fear of homosexuality, because it seems to them to threaten the family unit and, therefore, civilization itself. There is the fear of public education insofar as books assigned to children and ideas to which they may be exposed could undermine Christian beliefs and values or the family's influence. There is a fear of government, that is, secular government with humanistic values. The greatest fear that a fundamentalist has, though, is the fear of displeasing God or disappointing him and facing his punishment. Fear intensifies insecurity.

Fear-born insecurity manifests itself in certain symptoms. Some fundamentalist folks primarily direct their insecurities internally, and others direct them outwardly. Those tendencies are similar to what some psychologists would refer to as the depressive versus the paranoid position that people are predisposed to take.

Those who direct their insecurities inwardly are prone to feelings of guilt, shame, anxiety, and impatience, even anger with themselves. They will tend to live in a state of ennui to a greater or lesser extent, and/or to make recurrent heroic strides at self-improvement. I have already listed many of the forms that those strides often take, including more prayer, Bible study, repentance, fasting, time, and efforts at service. Yet those efforts often leave the practitioners still feeling a gnawing sense of personal dissatisfaction.

Those who direct their spiritual insecurity outwardly focus their concerns on others. Not surprisingly, though they are hardly the only ones, fundamentalist leaders are prone to take an other-directed approach. They will identify and concentrate their efforts on the needs for change in other people. This manifests itself in directing other fundamentalists, but also by striving to change those in the wider society in need of conversion, correction, or confrontation. People to be confronted are those who oppose the faith or those who enjoy positions of influence but do not share their beliefs about how wider society should operate.

Fundamentalist leaders tend to be distrustful of those who are different. One simple example of that propensity is that fundamentalist leaders will rarely participate in ecumenical meetings with other Christian leaders, and they will avoid interfaith gatherings altogether. Fundamentalist leaders are prone to be scrupulous about matters of doctrine. They are unwilling to engage in dialogue on an even footing with other religious leaders who embrace different beliefs from their own. They tend to need to be in control.

Fundamentalist leaders also direct their insecurities outwardly by needing to be seen as special and as especially blessed by God in their ministries. The need to see God's blessing usually takes either the form of quantitative or qualitative growth. The growth may involve more people, more religious experiences, more money, more programs, more buildings, more real Christians, or more influence in the wider society. That too is driven by fear. It is driven by the fear that God might not exist, might not approve, or that the leader won't be seen as "God's man."

There are examples of this need to be special. Very rarely will Christian fundamentalist leaders encourage their followers to participate in charitable efforts with the members of other churches. If their own church cannot receive special recognition, they passively discourage participation.

There was a mega church in the California town in which I lived for ten years. It was a fundamentalist church that had a dozen ministers on its staff. During the years I lived there, not one of those ministers attended any of the meetings with the other clergy in that town. They kept to themselves. They remained aloof from other clergy, even though several of them shared similar orthodoxy of Christian faith. I happened to speak with one of the associate ministers of that church. He allowed, "We know that your church has one program that's better than ours, and that your church has been growing. We always knew that the success of our ministries would help other churches grow too." I felt less encouraged than enlightened by his words. I was enlightened to his mind-set. Therein lies the need to be special and blessed perfectly illustrated.

You may notice an inherent symbiotic relationship between Christian fundamentalists and their leaders. Both are often driven by the same fears, but in opposite ways. Both seek the same assurances to assuage their restless insecurities. And each holds the promise for the satisfaction of the other's needs. When a leader offers a program in which participants feel closer to God, the fears of both are lessened and the needs of both for assurance are temporarily satisfied.

The secret in this ever-expanding need for assurance is that it can never fully or permanently be satisfied. The appetite for assurances is insatiable. There must always be more assurance in order to quell that restless insecurity about whether God really exists, really cares, that one really is worthy of God's blessings, or that one will really inherit eternal life. This leads many fundamentalists to be highly susceptible to the uncritical acceptance of trusted leader's assertions about God's will and leading in various matters. That's why this pattern so often manifests itself in the acquisition of more control, whether of one's own life or the lives of others.

Control is another flaw in efforts to establish God's kingdom on earth. Not only are imperfect people unable to accomplish God's perfection, but humans certainly cannot control God's kingdom into being. To assume that God would be in control if only right-minded people of uncompromising faith were in control is absurd. Human control is human control. Divine rule is divine rule. The two are not equivalent, no matter how much people of faith would like to think otherwise. Jesus said that the rule of God is a matter of the heart. God's leadership works from the inside out, not vice versa. By definition, greater human control, no matter how devoutly exercised, cannot achieve God's rule. It only serves to multiply the power of those exercising it and the dependency of those following it. Regardless of how orthodox, how faithful, how biblical, or how motivated by zeal for God, human control over others is not the same as God's leadership.

God's leadership is only accomplished by people's voluntary receptivity and surrender to God, not to other people who claim to represent God. It is an individual matter, which cannot be imposed on others by those who claim to know what God wants. That is where trust comes in. Trusting God means allowing God to be God. It means leaving up to God how other people think, act, or live, instead of trying to do God's work for him by controlling the citizenry of a state.

Chapter 10

⁓

The Spirit of the Pharisees

What Jesus Had against Fundamentalists

That was the essential problem in the approach of the Pharisees. They made every effort to advance God's rule by exerting greater control over others. Jesus warned his disciples about what he called "the leaven (yeast) of the Pharisees." He told his followers to avoid their ways (Matthew 16, Mark 8, and Luke 12). In fact, the twenty-third chapter of Matthew's Gospel is devoted to the subject.

The Pharisees were a Jewish sect that existed back in Jesus's time. They were one among at least five Jewish sects that existed in Palestine at the time. The Pharisees became prominent during a time of intense stress and fear in the history of the Jewish people.

Israel was an ethnic and religious kingdom, a tribal kingdom. It had neither the capacity nor the inclination to extend its influence. It was isolationist in its international stance, except for its trade with neighboring kingdoms. Like other tribal kingdoms, it had limited capacities to cope with the rise of empires. Its sovereignty was frequently jeopardized. Its vulnerability was worsened when it divided into the two rival kingdoms of Israel and Judah. Consequently, for more than five hundred years serial foreign powers dominated the Jewish people, from before the time of the Babylonian Empire through the rise of the Roman Empire. Those empires were polytheistic cultures. Their dominance over Israel was profound and included strong cultural influence. Devout Jews found the religious, moral, and cultural influences of alien societies extremely offensive and threatening to the integrity of their religious culture. The Pharisees came into being to resist those influences and to preserve the purity of Judaism. Some religious historians credit the Pharisees with holding Jewish faith and piety together from the time of the Babylonian Captivity through the Diaspora. Those were times of profound stress and fear for the Jewish people.

In general, fear shows itself. Fear has symptoms. It triggers physical tension and rigidity. Muscles become tense. Breathing becomes more rapid and shallow. Pupils dilate. Adrenalin levels and heart rates increase. Beyond physical changes, fear causes cognitive and psychological changes too. Fear can trigger cognitive rigidity and emotional tension, anxiety, anger, or aggression. Behaviorally, structure or control often reduces the painful feelings associated with fear.

Fear also manifests itself spiritually. Here are a few signs of fear-based, rather than faith-based, spirituality: rigidity, impulses to control, dogmatism, judgmentalism, defensiveness, and anger. Those symptoms, in turn, evidence themselves in efforts to correct and/or control the perceived wayward ways of others. It seeks control over the beliefs and behaviors of other people.

The degree of fear, rather than faith, in the motivation of those who claim to be doing God's good work can always be inferred from some of the aforementioned telltale signs. It is fairly simple to discern whether actions that are attributed to faith are inspired by the Sprit of God or a spirit of fear. You can almost feel the difference. There are basic signs of whether actions attributed to faith are really inspired by God. Jesus said, "A new commandment I give you: love one another … By this all men will know that you are my disciples, if you love one another" (John 13:34f). And again, "I was hungry and you gave me something to eat, I was thirsty and you gave me something to drink, I was a stranger and you invited me in, I needed clothes and you clothed me, I was sick and you looked after me, I was in prison and you came to visit me … Truly I tell you, whatever you did for one of the least of these brothers and sisters of mine, you did for me'" (Matthew 25:35–36, 40). St. Paul wrote them about the signs of faith-based spirituality too. They are temperamental in nature. He called them the fruit of the Spirit. St. Paul wrote, "The fruit of the Spirit is love, joy, peace, forbearance, kindness, goodness, faithfulness, gentleness, and self-control" (Galatians 5:22–23). Humble, need-meeting love demonstrates the Spirit of God and faith-based spirituality.

Are the symptoms of Christian fundamentalist efforts to reshape society characterized by those traits or others?

Several Jewish sects were active in Israel at the time of Jesus. Most of them came into existence in reaction to the intense and particular stresses of that time. Those stressors included external political domination, military occupation, extensive foreign cultural influence, economic depression, and inroads by alien religions.

These stress factors inspired the development of several Jewish sects. The Sadducees already existed. They were the official Jewish leaders, mostly comprised of the priestly class, the Levites, and were more concerned with ceremonial traditions and theological correctness. The Herodians were political supporters of King Herod, the puppet king of the Roman Empire. The Zealots were political activists, rebels, or insurgents. They sought to transform Gentile-dominated Jewish society by violently overthrowing the prevailing powers. They used terrorist tactics. The Essenes were an ascetic sect. They adopted extremely pious lifestyles of self-imposed deprivation and ritual purification. They reacted to the stresses of the time by sequestering themselves in the wilderness by the Dead Sea, withdrawing from the rest of society.

The Pharisees came into being sometime around the Babylonian Captivity, when the Jewish people were enslaved by the Babylonian army and taken to Mesopotamia. Pharisees distinguished themselves by their engagement with the common people of their times. They were largely middle-class Jews, unlike the Sadducees, who were mostly of the upper class. The Pharisees told the biblical stories. They taught the faith. They trained people in moral conduct. They advised people on how to live their lives with practical guidelines derived from strictly biblical instructions. They were extraordinarily devout Jews and were scrupulously righteous in their personal lives. Arguably, the Pharisees were the best of the Jewish sects during the time of the Roman occupation of Israel. The stress factors of the times added urgency to the Pharisees' mission to preserve the fundamentals of Judaism.

So why did Jesus warn his disciples to beware of the spirit (the leaven) of those upstanding and engaged Jewish leaders? It was their scrupulous adherence to the doctrines, disciplines, laws, morality, and religious practices, which set them apart. They were absolutely devoted to the Bible.

The Pharisees were the Jewish fundamentalists of their time. They were absolutely convinced that they were right and tried their hardest to make sure that others conformed to their ways. They were rigid. They were judgmental. They were controlling of others. They were coercive, manipulative, and politically conniving. But it was all motivated by devotion to God, in order to preserve the holiness of God's people in the face of Gentile (godless) influences. The Pharisees were presumptuous. Their confidence in their own approach to religion inclined them to be prideful and self-righteous. Religious pride was the leaven of the Pharisees, and it expressed itself in the audacity to control others. They were self-appointed watchdogs of God regulations.

Jesus warned against such attitudes and behaviors. He said, "Woe to you, teachers of the law and Pharisees, you hypocrites! You shut the door of the kingdom of heaven in people's faces ... You travel over land and sea to win a single convert, and when you have succeeded, you make them twice as much a child of hell as you are … You give a tenth of your spices—mint, dill and cumin. But you have neglected the more important matters of the law—justice, mercy and faithfulness. You should have practiced the latter, without neglecting the former … You clean the outside of the cup and dish, but inside they are full of greed and self-indulgence … on the outside you appear to people as righteous but on the inside you are full of hypocrisy and wickedness … You snakes! You brood of vipers!" (Matthew 23:13 ff).

Throughout history devout Christians have fallen into the trap of the Pharisees. That has been particularly true of those whose dedication has propelled them to positions of leadership. Largely motivated by zeal for God and the drive to protect God's children, such Christians have emphasized doctrinal correctness, precision of religious practice, and scrupulous moral conduct. They have all too often missed the spirit of Jesus's example and teachings for the sake of defending the letter of moral law and imposing it on others. That is the leaven of the Pharisees, and it remains rampant among modern Christian fundamentalists as a group.

Once again, remember that the intensity of the Pharisees' efforts was fueled by several then-contemporary stress factors facing the Jewish people. It was their way of doing God's will, as they understood it, to preserve God's people under stress. They were deeply devout but also highly rigid, controlling, and judgmental. That was triggered by fear, which was engendered by external stressors.

Chapter 11

~

What's Caused the Rise of Fundamentalism?

Stress Factors Contributing to Fundamentalism

As I've mentioned, some would claim that fundamentalism is a uniquely twentieth-century phenomenon. Though I disagree, certainly, the latter half of the twentieth century has seen an unprecedented spike in the expansion of fundamentalism across the globe. Fundamentalism has increased to such an extent that a new era seems to have dawned, an *Era of Fundamentalism*. During that same time frame, not coincidentally, there also has been an enormous increase in the number and severity of stress factors. Those stresses have contributed to the rise and evolution of modern fundamentalism in its various expressions.

I realize that fundamentalists are likely to resist the notion that there may be natural cause-and-effect reasons for the spread of their version of fundamentalism. Many choose to believe that their approach to faith has been inspired by God alone. Likewise, they are prone to interpret similarities in the intensity and spread of other forms of fundamentalism as counterfeit spiritualities, inspired by evil. They prefer to understand the increase of fundamentalism in its various forms as indicative of an intensification of spiritual conflict between God and evil. They see themselves on God's side in that cosmic conflict. But there are other variables to consider.

During the past generation, people in a number of nations have sought to reclaim and reinstitute the traditional principles of their respective civilizations. The core component of most civilizations is religion, whether Shinto, Hinduism, Buddhism, Islam, Judaism, Christianity, or others. Many of the reclamation efforts that have taken place have focused upon the personal conduct of individuals within particular nations. Fundamentalists, certainly Christian fundamentalists, are far more interested in personal and moral, one might even say sexually related, conduct rather than social justice. That is ironic, since the Bible has more to say about justice, the treatment of the poor, and use of money than about sex. Fundamentalists in several societies have also attempted to reshape political policies. They tend to harness feelings of disillusionment and fear or anxiety in the general public and the religious ideals of a critical mass of the citizens within those nations.

Much has been said of causes for the rise of fundamentalism. There are many contributing factors. I will mention several stressors.

Rapid change has taken place in most countries across a wide spectrum of human enterprises during the past century. They have included science, medicine, industry, technology, education, economics, government, communication, and more. That has triggered or been accompanied by an unprecedented number of serial social changes as well. Those changes have taken place at such a rapid rate that the traditional customs and values of nearly every culture have been left reeling. They have impacted most aspects of human life. Of course, not all change is bad. But all changes engender stress, no matter how positive their effects may be. Rapid change causes people to feel stress because they are dislodged from their customary moorings.

Disillusionment with modernity is another catalyst for the spread of fundamentalism. Many people across the globe have been disappointed that the implied promises of modernity have not materialized. It is not so much that science and technology have not improved peoples' lot in life. The contrary has been true. Albeit that access has been unequal; there has been clear and extensive progress in education, medicine, technology, communications, standard of living, quality of life, and longevity. And yet, even with all the progress that has taken place, many people seem to have become increasingly disillusioned.

One reason for that disillusionment has been the rise in the number of secular dictatorships during the twentieth century. Communist governments, claiming to better their citizens' lives, actually dominated their people even more comprehensively, systematically, and brutally than traditional monarchies had. Furthermore, secular dictatorships also removed hope from people's lives. During the twentieth century, secular regimes not only restricted individual freedom, but also suppressed religious expression, which had traditionally been the haven of hope for oppressed peoples. While many secular dictatorships were communist regimes, fascism also spread for a short time, and other secular regimes existed in so-called third-world countries. Some of them were left-wing totalitarian states. Others were right-wing dictatorships.

The secularization of government was not limited to totalitarian regimes, however. People of strong religious faith have identified the forces of secularization in democratic nations as well. That drift has been attributed to modernity.

On another level, the more strides that have been made in science, technology, and on other fronts, the more vacuous human existence seems to be to some people. The question "Is this all there is?" has plagued humans throughout history. The book of Ecclesiastes was dedicated to that question more than twenty-five hundred years ago. It is a question that seems only to become more widespread in the wake of advances in modern science. The question of the ultimate meaning of existence seems to have become more urgent. Modern science and technology cannot offer help in understanding the meaning of human existence. That is not their role.

Though it may seem ironic, it is also quite logical that the less people struggle to exist, the more they look for meaning in their existence. According to several psychologists, changes in human circumstances produce changes in human motivation. In his *Hierarchy of Human Needs,* for example, Herbert Maslow proposed that humans possess basic needs, which when satisfied give way to "higher" motives for behavior. When the need for survival is secured, safety becomes a more pressing motive for behavior. When safety is satisfied, affiliation with others in community becomes more urgent. When affiliation needs are met, self-esteem comes to the fore. Likewise, when self-esteem is accomplished, self-actualization may become a primary motive. Similarly, once the accomplishments of modern science and technology help to satisfy basic needs, humans are motivated to affiliate and then to do what they can to achieve meaning. Fundamentalism provides both close affiliation with others of shared core beliefs and a clear sense of ultimate meaning.

Whether the people subject to it realize it or not, uncertainty about the meaning of human existence gives rise to a feeling of **existential crisis**. Science is a tool for research, understanding, and innovation. Its many and varied pursuits do not give meaning to life, except perhaps to those directly involved in these pursuits. Inasmuch as people try to discover existential meaning through the natural sciences, the meaning they find may well be dissatisfying.

At this point in the advance of science, for example, we humans find that we are organisms that have emerged from the biochemical rudiments of this habitable planet. Insofar as scientific inquiry can determine, humans seem to have an instinctual prime directive. Like all organisms, that most basic human instinct is to pass on and preserve our own individual genetic code.

Some people find that raison d'être unsatisfying. Perhaps that is due to the mixed blessing of human frontal lobe development, which among other things causes humans to reflect upon such matters as existence and meaning. Fundamentalism is a reaction to the apparent indignity of the meaning that scientific description has to offer.

And yet that very drive to reproduce and preserve genetic codes provides another motive for the spread of fundamentalism. Humans need to **safeguard offspring**. Parents are powerfully driven, scientists might even say genetically hardwired, to safeguard their young at all costs. It is a (God-given) instinct. In the United States many parents have demonstrated their desire to exercise increased levels of control over ever widening parameters of their children's lives. One simple illustration of that escalating drive to safeguard offspring has been the compulsion of parents to plan, structure, and oversee children's discretionary time.

The malaise, the ennui abroad in the modern world has given rise to escapist behavior patterns. Fundamentalists would attribute those escapist behaviors to modernity. Whether that is valid or not, escapism is one of the contributing factors to various sorts of addictive behavior. One way in which humans escape the futility of existential uncertainty is through substance abuse.

Parents want to protect their young from substance abuse and other dangers as well. Many parents, particularly fundamentalists, want to exercise control over increasing aspects of their children's environment. That includes the few times their children are out of direct contact, such as while they are at school. It is not accidental that much of the tension between fundamentalism and wider society galvanizes around the education of children. They want more control over who teaches their children, what they teach them, and how they do it. That has triggered political battles in public school districts. It has also created a demand for and the proliferation of fundamentalist schools of various persuasions.

It is not coincidental that particular attention has been paid to matters having to do with the origins of life and sex education. They relate to faith and personal conduct. Those subjects have the capacity to cause cognitive dissonance between the fundamentalist mind-set of parents and their children. Many parents want their children to share their beliefs, values, and worldview. Public education may expose children to other ideas. That threatens some parents. Concepts pertaining to the origins of life and sex education bear most directly on the values and beliefs of a family. They are connected to the meaning of existence. The rearing of children is a contributing factor to the rise of fundamentalism. It promises parents more comprehensive control over their children's thoughts, values, safety, and well-being.

Globalization has also had a significant hand in fueling the fundamentalist agenda. As the world becomes smaller—that is, as people become more aware of the cultures and conditions of people in other parts of the world—they are immediately presented with questions such as, "What do I think about that: religion, custom, practice, lifestyle, or way of being in the world?" Entertaining other ways of being and thinking raises questions about one's own practices and beliefs. And that questioning increases the potential for cultural relativism. I understand relativism as a mind-set that is aware of cultural differences and that regards those differences as matters of preference. Relativism tends to respect differences. Relativism does not discourage consideration or even adoption of the practices of other cultures. It may encourage adaptation of traditional cultural beliefs and practices. Relativism contradicts absolutism. It creates a climate in which various cultural options may be considered on something of an equal footing.

Communications technology has increased the pressure of **relativism**. Segments of every society have become more keenly aware of new and different ways of thinking and living. Some people find those ways compelling, and others do not.

Consider the so-called "Arab Spring" phenomenon. Communications technology and social media exposed people to their own conditions compared to the rest of the world. The citizens of several Islamic nations were dominated by autocratic regimes. Citizens became aware that conditions in their countries were less desirable than conditions in other countries. They became more dissatisfied with the political and economic conditions in their own countries. New communications technology and social media made them aware of fledgling protest movements in other countries. That bolstered their courage to demand that changes be made in their own nations. Their newfound awareness exploded into mass protests against the status quo. Protesters throughout the so-called Arab world demanded democratic reforms in order to promote justice. The nations in which those protests took place fell into disarray within only a few weeks of each other, like so many dominoes. Several of them have collapsed, and efforts have been under way to develop new systems of government in those nations.

The new consciousness that modern technology raises does not always inspire acceptance of new or different ways of life. It threatens those who do not share fascination with culturally different ways. The threat of social change causes some people to react against it. There has been a backlash in many sections of the world against the diversity and cultural relativism that global awareness threatens to bring. The most basic way to resist social change is to reclaim core cultural traditions. Fundamentalism is the most thoroughgoing expression of backlash to globalization and cultural relativism.

A natural partner to globalization is **migration**. Human migration has always taken place. During the previous four centuries, it was most often Europeans who migrated to other civilizations. During the period of Western colonialism, Europeans migrated with the full confidence that their culture was superior. They ordinarily imposed their cultural standards upon the indigenous populations. Otherwise, they segregated themselves in expatriate enclaves and immersed themselves in familiar cultural norms, often more rigidly adhered to than in their homelands.

There were precipitous declines in colonial domination after each of the world wars of the twentieth century. Previously colonized nations often discarded many of the trappings of Western civilization. That cleared the way for indigenous peoples to reassert their own traditional cultural norms. That has incentivized the strength of fundamentalism, as indigenous people have appropriated their own cultural and religious heritage.

Population fluidity has given strength to fundamentalism. Currently, far more people migrate from other civilizations into traditionally Western nations. That has caused the same reaction in two opposing directions. Population fluidity predisposed immigrants from other civilizations and the indigenous citizens of the Western nations to adopt fundamentalist expressions of their respective religions.

Immigrants to Western nations feel dislodged from their native civilizations. They react as most immigrants always have. Immigrants act as Europeans colonists did. New immigrants cling to their own customs, often in intentionally rigid ways. They create havens for themselves in alien lands. That lends itself to fundamentalist tendencies.

That, in turn, threatens the indigenous people of the nations into which people migrate. The indigenous citizens frequently react by clinging to their own traditions in increasingly vigorous ways. It is a tribal urge by which people try to secure their customary identity in the face of alien alternatives or challenges to it. And that inclines Westerners to be more receptive to fundamentalist tendencies.

It may seem ironic at first thought, but **literacy** is another contributing factor in the rise of fundamentalism. Religious fundamentalism is almost always rooted in some body of sacred literature. One of the reasons that literacy has the capacity to promote fundamentalism is that sacred texts can be read by more people. For the preponderance of history many religious practitioners either did not have direct access to their sacred texts or they were unable to read them. They were unable to school themselves in the fundamental axioms of their particular faith. With the advancement of literacy many more people have been able expand their knowledge of the fundamentals of their religious traditions.

Throughout history, religion was passed on by word of mouth. Oral tradition was the normal way in which faith was passed on among pre-exilic Jews and for the majority of Christians for more than fifteen hundred years. Oral tradition is the spoken word. It is usually presented in story fashion or by repetition. When people listened to a story, they thought about the moral of the story or the symbolic meaning of the words. They used their imagination. Allegory and metaphor were normal ways of understanding much of the Bible. That was the way average believers heard God whisper to them through the words they heard. During much of the history of the Christian church, readers followed an approach called "lectio divina." It was also based on imagination. But that approach has largely fallen by the wayside in modern times.

In the modern world, people are trained to read in two different ways. Literature is broken down into fiction and nonfiction. If a book is fictional, it is made up. People read fiction for entertainment and inspiration. The right side of the brain is employed to a greater extent. If a book is nonfiction, it is factual. People read nonfiction to learn information that they can apply concretely. The left side of the brain is engaged to a greater degree. People trained in Christian fundamentalism are certainly not taught to read the Bible as fiction. They are instructed to read the Bible as nonfictional literature. Their education conditions them to approach it with the intent to gain information and to apply it concretely. Obviously, that has given rise to a literalistic way of interpreting the sacred scriptures. Whereas for many centuries, both in rabbinical and Christian tradition, allegorical and metaphorical interpretation were normal ways to understand much of the Bible, factual ways of reading are now in vogue. That lends itself to literalistic interpretation of sacred texts, and that feeds a fundamentalist approach.

Another contributing factor to the rise of fundamentalism is **cognitive overload**. It is connected with scientific advancement, relativism, and literacy. For most of history, educated people were actually able to read all of the literature available to them in the languages they spoke. During the past one hundred years there has been an enormous proliferation of information. It is available through various media. In fact, whether they want it or not, people are constantly exposed to information. They are saturated with data. People are overloaded with information. Not only is there more data than anyone can grasp, but experts disagree on the interpretation of the data. The average person feels overwhelmed and confused. Many people react to that information overload by trying to limit it. One way to limit information overload and to reduce the confusion it causes is to simplify the manner in which is received. People are increasingly prone to select media for receiving information that will help them organize and interpret the data from particular ideological points of view.

Fundamentalism offers people overloaded with information, overwhelmed by different interpretations of it, and cognitively confused a comprehensive and well-organized system for understanding the world. That has the benefit of reducing the volume of information, reducing confusion, providing an interpretive framework, and offering a system for integrating data and incorporating or rejecting new data. That approach reduces anxiety from overload and provides ultimate meaning.

Fear is probably the most compelling factor that has given rise to the sudden spike in the prevalence of fundamentalism. Everyone experiences fear. Fear and sadness are the most universal negative feelings that humans experience. Fear can be roused by any of a vast number of external factors, as well as by internal dynamics. There are all sorts of causes of fear in the contemporary world. To attempt to name all of them would be futile, and so I will simply mention a few. While the fear of nuclear holocaust is far less than it was during the Cold War, it still exists. The fear of economic insufficiency is as widespread as ever. The fear of change is everywhere. There is a pervasive fear of the loss of rootedness and identity. But there are even more basic fears at work these days as well. There are real dangers facing humanity, now more than ever. Some people are terrified by those threats.

Overpopulation is an imminent threat. The world's population exceeds seven billion. It has been growing inexorably. The impact of that growth will continue to increase demand for what will likely be diminishing supplies of available resources. Increased numbers of any species most certainly always has an increased impact on habitat. That is especially true of humans.

Humans are higher maintenance than any other species. Most other species adapt themselves to their environments. We humans have the capacity to adapt our environments to ourselves. That capacity has lowered our tolerance for discomfort and inconvenience. When we want shelter from the elements and from others, we create new surroundings by building shelters. That takes resources. When we are cold, we heat our surroundings. That takes resources. When we are hot, we cool our surroundings. That takes resources. When it is dark, we light our surroundings. That takes resources. When we want to travel, we use contraptions to transport us. That takes resources. When we want to preserve our food, we use containers and contraptions to keep it fresh. That takes resources. When we want to communicate with others, we use technology to traverse distance. That takes resources. These have engendered an insatiable appetite for the resources we use to meet our needs for comfort and convenience. One could say that we have become the species best known for our consumption of resources. We have come to rely upon resources for comfort and discretion as well as for survival.

The more of us there are, the more the impact will be. According to the United States Census Bureau and the United Nations Population Fund world population never exceeded one billion people from the beginning of human existence until 1800 AD. By 1927, only one hundred and twenty-seven years later, the world's population doubled to two billion. Human population increased to three billion in 1960, only thirty-three years later. On average world population has increased by one billion people every thirteen years since that time. The population of the world has nearly quadrupled in less than one hundred years and is predicted to increase to more than nine billion, by approximately twenty-eight percent, by 2046. There are obviously far more humans living on earth in the current generation than ever before and our numbers will only increase. In 1993, representatives of the academies of science from nations all over the world gathered for what has been called the New Delhi Summit. They agreed that increased population will inflate demand for resources and will hasten the depletion of the basic natural resources upon which all life depends.

The threats attendant to **climate change** generate widespread fear. Climatologists warn that Earth has been reacting to human overpopulation, consumption, and industry. Human impact increasingly threatens to compromise the environments in which people live and the natural ecosystems for all life. Global warming threatens to cause resource depletion. Potable water will become insufficient for human needs and the needs of other forms of life. Widespread droughts will decrease the availability of land for agricultural use. The oceans will become so over-fished and compromised by pollutants that saltwater food sources will be dramatically reduced. The polar ice caps will melt, causing sea levels to rise, jeopardizing the current habitats of a critical mass of humanity. It is likely that there will soon simply not be enough natural resources to go around.

Worldwide drought, flooding, dislocation, homelessness, malnutrition, famine, and poverty are overwhelming prospects. Such threats seem not only frightening, but also nearly inescapable. What are people to do? Humans must radically change their ways, or their lives will be radically changed. The threats of environmental disaster and depletion of essential human resources hang over the collective head of humanity like Damocles's sword. Denial is one psychological defense against it. Fundamentalism is another.

The **pattern of destructive human behavior** is threatening as well. Like many species, humans compete with each other for food and habitat. Albeit that we have the cognitive capacities to solve the problems connected to resource distribution in other ways, humans have resorted to violence more efficiently during the past one hundred years than ever before. During that time frame, more than half a billion people have been killed by warfare, genocide, and disease or starvation resulting from inequitable resource distribution.

The record of collective human behavior does not engender confidence. The brutality of the human treatment of others, even of our own species, has been all too consistent. Self-interest and counterproductive levels of competition have significantly impeded the human ability to resolve conflicts. People's capacity to cooperate, collaborate, and solve pressing problems has been inadequate. And that has given rise to greater cynicism about the human capability to work together to avert the dire threats that face the world.

In part, it is precisely because we are conscious of declining resources that human behavior has become radicalized during the past generation. Competition has reached a fever pitch. Madness is abroad among humans throughout the world, and I suspect that it is rooted in desperation. It is the fear of threat to safety and survival. Humans are violently acting out their fears in some parts of the world.

Africa has been the most obvious stage upon which the drama of competitive violence has been played out in recent years. Sub-Saharan Africa has been embroiled in a continental war for more than ten years with more than five million casualties. The region of those conflicts occupies an area larger than all of Western Europe. While its identified focus is largely tribal and religious, its underlying cause is fear. Africans are engaged in competitive struggles for dominance and for power over the resources needed for survival.

Nations throughout the West and Asia, to a lesser extent, have been riveted by **economic and energy crises**. Those crises have been prolonged. Large segments of populations in Europe and North America are suffering from reduced standards of living and higher levels of unemployment.

The current global economic upheaval has begun to call into question the long-term viability of the economic systems upon which standards of living in the so-called developed world have been based. Current economic conditions have dealt serious blows to the financial solvency of governments in several of those nations. Greece, Iceland, Portugal, and Ireland are in jeopardy. Spain and Italy are in danger. That, in turn, has undermined the ability of Western nations to provide basic social programs for the citizens most in need of them. Panic has gripped citizens who depend upon the social safety nets provided by those nations.

It is also increasingly apparent that carbon-based sources of energy will become insufficient. Traditional carbon-based energy sources cannot indefinitely continue to provide the power for increasing demands for heat, light, cooling, communications, and industry, upon which modern life and commerce depend. The rise of Asian economies has compounded the problem. Both China and India are populated by more than one billion people. The level of their competition for jobs and energy sources has increased. Both monetary and energy supplies have been depleted by overextension.

Economic crisis breeds uncertainty. Energy shortages breed uncertainty. When people feel uncertain, they feel vulnerable. They try to find something certain to rely upon. Fundamentalism specializes in certainty.

Several democratic nations, including the United States and some member nations of the European Union, have **dysfunctional governments.** Some of them seem to have been rendered incapable of effectively responding to pressing economic and social problems. Democracies appear impotent, not so much for lack of possible strategies as by political polarization. Under stress, they have been torn apart by political and ideological differences. Belgium, for example, was unable to form a functioning government for more than a year. For the first time in its history the United States government was nearly unable to reach agreement to pay the bills that it had already incurred. Power politics have replaced pragmatic compromise, even in the most basic legislative matters. Defeating those of differing political or ideological perspectives has replaced practical problem solving as the central goal of elected leaders. People of differing perspectives dehumanize each other and seem to be unwilling to achieve compromised settlements. Their goal seems to be to gain power for their respective positions.

When there is no effective and benevolent power that can be relied upon to solve problems in this world, people are inclined to find it beyond this world. Faith in God provides a real alternative to faith in government. God is the ultimate power, completely benevolent and effective. Fundamentalism offers an unequivocal belief system, which promises that God will be on the side of whoever is on his side.

Moral decay is a shared concern among Christian, Islamic, Jewish and other renditions of fundamentalism. Fundamentalists of various denominations identify moral corruption as the most urgent problem facing their cultures. More than that, it is their most highly motivating shared concern. The issues about which they are most concerned are sexual in nature. They include profound consternation about premarital sexual activity, extramarital sexual involvement, personal physical exhibitionism, immodesty, feminism, divorce and remarriage, pornography, pedophilia, homosexuality, abortion, and contraception. They are seen as the primary symptoms and agents of immorality.

Fundamentalists also see them as the basic catalysts of social disorder and decadence. They believe that sex undermines religious faithfulness more than anything else. They regard sexual issues as primary causes of everything from cultural devolution to economic destitution. Each sect of modern fundamentalism identifies sexual moral corruption as the central problem facing its own civilization. Each one considers it to be the single most dangerous factor contributing to the potential fall of civilization itself.

The peoples of the world have rarely been confronted simultaneously by so many and such serious changes or threats. All of these factors are common knowledge. And it is precisely because they are common knowledge that they trigger strong human reactions. The net effect of all those factors, taken together, has been to create intense stress, which fundamentalism offers to relieve.

An historic confluence has taken place. The convergence of so many different overwhelming stress factors has engendered within many people a profound craving for certainty and solutions. The peoples of the world, glutted with problems, are desperately looking for certainty and solutions. Fundamentalism has certainty to offer and solutions looking for problems to solve. The question is less one of why fundamentalism has proliferated during the past forty years as opposed to why it would not.

Chapter 12

—

Stresses and Defenses

How Humans Defend against Stress

Beyond the understandable need to find certainty and solutions, threats and stress trigger a variety of human defense mechanisms. Defense mechanisms both lend themselves to the appeal of fundamentalism and to the current politicization of fundamentalism.

Many are familiar with the results of behavioral experiments with laboratory rodents. One of the best known was conducted by John B. Calhoun in 1968-69 under the auspices of the United States National Institute of Mental Health. In the study four pairs of male and female rats were confined to a large, eighty-one square foot case containing all the resources that they required. The population of rats doubled by normal reproduction every fifty-five days until space and resources were insufficient to the population. When the number of rats in the container multiplied to six hundred and twenty the rodents' behavior changed dramatically. They became uncharacteristically isolated from one another. Alpha males abandoned protective functions. The behavior of the females generally became more aggressive. Beta males became reclusive. Adults rejected, prematurely weaned, and physically wounded newborns. Reproduction decreased, offspring died off, and the rat population declined precipitously. Under the stresses of population density behaviors changed and new defense mechanisms were triggered.

Stress significantly affects all creatures. Stressors trigger defensive reactions in most species. Some of those defenses are helpful. Stress causes some clustering creatures to behave in altruistic, self-sacrificial ways in order to divert threats away from their offspring and others in the group. When a goose becomes ill or injured and is forced to ground, two others will remain with it until it has recovered or died. Many creatures will become uncharacteristically aggressive toward predators or serve as decoys to preserve their young. Then again, some defense mechanisms are not helpful. Deer are famous for freezing in the headlights of oncoming cars. Confronted by predators, some goats become paralyzed and actually collapse. Under stress, creatures react in exaggerated ways. Some defensive behaviors are effective, and some are not.

While we like to think of ourselves as different from "lower" forms of life, humans react to stress as well. Stress is ordinarily experienced as interior agitation. That agitation often takes the form of anxiety or fear. Anxiety and fear are emotionally painful. Psychological pain evokes psychological defense mechanisms. Stress frequently triggers behaviors patterned by those defense mechanisms. Over time, unrelenting stress raises the general level of felt, free-floating agitation. Those feelings can cause both individual and collective patterns of defense. Some of those defensive patterns can be productive, and others can be counterproductive.

Defensive patterns of behavior are most often individual in nature. Sigmund Freud postulated a number of defense mechanisms. He identified psychological defenses that individuals employ to defend the ego from the harsh reactions of the superego to impulses from the id. In other words, Freud observed and named ways in which people protected their sense of self from feelings of disapproval in reaction to their own unacceptable thoughts, emotions, or actions.

Insight into defense mechanisms has expanded considerably since Freud's initial hypothesis. In his book *Adaptation to Life*, George E. Vaillant proposed different levels of human defense mechanisms. I will attempt to distill and summarize in my own words Vaillant's four categories of defense. They include what he called pathological defenses, immature defenses, neurotic defenses, and mature defenses.[vi]

Vaillant has identified five **pathological defense mechanisms**. One is *delusional projection*, in which individuals project dangerous motives or actions onto others in ways that may be understood to be paranoid or unrealistically malevolent. Another is *denial*, which is simply refusal to accept external reality. A third is *distortion*, which involves reshaping external reality to meet internal needs. *Splitting* involves dichotomized thinking, a propensity to attribute goodness to some and evil to others, thinking simply in black and white terms. *Extreme Projection* is an exaggerated version of projection, which is the displacement of internal thoughts and feelings to other(s). These mechanisms are always seriously counterproductive and self-defeating.

Under stress, people may react by regressing emotionally and/or physically. According to Vaillant, there are six **immature defense mechanisms**. One is *acting out*, which is physical behavior that directly expresses internal wishes or impulses. *Fantasy* is a way to escape from stress by retreating into imagination to relieve conflicts. *Idealization* is conceiving of another in grandiose terms and behaving in ways that are congruent with those thoughts. Another is *passive-aggression*, in which a person diverts negative feelings into unrelated negative actions. *Projection* is displacement of internal thoughts or feelings outside oneself and onto others. *Somatization* is the experience of negative feelings manifested in physical symptoms. While not often as out of touch with reality as pathological defenses, these defenses are also self-defeating and often quite counterproductive in their outcomes.

The number of ordinary neurotic defenses is so extensive that listing them will have to suffice. **Neurotic defense mechanisms** include displacement, dissociation, hypochondria, intellectualization, blaming, rationalization, isolation, reaction formation, regression, repression, undoing, and withdrawal. Neurotic defenses are less unproductive and more commonly employed than either pathological or immature defense mechanisms. But they do not ordinarily promote higher levels of functioning or positive outcomes.

It is important to note that Vaillant also identified several far more positive defense mechanisms. Reminiscent of some of the effective defense mechanisms of other creatures, humans also have what Vaillant calls **mature defense mechanisms**. One is *altruism*. Altruism is the capacity to conceive of hardship as serving a higher good and to act self-sacrificially for others in the service of that higher good. *Anticipation* is the ability to calculate future stress or hardship and to develop plans to address it. *Humor* is an ability to apprehend comical elements in painful conditions and to communicate them in ways that cause others to laugh so as to reduce the pain for others and oneself. *Identification* is the process of connecting personally with the positive attributes or actions of others and seeking to emulate them. *Introjection* is the act of internalizing positive experiences or the positive attributes and actions of others, and personally drawing them within oneself. *Sublimation* is the exercise of self-discipline. A person is able to refrain from or postpone the pursuit of thoughts, feelings, or actions that are unhelpful when they arise. *Thought suppression* is the active discontinuation of a thought that would be counterproductive. Humans may employ mature defense mechanisms to deal with stressors and the agitation they trigger. They are effective and often produce positive outcomes.

According to the Bible and Christian tradition, faith is meant to be the primary defense against stress. Faith is the means by which what Vaillant calls mature defense mechanisms are activated. St. Paul called those mechanisms "the fruit of the Spirit." He listed nine of them, including love, joy, peace, patience, kindness, gentleness, goodness, endurance, and self-control. Vaillant identified self-sacrificial service, humor, anticipatory planning, emulation of good qualities, internalization of positive attributes, sublimation of inappropriate actions, and suppression of negative thoughts. The parallel is remarkable, given the two thousand-year interval between the two lists.

Stressors can prompt collective defense mechanisms as well as individual ones. Most of us have heard terms like mob mentality to try to explain spontaneous incidents of destructive behavior involving groups of people. Lynch mobs, massacres, and riots fall into this category.

The study of history includes heinous patterns of collective behavior, which mob mentality simply does not seem to explain. They have been premeditated and systematized. Recent history has witnessed extreme examples. The Holocaust, in which more than ten million European civilians were exterminated during World War II, was the most notorious. In Southeast Asia hundreds of thousands were slaughtered following the withdrawal of US forces. Another instance was the Rwandan genocide, when more than eight hundred thousand civilians were massacred during a span of merely three months. Most of them were Tutsis killed by Hutus. Yet another was the so-called ethnic cleansing perpetrated by Bosnian Serbs against Muslims, which took place during the Bosnian War. Those were not incidental or spontaneous, but were prolonged, systematic, and extreme patterns of malevolent group behavior.

Professor Vamik Volkan of the University of Virginia, in collaboration with others, has proposed a number of group defense mechanisms. They are symptomatic of "group regression." In *Blind Trust: Large Groups and Their Leaders in Times of Crisis and Terror,* Volkan describes group regression as a process whereby large groups of people or critical masses of populations revert to immature patterns of behavior in defense against real stressors and perceived threats.

Group regression may involve a number of defense mechanisms. They include the following: *rallying* around a leader to an exaggerated degree takes place when people surrender their individuality to a group or the leader(s) of a group. *Splitting* involves adopting an us/them, black/white mentality. It identifies those within the group as good and others, outside the group, as bad. *Paranoia* perceives evil foes that do not actually exist. *Narcissistic preoccupation* involves convictions of the exceptional superiority of the group in the past. *Magical thinking* is the belief that an individual or new societal pattern will save the group. *Perennial mourning* is a condition characterized by the group becoming stuck in grief over what the group has lost. *Reactivation of chosen past glories* involves remembering when the group was great. *Reactivation of past traumas* involves remembering when the group was victimized. *Ruining basic trust* is the practice of teaching members of the group to distrust others outside the group, especially identified adversaries. *Heightening leaders' importance* idealizes the identified leaders of the group and how important they are to the future of the group. *Magnification of minor differences* emphasizes any differences that exist between the group and others and inflates their importance. *Dehumanization* is the process of negating the shared humanity of identified enemies. These patterns of group behavior were inferred from past instances in which populations perpetrated heinous acts over prolonged periods of time.[vii]

My purpose in mentioning defense mechanisms is to point out that periods of intense and enduring stress are liable to trigger both individual defenses and group regression. As the previously mentioned stressors continue and perhaps intensify, it is likely that there will be increased tendencies to employ defense mechanisms, both individual and collective ones.

Collective defense mechanisms may cause dysfunction in government and society at large. Politicians in the United States have employed some of those identified regressive group defense mechanisms. Splitting has certainly taken place. During such critical times as these, it is clearly regressive for elected leaders to resort to fueling us/them, black/white thinking in dealing with extremely serious problems for which no one has proven solutions. Narcissistic preoccupation has begun to take place. The term "American exceptionalism" has frequently been used in public discourse lately. It is an obvious way of emphasizing the nation's exceptional superiority and is regressive. Magical thinking happens when unproven economic theories are raised to a level of social salvation, and that is regressive. When politicians magnify minor differences among their various points of view, regression is taking place. Regression is also taking place when those of different political points of view dehumanize each other and show signs that they have come to conceive of each other as objects of threat or evil.

These phenomena illustrate several points. Stressors exist. Stress has been experienced. Stress evokes painful feelings. Humans react to painful feelings by employing regressive group defense mechanisms as well as individual ones. These patterns of regressive group defense promote dysfunctional outcomes. Group leaders are as vulnerable to these dynamics as anyone else. Worse still, they can also harness these dynamics to manipulate others to support their positions and power.

Fundamentalism is a comprehensive way whereby individuals may defend themselves from overwhelming stressors and fears. It provides a ready means of denial, simply by focusing attention on the axioms of belief or values rather than on emergent universal problems and how to solve them. Denial is neither a mature defense mechanism, nor is it born of faith. Fundamentalism claims to offer certain rescue from those very real dangers, which will save the world or will, at the very least, save the faithful from it. It provides objects to be blamed and scapegoats to be driven away. These objects may be Satan (the force of evil) or ideological adversaries, citizens of different persuasions or who lead objectionable lifestyles from their point of view.

The 9/11 attack on American targets by Islamic fundamentalist terrorists was one of the most traumatic events and significant stressors of this generation. Arguably the two most influential Christian fundamentalist leaders in America at that time responded to the attack almost immediately. The Reverend Jerry Falwell and Pat Robertson engaged in a televised conversation. I followed their discussion. The two agreed completely. As notable as what they emphasized was what they neglected to emphasize. They did not labor at any length on why God lets terrible things happen to innocent people. They did not discuss the importance and difficulty of following Jesus's teaching to forgive those who hurt us. They did not emphasize how Christians might help the people directly involved.

Instead, Falwell and Robertson agreed on the cause of the success of the 9/11 attack. They believed that the attack was a message from God to America. They agreed that the success of that attack was God's judgment on America. What was the focus of God's judgment? It was not judgment for any of the direct complaints of al-Qaeda, which had motivated that deplorable terrorist attack. It was not for American materialism, which al-Qaeda despised for its supposed infection of Islamic civilization. It was not for American military forces occupying Saudi Arabia, which al-Qaeda deplored because armed infidels were present in their holy land. It was not for unequivocal American support of Israel against Palestinians, which outrages radical Muslims.

Instead, Falwell and Robertson agreed that it was God's judgment of America for accepting homosexuality and abortion as permissible alternatives. Although President George W. Bush appropriately quashed their comments, many Christian fundamentalists inwardly agree. The analysis of those two fundamentalist leaders was extremely revealing.

Surely, stress of the magnitude engendered by 9/11 triggers defense mechanisms. But consider what mechanisms were generated. None of them were the mature ones described by St. Paul or Dr. Vaillant. On the contrary, consider the pathological defense mechanisms that such a response betrayed: denial, distortion, blaming, and splitting. Consider the regressive group defense mechanisms of splitting, ruination of basic trust, and dehumanization of others that it betrayed. The reaction of Falwell and Robertson was to blame and scapegoat segments of

American society. It hardly followed the pattern of behavior that Jesus demonstrated. Their reaction was as devoid of the fruit of the Spirit as it was of mature defenses. Jesus told his disciples to pay attention to the fruit of would-be leaders. Pay attention to the fruit of fundamentalism.

Christian fundamentalists and their leaders are subject to the same negative impulses and defense mechanisms as anyone else. They are only human, after all. But to represent those defensive mechanisms and the words or actions they prompt as God's inspiration, God's Word, or God's will is delusional at best, or worse, intentionally deceptive.

Each fundamentalist sect has plenty of adversaries to blame and demonize. Islamic fundamentalists demonize the West, especially the United States and Israel. Christian fundamentalists demonize liberals, humanists, proponents of gay rights, and pro-choice advocates. Israeli fundamentalists demonize Islamists and secular Jews. Those enemies provide diversionary escape from besetting universal threats. They provide causes to pursue instead of effective, collective problem solving for the tangible dangers facing humanity. They frequently follow negative defensive patterns and not positive ones.

All of the aforementioned stressors to humanity automatically trigger another defensive reaction among Christian fundamentalists. They turn to escapism, what some might call regressive fantasy. People can make efforts to escape painful thoughts, feelings or experiences by shifting their thoughts to fantasies. We have all done that as children, when we engaged in daydreaming instead of paying attention to our schoolwork. Adults allow themselves to regress to that defensive occupation when they engage in pipe dreaming. It is regressive behavior, used to escape unpleasant circumstances and feelings. It is ordinarily harmless, except insofar as it avoids work that needs to be done.

There is an apocalyptic thread that runs through the Bible, particularly prominent in the Christian scriptures. Jesus said: "When you hear of wars and revolutions, do not be frightened. These things must happen first, but the end will not come right away. Nation will rise against nation, and kingdom against kingdom. There will be great earthquakes, famines and pestilences in various places, and fearful events and great signs from heaven … There will be signs in the sun and moon and stars. On earth, nations will be in anguish and perplexity at the roaring and tossing of the sea. Men will faint in terror, apprehensive of what is coming on the world …" (Matthew 24, Mark 13, and Luke 21). These are among the images of the apocalypse (the end-times) scattered throughout the Christian scriptures.

The list of stressors that exist in the contemporary world resonates in the minds of many fundamentalists with some of these apocalyptic signs. Is it any wonder that many Christian fundamentalists are largely convinced that the end is near? Is it any wonder that people would turn to Christian fundamentalism for escape from the complex threats currently facing humanity?

Presently, apocalyptical thinking is more prevalent than at any time in modern history. It is a defense against overwhelming threats and fears. While most other world religions do not officially possess the concept of apocalypse, Christianity does. The apocalypse is a particular conceptualization of the end of human history. It involves deplorable universal conditions and traumatic events leading up to a cataclysmic end. Apocalypse is part of the Christian theological subcategory called eschatology. Most Christians believe in Christ's return and life in God's heavenly kingdom hereafter. It is the core element of Christian eschatology. That is the Christian hope. And it is one well worth having. Apocalypse is not integral to that Christian hope, however. Its overemphasis is characteristic of modern Christian fundamentalism.

Apocalyptic thinking has reached a fever pitch in recent years. In part, it is promoted by the enormous dangers facing this generation and the absence of hope that humans will be able to avert them. Christ's imminent return provides an escape mechanism from those dangers and the stress they would otherwise inspire. But it apparently also adds urgency to the practice of uncompromising fundamentalist agendas to reform the world before the end comes. The goal is not so much perhaps to achieve the kingdom of God on earth as to work for it in order to be found worthy to be admitted into it when Christ brings it into being.

Students at the several Christian institutions of higher learning that I attended often had occasion to speak of the end, with hopes for Christ's imminent return. It was never during vacations, social events, or in pleasant weather. It was always during final exams, and when students faced tests or term papers for which they felt unprepared. That tendency testifies to the idea that apocalyptic thinking offers a psychological defense against stressors and the anxieties or fears they cause.

There are two problems with contemporary Christian fundamentalist apocalyptic thinking. It disregards the point of Jesus's teaching about it. Jesus made it very clear that no one would ever know when the end will come. To claim otherwise is contrary to what he said. It also divorces the intent of the biblical references to it from practice. The intent of his mention of it at all, and of references to it by St. Paul or in the book of Revelation, was simple. Their intent was for people to understand what was happening when the end would come and to incentivize greater faith and love in the meantime. It was not to escape or to incite political power tactics to gain control over others in the meantime.

Defense mechanisms have an appropriate place in the face of real dangers. But the most effective are positive or mature ones, including altruism, anticipation, humor, identification, introjections, sublimation, and thought suppression. Under stress, during the past thirty years, Christian fundamentalists have resorted to power politics instead. That shift to achieve political power to try to control people through government is the primary distortion that has crept into Christian fundamentalism. It has been inspired by defensive patterns of behavior in reaction to stress and frustration.

Chapter 13

～

Fundamentalism in National Practice

The Motivations and Means of Fundamentalism's
Spread in Four Nations

Fundamentalists have used the principles and processes of democracy to try to institute the strict practices of their faith in several nations. The much-heralded "Arab Spring" has inspired the removal of dictatorships in several Muslim nations. Those dictators, while Muslim, have functioned as secular leaders. Their regimes were inclined to suppress Islamic fundamentalists and to promote secular laws to serve their own interests. The current democracy movements in Islamic nations, which once labored under dictatorship, have removed some of the previous restrictions on fundamentalist practices. It is noteworthy that it has resulted in increased fundamentalist influence in more than one of those countries.

Egypt is the most obvious example. Egypt's recent parliamentary elections have catapulted members of the Islamic Brotherhood to an unprecedented level of influence. It remains to be seen how greater fundamentalist participation in government will play itself out in Egypt and in other nations influenced by the Arab Spring.

There are several previous instances that reveal something of a track record for fundamentalists in nations that have undergone significant change. Let's look at each of four nations in which fundamentalist dynamics have been in play for some time. Those four nations are Iran, Afghanistan, Israel, and the United States. In one of those nations, the fundamentalist movement gained power and brought change by means of revolutionary process, and in three of them it has happened by means of democratic process. But all of them have employed the tactics of power politics.

Iran has always been a unique nation. It descended from the ancient Persian Empire. It is a nation in which the vast majority of people have been Muslim for more than twelve hundred years. It is a nation steeped in Islamic civilization. Nevertheless, Iran has held a different position relative to other nations within that civilization. Iranians are largely Shiite rather than Sunni Muslims. Iranians are Persians, not Arabs. They speak Persian rather than Arabic.

During the Cold War, in an effort to secure oil suppliers, the United States made efforts to strengthen ties with the Iranian government. It supported the reign of Shah Mohammed Reza Pahlavi with monetary and military supplements. Under his regime, the shah instituted what was called the "White Revolution." It consisted of a series of progressive reforms, which he hoped would strengthen Iran. Among other proposed reforms, the shah made efforts to privatize public business enterprises, extend the right to vote to women and non-Islamic citizens, and offer public education to all children.

Ironically, those progressive policies and programs alienated many of the Iranian people. Popular opinion, fueled and guided by clerical criticisms, perceived the shah as enamored of Western civilization and as currying favor with America. His adoption of Western styles seemed to confirm their suspicions. That further alienated the people and radicalized Iranian clergy. Muslim clergy were the shah's most outspoken critics.

His most severe critic was Ayatollah Ruhollah Khomeini. In reaction to his increasingly hostile criticisms, the shah's government exiled Khomeini. But the ayatollah remained an even more comprehensive critic of the regime during his exile. Khomeini developed his political thoughts during that time, basing them on the Quran and Shari'a law. In *Islam and Revolution*, Khomeini wrote that the laws of society should be constituted of the laws of God, Shari'a, which cover "all human affairs ... and provide instruction and establish norms [for every aspect of human life]."[viii]

Meanwhile, back in Iran, frustration with the regime's incompetence and the shah's reform policies grew increasingly widespread. Popular demonstrations broke out across Iran in 1977 and 1978. The nation was crippled by widespread strikes. And in January 1979, at the urging of his supporters, the shah and his family left the country. Khomeini returned to Iran soon after, greeted by millions of supporters. He returned at a high-water mark of Iranian discontent and immediately became the icon of resistance to the status quo. Supported by most segments of Iranian society, Khomeini became de facto interim head of state after the shah's regime fell.

Ayatollah Khomeini immediately set to work to overhaul the government and Iranian society. Within three months, Iran held a national democratic referendum, in which Iranians were asked to vote for their country to become an "Islamic Republic." By the end of that same year, 1979, another national referendum was held to approve the new "theocratic constitution" and to elect Ayatollah Khomeini as the supreme leader of the nation. Using democratic processes, the government was completely restructured within a matter of months.

That political and legal reconfiguration has been used to dominate the people of Iran and suppress dissidents ever since. It has also served to make Iran so intransigent that it remains a renegade state within the community of nations and a threat to world peace. Iran is unable to negotiate with other nations or to find moderation within its own society, precisely because compromise has been regarded as tantamount to unfaithfulness to God as his will is set forth in the Quran. It is important to keep in mind that Iran instituted those Islamic fundamentalist ideals by means of democratic processes.

Scholars have struggled to comprehend what happened in Iran, what caused that Islamic fundamentalist revolution. Most see the Iranian Revolution as historically unprecedented simply because it was not inspired by the usual stressors: political oppression, war, extreme economic hardship, or any of the other usual causes of revolution. Scholars seem to underestimate the power of fundamentalism per se.

There was a pattern to the fundamentalist revolution in Iran. Rapid changes were made by the government. Those changes departed from traditional values and practices. There was general frustration among the citizens. That frustration focused on the rapid and multifaceted changes and government incompetence. A hard-core and well-organized religious minority provided a clear and different vision. Those religious hardliners harnessed the widespread frustrations within the general population. They relentlessly criticized the government for the changes made and its incompetence. They offered promises of reform. Then they used existing democratic institutions and processes to transform Iran into a theocratic state. Under that combination of conditions, or some variation of them, fundamentalism can and will often use democracy to advance its theocratic aspirations. Those aspirations involve the specific goal of limiting pluralism by legislating religious regulations and executing them in authoritarian ways.

This is no new recipe for radical government shift from democracy to totalitarianism. The Fascists employed similar tactics during the 1930s. One difference was that at that time the democratic societies that turned to fascism were grappling with a worldwide Great Depression. Germany was also gripped by hyperinflation, as well as government inability to remedy the situation. Another difference, of course, was that the Fascist revolution was secular in nature but quickly adopted a fundamentalist mind-set and adorned itself with quasi-religious trappings. In Iran, it was simply rapid social change coupled with government incompetence that created the unrest and resulted in a fundamentalist revolution.

Afghanistan also underwent a fundamentalist metamorphosis within the past generation. Like Iran, it was a country steeped in Islam. Unlike Iran, Afghanistan followed Sunni Muslim doctrines and traditions. And yet, like Iran, it was also taken over by leadership that was perceived to be hostile to those traditions. It wasn't a Westernized king, as it was in Iran, but worse. Communism, inspired by an outside power, came to dominate Afghani society. Later, forces from the Soviet Union invaded Afghanistan. The Soviets tried to control the Afghan population. The Afghanis resisted by employing tactics of guerrilla warfare, as they historically had.

Afghanistan has always been a tribal society. Strong tribal leaders have long participated in the regional governance of a loosely confederated monarchy. According to the archives of the British Broadcasting Company, after the British retreated from Afghanistan, it returned to its customary monarchy. In 1964, Afghanistan became a constitutional monarchy, but the society was polarized. Power struggles among tribes and ethnic groups existed in various segments of the country.

There was a coup d'état in 1973. Former Prime Minister General Daud seized power and ousted Zahir Shah. By 1978, Daud himself was overthrown by the leftist People's Democratic Party. The new regime imposed social changes, which lessened the importance of Islamic tradition. Afghanistan's cohesiveness was further compromised by even more intense internal power struggles. Simultaneously, and largely in reaction to secular social changes, Islamic fundamentalist and ethnic tribal groups strengthened their resistance. They engaged in armed revolt in various regions of the country.

The Soviet Union began to intervene in 1979. Ostensibly, it sought to support the People's Democratic regime. But despite Soviet support in finances and armaments, the Afghan army collapsed. The Soviet Union responded by sending troops into the country to stabilize the situation and support its leftist government. In 1980 Muhammad Karmal was installed as head of state. The Soviet army supported the government by making every effort to suppress revolt. Mujahedeen groups increasingly rallied to resist. They received financial support for their resistance from an odd collection of outside nations, including Saudi Arabia, Iran, China, and the United States.

The struggle intensified. By 1985, the conflict displaced half the population to neighboring Pakistan and Iran. Also by that time, the various rebel groups of the Mujahedeen joined forces. In 1986, the United States began to provide the Mujahedeen with more sophisticated weapons. They gained momentum. And so, by 1988, peace accords were signed by Afghanistan, the Soviet Union, the United States, and Pakistan.

Although Soviet forces withdrew from Afghanistan in 1989, the fighting continued. It shifted from a war of resistance to civil conflict. By 1992, the Mujahedeen took control. Rival militias continued to vie for power, however. In 1993, its disparate groups agreed to form a government. A Tajik leader, named Rabbani, became president, but the ethnic Pashtu-dominated Taliban presented a major challenge to the Rabbani government.

In 1996, the Pashtu fundamentalists of the Taliban seized control of Kabul. The Taliban immediately set to work to reverse the social and political reforms that had been instituted by previous administrations. They imposed strict Islamic laws, enforced by brutal punishment of nonconformity. Islamic fundamentalism dominated Afghanistan from 1996 until the American-led invasion ended Taliban rule in 2001.

Very different powers have controlled Afghanistan's people in rapid succession. In the twentieth century, Afghanistan has been ruled by governments dominated by the British, ethnic monarchs, a right-wing secular military dictator, a left-wing political party, the Soviet Union, a Tajik president, a Pashtu Islamic fundamentalist regime, and the Taliban.

Change was constant. Instability was Afghanistan's normal condition. Note that fundamentalists were able to use that very instability to their own ends.

Fundamentalism offers such a degree of zealous single-mindedness that it can provide organization and rigid focus where none exists. Note also that social change provides a catalyst to forge both impetus and focus for fundamentalists. Notice that fundamentalists, both in Iran and Afghanistan, have used religious laws to dominate those populations. They employ often brutal force to administer those laws. In both cases nonconformity has been impermissible.

As it happened, Taliban leaders were not content to limit their fundamentalist efforts to their own nation, but also sought to correct the wrongs of the world from their perspective. And so the Taliban provided a center of operations for al-Qaeda and, thereby, supported its terrorist exploits around the world. Fundamentalist ideals tend to be relentless, but expansive as well.

Fundamentalism has also been on the rise in Israel during the past generation. Increasing numbers of Israelis have adopted forms of Jewish fundamentalism.

The modern state of Israel came into being during the years following the Holocaust. Israel was originally formed as a secular democracy. Part of the reason for that was the backlash of Jews to the experience of the Holocaust. The unrelenting evils of that diabolical policy understandably raised questions about the existence of God for many of its survivors. Key leaders of the Zionist movement were not only secular Jews, but socialists as well. Recent years have seen secularism increasingly come under fire in Israel.

Jewish fundamentalism has been growing for forty years. Part of the rise can be attributed to the tremendous influx of Jews from the former Soviet Union and Africa. With the ongoing flow of immigrants, there has been a crisis in available residential space. That has intensified the need for additional land. The need for more land has increasingly caused

Israel to encroach into Palestinian territories. The Israeli government has built numerous settlements in the Palestinian territories simply to house increasing numbers of immigrants. That has further radicalized desperate Palestinians. Obviously, their location in Palestinian territories intensifies the felt insecurities of Jewish settlers in those territories.

Jewish fundamentalism helps Jewish settlers counteract their justifiable fears. But it also helps them find justification for Israel's unilateral acquisition of Palestinian lands by providing them with the sense of mission. Adopting a Jewish fundamentalist framework enables them to claim that the Hebrew scriptures give Israel entitlement to more land than it previously possessed. That has intensified the animosity between Jewish settlers and Palestinians. The resulting dangers help Jewish fundamentalists gain even greater influence among people throughout Israel. Since Israel is a democratic state, the more Israeli fundamentalists there are the more influence they have to accommodate their passions, principles, and sensibilities.

Simultaneously, and perhaps just as significantly, the rise of Jewish fundamentalism was triggered by the outcome of the Seven-Day War in 1967. Something of a movement was born when Israel so dramatically and completely, one might say miraculously, defeated the military aggressions of its Muslim neighbors within just one week. And that movement has grown both in numbers and zeal.

There is a messianic thread embedded within a few of the Hebrew scriptures. They include the books of Daniel and Isaiah. They allude to a coming Messiah, who would not only set his people free from oppression but also would usher in an age of unparalleled peace, justice, prosperity, and righteousness for the Jewish people and for the world.

From before the time of Judas Maccabeus until after the time of Jesus, a critical mass of the Jewish people believed that God would send a liberator, a messianic king, to save them. That conviction was advanced by the inroads of Hellenistic culture on Jews living abroad and at home. It was fueled by Israel's occupation by foreign forces. It was intensified by Gentile influences, laws, and customs within Israel. The messianic king would intervene to change all that. The Messiah would be indomitable, like David. He would drive out pagan forces. He would inspire Israel's faith. He would reform Israel and restore its former glories. He would inaugurate God's kingdom on earth.

Several presumptive messiahs arose and failed. The consequences of their failures were invariably disastrous. Far from accomplishing the desired outcomes, the failures of those messianic revolts worsened the conditions they sought to remedy. Uprisings led by presumptive messiahs caused the Roman occupation of Palestine, which Jews found abhorrent. Conflicts culminated in 70 AD, when the Roman Empire reacted to yet another Jewish rebellion by destroying the temple, defeating the last Jewish stronghold at Masada, and then forcibly dispersing the Jewish people throughout the Roman Empire (the Diaspora).

Understandably, those serial failures created a backlash among members of the Jewish priesthood, rabbis, and other leaders. Before the Diaspora took place, in 70 AD, Jewish leaders wanted to stave off the destruction of Israel by Rome. That explains the religious establishment's reaction to Jesus to some extent. In any case, it became accepted rabbinical practice to explain the concept of Messiah in collective terms. Priests and rabbis alike taught that Israel was the messianic hope. God would institute the messianic age, not through revolt led by an individual, but by making Israel the Messiah.

The modern Jewish messianic movement largely embraces that concept, that Israel will be the Messiah. They believe that God has called Israel to establish God's reign, which will eventually spread throughout the world. That view has been supported and advanced by multiple Jewish fundamentalist sects. Many of the settlers in the Palestinian territories share that conviction. This concept lends credence to Jewish fundamentalism.

The increased numbers of Jewish fundamentalists has affected Israel's political climate. More than one conservative political party has sought to appeal to fundamentalist voters. Consequently, there have been increasing numbers of political efforts made to institute regulations from the Torah in modern Israeli society. Sabbath regulations have been instituted to restrict commerce and travel. Marriage and divorce laws have been reformed. Laws curtailing the availability of abortion have been put forward. Modesty laws have been proposed. Modesty patrols comprised of Jewish fundamentalists have accosted women for immodest behavior or attire. They have assailed women for eating ice cream cones or hot dogs in public. They have vandalized stores in Jerusalem that they accuse of promoting such immodesty. Many of the settlements in the Palestinian territories have been populated by zealous Jewish fundamentalists, who believe that they have been given a mission to possess the historic boundaries of the ancient kingdom of Israel before it divided into two kingdoms.

According to a BBC News report on December 27, 2011, President Shimon Perez said that Israeli democracy is threatened from within. He stated that Israel is involved in "a fight for the soul of the nation and the essence of the state." The basis of the internal war, which he believes threatens the very nature of democracy in Israel, is a clash of civilizations. Ultraorthodox Jewish sects are in the process of making every political effort to impose stricter codes of moral regulation on the personal conduct of the general public in Israel. Other Israelis experience Jewish fundamentalists as engaging in a religious war against Jews of different persuasions. They are extreme in their convictions and intransigent. Israelis have come to recognize those fundamentalist traits. They also recognize that fundamentalists are using democratic processes to accomplish their goals. Some, like Perez, regard Jewish fundamentalism as jeopardizing the balance between democracy and religion.

Over the years Jewish friends have led me to believe that there has always been a core element to traditional Jewish thinking. It goes something like this: "Jews will argue with each other over everything, except that we are all Jews. That's what unites us beneath all our disagreements."

That view seems to have changed in recent years. Jewish fundamentalists contend that it is not sufficient to be ethnically Jewish. They believe that secular Jews are not entitled to claim that they are actually Jews at all. But it goes further. Jewish fundamentalists go so far as to question whether religious Jews of more liberal inclinations are legitimate Jews. Jewish fundamentalism has influenced the Rabbinate Council in Jerusalem. It has expressed less tolerance for variations in Judaism. The recognition of converts admitted to Judaism by liberal synagogues has been called into question. In essence, that threatens to discriminate against synagogues of more liberal orientations (whether reformed or conservative synagogues). It is a radical departure for Jews to question the Jewish identity of other Jews. And yet, that is one of the benchmarks of fundamentalism. It seeks to segregate, discredit, and ostracize those who do not share or conform to its rigid mind-set.

In Israel, as in Iran and Afghanistan, social changes and circumstantial stressors have been instrumental in fundamentalism's growth in numbers of adherents and their political influence. Because of the nature of fundamentalism, increasingly, social influence must give way to political dominance. Fundamentalists seem unable to content themselves with enjoying the right to practice their faith or even to influence others in society. They seem compelled to gain political dominance in order to control their environment and others in society.

The United States has undergone its own movement to reclaim traditional values. Of course, in its case they are not Islamic or Jewish values but traditional values of Western civilization. Conservative Christian values and beliefs are the ones around which that movement has configured itself. Advocates for reform have inevitably appealed to the Bible for their authority as much as Muslims in their countries appeal to the Quran and Jews in Israel appeal to the Torah.

Like Iran, the United States underwent an enormous shift from its religious and cultural roots within a relatively short period of time. Huge social changes took place at a rapid pace. World War II uprooted large segments of the population even more than World War I had done. People were separated from their traditional communities. Women were thrust into the workplace in ways that they never had been before. The stresses of the war caused certain moral taboos to be relaxed. Customary patterns of courtship changed. Following the war, the GI Bill provided hundreds of thousands of veterans with a college education. Advanced education inspired questions about traditional beliefs. It propelled many into the ethos of a new middle class. That created a new suburbanization, which further separated people from their traditional ethnic and religious roots. The availability of new methods of birth control gave rise to a sexual revolution. Peer groups seemed to have more influence on young people than their families or their traditional institutions. Radio and television gave people access to new issues, styles, behaviors, mores, and values. They suddenly had more impact than customary influences did.

Amidst those social shifts, new movements for human rights emerged. They were pushed forward as if lined up along some inexorable conveyor belt. American society reeled over one liberation movement after another. The civil rights movement for Americans of color and the anti-war movement hit America in tandem. The women's rights movement came next. That was followed by the gay rights movement. One change came after another—migration, subcultural displacement, relaxed sexual behavior, racial integration, gender equality, and acceptance of diversity in sexuality, and with all these also came a growing tendency to question traditional customs and authorities. Change was everywhere.

Simultaneous with those changes, and somewhat motivated by them, there was a surge in Christian fundamentalism. It coincided with the expansion of Islamic and Jewish fundamentalism. It also portrayed a similar mind-set and adopted similar strategies. While Christian fundamentalism is certainly not the only expression of fundamentalism extant in the United States, it is unquestionably the most widespread and influential. At first, the focus of Christian fundamentalist efforts was exclusively spiritual in nature. It emphasized restoring orthodox faith, saving the unregenerate, renewing the apathetic, teaching biblical principles, and training disciples for ministry. As felt pressures from a changing society alarmed leaders, the mission expanded. Christian fundamentalism began efforts to reform what it considered to be negative social currents and the structures that were identified as supporting them.

This has not been the first time in American history that evangelical Christians have spearheaded efforts to reform social evils. In the eighteenth century, British evangelicals and, inspired by them, nineteenth-century American evangelicals were very active in the movement to abolish slavery. In the latter decades of the nineteenth century and early decades of the twentieth century, evangelicals were equally engaged in the temperance movement to abolish alcohol consumption. Both efforts resulted in conflict, violence, and social upheaval. But the modern version of faith-inspired social reform is by far the most comprehensive in its agenda, and is more politically far-reaching.

I must be quick to differentiate evangelical and conservative Christians from Christian fundamentalists. While there is some overlap, of course, not all Christian fundamentalists are evangelicals, and not all evangelical or conservative Christians are fundamentalists. Evangelicals and conservative members of various Christian denominations do not necessarily share the intolerance for others, demonization of those who are different, intransigence, dogmatism, and judgmentalism, or willingness to impose their ways on others that Christian fundamentalists do. Diversity of perspective is accepted, and those of differing perspectives are respected, without the need to control or ostracize them. They are characterized more by the Christian values of faith and love than by the drive to control others through power politics.

Chapter 14

~

Fundamentalist Strategies in America

Fundamentalist Strategies and Goals in the United States

Over the course of time, evangelistic efforts in the United States have become increasingly widespread and their methods ever more sophisticated. Evangelistic crusades and Christian revivals have been commonplace in America. They have included the preachers of the "Great Awakening" during the eighteenth century, the "prairie revivals" of the nineteenth century, and the so-called "sawdust trail" evangelistic circuits of the earlier part of the twentieth century. Many of those evangelistic "crusades" were limited to rural areas and cities in the central and southern United States, what has become known as the "Bible Belt." From the 1950s, Billy Graham did an extraordinary job of evangelistic ministry by expanding his crusades across the nation and by means of television. Untold numbers were converted to a vibrant Christian faith.

Since that time, many more sophisticated methods and nuanced approaches have been employed. Not unlike Jesus, churches and nondenominational organizations have identified and focused their attention on insecure segments of the general population. People with particular needs have purposely and strategically been targeted for evangelization and discipleship. Teens, college students, singles in urban areas, newly divorced persons, new parents, parents of teens, the newly unemployed, men under fire, people in recovery from various addictions, and prisoners have been among those specifically identified as prospects. They have been seen as people in need—in need of support, community, and identity.

Those target groups have at least one thing in common. They are people in transition. They are people with often desperately felt needs. They are people whose circumstances cause them to feel a greater degree of insecurity and loneliness. They are people looking for identity, personal support, community, and hope. They are more receptive and open to root change.

Christian fundamentalist enterprises, like their Islamic counterparts, have identified people in transition as particularly suitable for outreach. Their needs not only make them appropriate recipients of charitable acts, but also make them most likely to be receptive to a significant change of life and of core beliefs. The strategy has been extremely effective. The focus on people's needs is positive. It was Jesus's strategy. He said, "Come to me, all you who are weary and burdened, and I will give you rest" (Matthew 11:28). With the successes of evangelism the number of Christian fundamentalists has increased dramatically in America during the past few decades.

Another very effective strategy that has been used to attract converts has been what I will call the rise of "tootsie pop" mega churches. I define a tootsie pop church as one that initially sparkles and seems sweet but which offers a different experience at the core as people become increasingly involved. It is common for many modern fundamentalist churches to gear the style of their public services and events to attract, engage, and energize people, to sweep people into exciting community. Worship services are crafted to have an emotional impact. To accomplish that objective, the church will offer lively contemporary music, accompanied by rock bands, instead of hymns accompanied by an organ. They will offer multimedia presentations to complement sermons. They will offer power-packed and moving testimonials and prayer forms. Some will even offer television monitors to enable those more accustomed to staring at a computer or television screen to watch the service in the church.

These have their purpose in engaging participants on an emotional level. The style seems lively, contemporary, open, and accepting, not boring like traditional church. The core of their ministry is to draw people energized by public services into smaller groups of every kind. As people become more involved at a personal level, they naturally bond with others. As that happens they become influenced more strongly by peer pressure and the approval of recognized leaders. Gently and gradually, as people become more active in the church, it becomes far more dogmatic and personally controlling. Conformity becomes increasingly important, and that can include conformity not only to doctrines, conduct, and values but to political ideology as well.

During the past thirty years, with increased numbers and enthusiasm, it became clear to many fundamentalist leaders that, while spiritual conversion was most important, it was not sufficient. The mission needed to expand its vision. Serious Christian disciples needed serious missions beyond themselves. Not only should men's souls be saved, but so should the values and systems of society and the world. That has been the case in history but was focused upon charitable missions. Mission has become far more political during the past generation.

Certain compelling emotional issues have galvanized the growing Christian fundamentalist movement as targets for reform. They have included not only abortion, extramarital sexual behavior, and homosexual rights, but also public school curricula and public displays of faith among others.

Fundamentalists adopted and utilized the same methods that they identified as having contributed to social problems. They organized as liberal protest movements had done in the past. Like liberal movements, they mobilized. They demonstrated. They protested. They developed publishing companies, television networks, radio stations, and strategic political organizations. New broadcasting media were founded to disseminate the news, produce talk shows, and provide entertainment from a Christian fundamentalist vantage point. Organizations such as the Moral Majority were created to promote Christian fundamentalist values and a political agenda for the nation. Additional fundamentalist Christian educational institutions were established to reverse humanist thought with law schools to reform secular laws. The vision soon became far more comprehensive reform.

America needed to be reformed along more strictly biblical lines. This has been called "Reconstructionism." An increasingly comprehensive fundamentalist Christian effort has been under way to restore America as a Christian nation. I say to "restore" America as a Christian nation because that is how many leaders of the movement have framed it. Widespread historical revisionism has been characteristic of some prominent fundamentalist leaders.

A classic instance of Christian fundamentalist revisionism is the tendency to recast the Founding Fathers as like-minded fundamentalist Christians. This tendency includes the insinuation that homogeneity of faith existed among the Founding Fathers and framers of the Constitution. It is not surprising that American fundamentalists should assert that their homogeneity of faith was both Christian and biblically literalistic. This reflects their own faith.

Revisionism has been a long-accepted scholarly enterprise. It is integral to intellectual progress and integrity. At its best, revisionism is necessary when new facts demand that previous paradigms be adjusted in order to make them more accurate. At its worst, revisionism is ideological. It selects, manipulates, and fabricates evidence to justify preconceived ideas. That sort of revisionism involves a purposeful redaction of history. It takes place when people claim something to be true that was not true or claim that something is not true that was. It is a process that makes selective or distorted use of historical evidence to advance a viewpoint or to negate the views of others.

Wordiq.com identifies several techniques used by ideological revisionism. They include the following: selective use of historical facts, denial or derision of known facts, assumption of unproven facts, obfuscation of facts, fabrication of facts, and constant attack of those who oppose their manipulated facts. The propaganda machine in Nazi Germany used revisionism freely. Communist authorities have done so as well. Revisionism in service of ideology is an integral part of propaganda.

I believe it was Senator Daniel Patrick Moynihan who said that everyone is entitled to his own opinions but no one is entitled to his own facts. Facts are objective, empirically proven to be true. Opinions, convictions, and beliefs, no matter how firmly held or well-intentioned, are subjective and are not necessarily empirically verified. It is important to differentiate between the two and to identify them as such.

Revisionism is currently used with great license in modern-day America. Quite a number of currently active and popular media commentators and personalities seem to specialize in revisionism. Their presumed objective is to make their subjective convictions seem to be objectively true. And many folks are eager to accept it. As I've mentioned, the overload of data overwhelms many people. And so, all too many people select means of packaging information that reduce their stress and lighten their own intellectual workload by interpreting the information for them. The greatest ally of ideological revisionism is a poorly informed and intellectually undisciplined population.

One such commentator, Glen Beck, recently identified George Whitefield with the Founding Fathers of the nation. I listened to the radio broadcast in which he featured Whitefield. The reason Beck insinuated that Whitefield was associated with the circle of the Founding Fathers is that Whitefield was an evangelical Christian minister. Beck's intent seems to have been to lend credence, by association, to the idea that Whitefield's mind-set was representative of the Founding Fathers and framers of the Constitution. That would be tantamount to saying that since Billy Graham visited England to lead evangelistic revivals and was received by the queen, modern England is an evangelical Christian nation of Southern Baptist persuasion. It is blatant revisionism in service of propaganda.

Whitefield was an evangelical minister of the Church of England who came to evangelize colonists in North America. He was not an American. He died in 1770, before America was a separate nation from Great Britain. He was not among the entourage of the Founding Fathers. The truth is that the Reverend Mr. Whitefield was a very effective British evangelist who revived the Christian faith and stirred the moral sensibilities of a large number of colonists. There is no need to make more of his contributions to America than that.

Whitefield also happened to have been friendly with Benjamin Franklin. Franklin was not like-minded or even a devout Christian. He was an eighteenth-century humanist. In *Poor Richard's Almanac,* Franklin wrote, "Lighthouses are more helpful than churches." He also wrote, "Revelation had indeed no weight with me." And again, "I have found Christian dogma unintelligible. Early in life I absented myself from Christian assemblies." Nevertheless, even though they disagreed on religion, they were friends. That bears witness to the importance of never allowing religion to create enmity between people of different viewpoints.

Such vocal American broadcasters as Glen Beck, Rush Limbaugh, and others, as well as increasing numbers of American politicians, continue to engage in ideologically or religiously inspired revisionism. It is a way of using God to promote ideological propaganda. There is a danger of violating the Third Commandment in that practice. "You shall not use the name of the Lord your God in vain." Such public figures, together with some televangelists, imply that the Founding Fathers were virtual fundamentalist Christians of a modern type.

Recently, one candidate for the presidency of the United States, Representative Michele Bachmann, credited John Eidsmoe's book *Christianity and the Constitution* for inspiring her political thought. That text claims that the Christian faith inspired the efforts of the Founding Fathers and framers of the Constitution. Eidsmoe does a thorough job drawing upon the personal writings and actions of thirteen members of the founding circle. Although most of the representatives to the Constitutional Convention were Anglicans (Episcopalians), Eidsmoe claims that Calvinism was the strongest theological influence over the framers of the Constitution. Eighteenth-century Episcopalians were not Calvinists. They had been influenced strongly by the Enlightenment. The majority of the individuals that Eidsmoe chose to concentrate upon largely held a fervent biblical faith. But Eidsmoe failed to prove that their personal faith explicitly evidenced itself in the public documents of the founding of the nation. As I will indicate later in greater detail, the foundational documents of the United States conspicuously omit statements of Christian faith. And so, insofar as any of the Founding Fathers may have been devoutly Christian, they certainly compartmentalized their private faith from their collective statements of political philosophy. Eidsmoe seems to insinuate that it is appropriate to reform the laws of the United States to continue the spirit of the Founding Fathers' intent. He suggests that it is appropriate for the laws of the United States to be aligned more fully with biblical standards. His rationale seems to be based upon the proposition that many of the Founding Fathers and framers of the Constitution would have intended it that way because they were devout Christians. His scholarship seems selective and inspired by his ideological perspective.

The truth is that some in the American Founding Circle were orthodox Christians, perhaps even evangelical, and some were not. Some had been affected by the First Great Awakening, either directly or indirectly. Virtually all of them had been exposed to orthodox Christian doctrines, and their consciences were shaped by ethical ideals inspired by Christianity. Nevertheless, some were not inclined to orthodox Christianity, let alone an evangelical faith. They were freethinkers. To illustrate the point I will quote a few of the most prominent leaders of the time, those with universal name recognition.

George Washington wrote, "It is impossible to rightly govern without God and the Bible." Nonetheless, addressing the United Baptists of Virginia in 1789, he said, "No one would be more zealous than myself to establish effectual barriers against the horrors of spiritual tyranny, and every species of religious persecution." And in a letter to Sir Edward Newenham, in 1792, he wrote, "Religious controversies are always productive of more acrimony and irreconcilable hatreds than those which spring from any other cause." Notice the balanced quality of his words. Such moderate wisdom has been the basis of the separation of church and state in the United States.

Not all of the Founding Fathers were quite so temperate in their perspectives. John Adams wrote, "This would be the best of all possible worlds without religion." In 1816 Adams wrote a letter to his son in which he said, "Let the human mind loose. It must be loose. It will be loose. Superstition and dogmatism cannot confine it." And again, "The government of the United States is not in any sense founded upon religion." Thomas Jefferson was harshest of all. He was convinced that Christianity was responsible for deplorable acts of evil. He wrote this in his *Notes from the State of Virginia*: "Is religious uniformity attainable? Millions of innocent men, women, and children, since the introduction of Christianity, have been burnt, tortured, fined, and imprisoned. Yet what has been the effect of coercion? To make half the world fools and the other half hypocrites." And again, "The way to silence religious disputes is to take no notice of them." And again, in 1814, in a letter to Dr. Thomas Cooper, he wrote, "Christianity neither is, nor ever was a part of the Common Law. It must not be part of the Common Law."

You see, there was diversity of perspectives among the Founding Fathers. Certainly there were voices that advocated a semblance of

Christian fundamentalism appropriate to that era. Some were Puritans, Presbyterians, or members of the Dutch Reformed Church. They were influenced by Jean Calvin, and may have shared his disposition toward theocracy. But more than half of the representatives to the Continental Congress and those involved in shaping the Constitution were Anglicans (Episcopalians). Eighteenth-century Episcopalians were extremely reserved about their personal faith and highly averse to imposing it upon others. There were also deists and humanists, who had no interest in shaping a Christian state. The founding circle was able to find compromise and common ground. If they had not been, then the American democratic experiment of the eighteenth century would have failed. It would have become a continent of many miniature nation-states, each dedicated to different religious or no-religious ideologies.

Aware as the Founding Fathers were of the potentially violent excesses of religious enthusiasm, they wanted to circumscribe the dual threats of the state controlling religion and religion dominating the state. They were well aware of the devastating religious conflicts throughout Europe during the sixteenth and seventeenth centuries. They were also keenly aware of the more recent phenomenon of the witch trials in Massachusetts Bay Colony and of religiously based persecution in some of the colonies. It was religious persecution that gave rise to the creation of the colony of Rhode Island. Rhode Island was founded upon religious freedom in reaction to the dogmatism and persecutions that characterized Puritan fundamentalist Massachusetts Bay Colony.

The colonial leaders of the American Revolution were abundantly aware of prospective problems between religion and the state. They were extremely disinclined to replicate those situations in a newly formed American nation. Although some of them were orthodox Christians, when it came to ideas about government, many of the Founding Fathers and framers of the Constitution were even more strongly influenced by the Enlightenment and its religious expression, deism, than they were by the Bible. In *Of the Religion of Deism Compared with the Christian*

Religion, Thomas Paine wrote, "The religion of Deism is superior to the Christian religion. It is free from all those invented and tortured articles that shock reason or injure humanity, with which the Christian religion abounds." Let me make it clear that Paine was not a Founding Father, nor was he a framer of the Constitution, but he was the most influential spokesman of that time for the cause of liberty. Such leaders of the Revolutionary War were influenced by the rediscovery of the pre-Christian classics, Freemasonry, and the writings of contemporary thinkers more than a fundamentalist reading of the Bible when it came to building the government of a new nation. Several of them were self-styled eighteenth-century intellectuals. Intellectualism was one of their values, and their writings reflected it.

The truth is that the most significant documents written by the members of the founding circle were all but completely devoid of statements of faith. There is a conspicuous absence of theological reflection, doctrinal statement, and religious affirmation in their writings. Most would agree that the essential documents composed at the founding of the United States were the Declaration of Independence, the Constitution, and the Bill of Rights. Some might add others, but most would place these three in an exclusive position of authority with respect to enshrining the highest ideals of the Founders and framers of the nation and their justifications for them. In those essential documents only one sentence stands out as offering any affirmation of religious faith whatsoever. And that sentence is not explicitly Christian or biblical, let alone fundamentalist in nature or tone.

The faith statement that I am referring to is found at the outset of the Declaration of Independence. It says, "We hold these truths to be self evident, that all men are created equal, that they are endowed by their Creator with certain unalienable rights, that among them are life, liberty and the pursuit of happiness …" Embodied in this statement is the belief that humans were created and are equal, therefore. It affirms the existence of a single Creator. That is an affirmation of general theistic conviction, not explicitly Christian at all. Also incorporated in the statement is the theological proposition that the Creator conferred upon all people certain basic rights. Three of them were named. They were life, liberty, and the pursuit of happiness. Only one of those three, life, is referred to in the Bible. Liberty might have been inferred from the story of the Exodus, but the Bible never states that liberty is a universal right. The pursuit of happiness was an innovation of the authors of the Declaration. The Bible makes no assertion that God made humans to pursue happiness or, generally, to be free. St. Paul wrote that faith in Christ offers freedom. His epistles to the Romans and Galatians emphasized that theme. He spoke of freedom from sin, death, and Jewish law. The freedom of which he spoke was spiritual, not political liberty.

My point is that there is nothing explicitly Christian, let alone expressive of Christian fundamentalism, in any of those sentiments. They are generally theistic and could reflect concepts of any belief system that allows for a single Creator, including the deism of the time. That statement in the Declaration of Independence was addressed to the King of England. It may have been inspired more by the desire to appeal to an authority superior to the king to advance their position against him than by shared Christian faith. For modern Christian fundamentalists to propose otherwise is merely an exercise in ideologically inspired revisionism. It is born of a desire to find one's own faith in the founding of American democracy.

In the libraries of the Founding Fathers and their circle of collaborators were many texts. They sought to be educated men, and we would do well to emulate their intellectual discipline. The Bible was there, of course, especially St. Paul's writings on spiritual freedom. Their libraries were also filled with humanist authors such as Montesquieu, Hume, Blackstone, Locke, Bacon, Rousseau, Voltaire, Machiavelli, and Hobbes. They also read the classics: Plutarch, Aristotle, Plato, and Shakespeare.

Recasting members of the founding circle as Christian fundamentalists has a dual purpose. It serves to project current fundamentalist thinking onto the founders of the nation. And it seeks, thereby, to justify modern fundamentalist proposals for reform in American society along the lines of their own beliefs. That is the purpose of historical revision of this sort, and it is merely propaganda. It is not worthy of sincere followers of Christ, who never resorted to deception or employed political power tactics.

I have had occasion to notice the number of books that have been devoted to the faith of the Founding Fathers during the past twenty years. I have wondered why so many fundamentalist and politically conservative authors have invested so much time and effort in such an obscure subject. Then it occurred to me that it was necessary to do so in order to attempt to construct some sort of legitimate foundation for the political ideology that they already embrace. You see, since the Bible has nothing to say about democracy, no one can build a political philosophy that claims to be democratic on the Bible. Hence, it has been necessary to build the case that the founding circle were largely Christians of a fundamentalist sort. From that questionable premise, it can be further argued that they intended to build a Christian nation. And that becomes the portal through which fundamentalists can back into the idea that biblical teachings should be the basis of civil laws. It is really an exercise in circular argumentation. Their argument seeks to build an authoritative beginning point for preestablished political end goals. But that beginning point comes neither from the Bible nor from the Founding Fathers and framers of the Constitution. That is the way revisionism of that sort works.

I would argue that the extent to which members of the founding circle embraced orthodox Christian faith and possessed vital Christian spirituality proves an entirely different point. It is a point that fundamentalists avoid. Some of the Founding Fathers and framers of the Constitution seem to have expressed forms of deeply spiritual, orthodox Christian faith in other documents, personal letters, and private diaries. And yet, they certainly did not express their Christian faith in the public documents that I have mentioned. That indicates that they differentiated between political philosophy and private or personal faith. They intentionally compartmentalized the two. And that dramatically underscores the importance of separating religion from government in the nation that they created.

Concurrent with historical revisionism, and partly based upon it, there has also been a tendency among some fundamentalist leaders to imply that the Constitution should be restructured along more strictly biblical lines. In that sense, there has been a propensity by such fundamentalists to stress increased regard for the Constitution, to cast its framers as fundamentalist Christians, and to insinuate that they were divinely inspired. And yet, they also suggest the Constitution's incompleteness. They advocate a need to reform the Constitution by means of amendments to it along more strictly biblical lines. That calls for a "biblical reconstruction" of the Constitution.

Naturally, that begs all sorts of questions. Those questions include: Which laws shall we institute along more biblical lines? There are more than six hundred laws in the Bible, including Sabbath laws, laws against idolatry, cultic laws, sacrificial laws, moral laws, crimes, agricultural regulations, charitable regulations, dietary laws, laws about disease and personal hygiene, and many more. Where are the boundaries? What are the limits? Is the consumption of pork or shellfish to be outlawed? Must brothers-in-law marry their widowed sisters-in-law even though they may already be married to someone else? Should adultery be a capital offense? How should work on the Sabbath, including participation in sports, be punished? How should making graven images, including images on currency, be punished as a form of idolatry? Should women be required to be segregated during menstruation? Who gets to decide which biblical laws are to be adopted by the United States and how those laws would be enforced? Why should intimate relations between monogamous, same-sex partners be prohibited and not between spouses during menstruation? Is that a personal intrusion? Why would that be true in one situation and not the other? To what extent should judgment of moral conduct be left up to God, and to what extent should it be legislated and enforced by government? What and who should determine the difference? These are all pertinent questions when it comes to aspirations to theocracy because it has to be mediated by humans.

Theocracy is a compelling mission. One element of that mission is evangelistic, to save souls by converting as many people to following Christ and the teachings of the Bible as humanly possible. A second element is to reform or even to restructure the nation using the electoral and legislative processes of American democracy. Under extreme stress, it is as possible to restructure a nation along more fundamentalist lines in a seasoned democracy, such as the United States, as it is in a new democracy, such as Iran. It simply requires harnessing general unrest and agitation to use democratic processes to impose fundamentalist values in authoritarian ways.

The simple fact is this: The Bible offers no basis for democracy. Even though most of the members of the founding circle were affiliated with some Christian church and were Christians of one sort or another, they were not interested in creating a religiously specific nation of any kind, including a Christian nation. During their time, the prevailing culture was far more implicitly infused with Christian values, and so the government did not need to impose them. Peer pressure sufficed. Time has passed, and things have changed. American culture has changed. The prevailing culture is no longer infused with as many implicitly Christian values as it once was. Peer pressure no longer functions as it once did. Many Americans, especially Christian fundamentalists, are deeply disturbed by that, and want to recapture the culture of a previous era. They have been frustrated by resistance to their efforts and their ideals, and so they have been trying to determine how else to accomplish that goal. They have resorted to this new strategy. But revisionism based on distortion is no proper basis for a democratic state.

The fact that cultures change raises other questions. Eighteenth-century America was very different from twenty-first-century America. Many of the Founding Fathers may have had negative, conscientious objections to changes that have taken place. That is pure conjecture. Is it the appropriate province of democratic governments in pluralistic societies to preserve certain historic cultural norms? Insofar as some may believe that it is, what cultural norms should democratic governments preserve and from which eras? Should they include fashion, artistic and musical style, etiquette, patterns of courtship, age of marriage, linguistic style, transportation or communication media, facial hair, medical or business protocols, or particular standards of social or moral conduct? We all have our personal preferences in some of these matters. Which cultural norms should be reinstituted or standardized by the government? Why? What should be the basis of those decisions? How should the government enforce them?

In democratic societies, fundamentalists have the freedom, indeed the sense of heartfelt duty, to advocate and to use the legal avenues at their disposal within the political process to institute their convictions. And yet, since fundamentalism is absolutist, it is also exclusive in its claims to truth. Exclusivity and absolutism leave no room for pluralism under a system of laws shaped by fundamentalist ideals.

Chapter 15

⁓

The Seeds of Unrest

*Origins of the Recent Politicization of Christian Fundamentalism
in the United States from a Personal Vantage Point*

Christian fundamentalism has not always been so ambitious. Historically, most Christian fundamentalists have had two political priorities. They have been deeply committed to political freedom, the freedom to follow their faith as they felt inclined. Closely connected to that has been their commitment to the freedom to share their faith with others so that they too might enjoy the same relationship with God.

That changed and became far more political within the past forty years. I was there when it began to change. It was 1974. I was on spring holiday from the evangelical seminary that I was attending in England. I was visiting L'Abri Christian Fellowship in Switzerland at the time. L'Abri was a Christian intellectual community, founded in the Swiss Alps by Dr. Francis Schaeffer. It was a ministry geared toward educating budding young Christian intellectuals. Dr. Schaeffer was an exceptional Christian philosopher and devoted many of his efforts to Christian apologetics.

In one of his talks, Dr. Schaeffer became even more passionate than usual. He was lecturing about the downwardly spiraling effects of humanism on Western civilization. He spoke of the ironically dehumanizing effects of humanism on modern society. He identified some of its effects on medicine and laboratory experimentation. When it came to abortion and experiments in cellular and genetic biology, he concluded his presentation with the words, "So drop the bombs; drop the bombs!" He was alluding to nuclear holocaust. He suggested that if human life has lost its dignity to such an extent, then we humans should end our collective misery. That's how passionately he felt about what he believed were the dehumanizing effects of humanism on Western governments. It seemed a clear call to corrective action. Humanism had so eroded the dignity of humanity in Western civilization that nothing was off limits. The call to reform society was clear.

It was 1976, and I was visiting with my then father-in-law, now deceased. He was a gifted man of passionate Christian commitment. He had just written a book about one of the Democratic Party's candidates for the presidency. He had discovered that Jimmy Carter was a born-again Christian. And that inspired him to write the book, *The Miracle of Jimmy Carter*. His heart's desire was to have a Christ-centered man in the presidency. He believed that it not only would help the nation but also would serve to lend credibility to evangelical Christianity. That would perhaps, he thought, remove barriers to some people's reticence to believe in Christ.

Jimmy Carter was elected president of the United States. While devout, highly intelligent, and compassionate, he never instituted many changes, certainly not ones based upon fundamentalist Christian values. Moreover, he seemed to have been stymied by the economic troubles of the time. He seemed helpless to effect the release of Americans who had been taken hostage at Entebbe Airport. Oil and gasoline prices skyrocketed during his tenure. America was gripped by double-digit inflation during his term of office.

Some felt that his leadership had not been particularly inspired. Born-again Christians were disheartened. They were discouraged. But their frustration motivated some to try to find a more intentional and strategic Christian fundamentalist political ideology.

One of my then father-in-law's close friends was Pat Robertson. He, too, was a man of passionate faith. It was his passion of faith that prompted him to turn his garage into a fledgling radio studio so that he could broadcast Christian messages and faith-based ideas about the news. It was his passion of faith that prompted him to build a broadcasting company, the Christian Broadcasting Network. It was his passion of faith that roused him to build a new Christian university, now called Regent University, complete with a school of law, to train Christians to take leadership roles in the nation.

It was not only his passion of faith, but also his inner drive to do great things for Christ. His father had been a US senator from Virginia, and he had achieved a measure of prominence through his political influence. That urged Pat Robertson's actions as well, I suppose. He could accomplish great things too. He could achieve influence in different ways, in God's ways. He had a passionate faith and an inner drive of ego to influence things for God. Passion of faith and ego can go hand in hand and aren't often discernible, particularly to the individual.

Robertson's passion of Christian faith began with evangelistic zeal. But from the 1980s to the present, it has become increasingly political. His efforts were rewarded with greater notoriety. That greater notoriety constructed a larger public platform. And on that platform he has increasingly wedded politics with evangelism and conservative values with spiritual guidance. Politicization of religion has always been a temptation to people of vigorous faith. It began with Christian leaders at the time of Constantine, and that may have been the church's greatest temptation. But the politicization of religion has always eventually given rise to cultural religion more than personal piety. As the adage affirms,

"God has no grandchildren." There has always been a paradoxical relationship between Christian faith and political power. Historically, Christians have been at their best when they have had no political power. The more political power organized Christian groups have gained, the uglier the outcomes have been.

In retrospect, I can see the beginnings of the contemporary Christian fundamentalist shift into the American political arena. It was a time when political discouragement met passionate faith, when a sense of frustration and urgency, social change, politics, and communication converged.

Chapter 16

Been There, Done That

The Ways Previous American Revivals Affected Politics and Society

As I have mentioned, this is not the first time that America has seen such a dramatic tandem shift in religion and politics. Some have drawn parallels between the current religious climate and that of the nation's Great Awakenings. A Great Awakening is a social condition in which there have been widespread religious, specifically Christian, revivals. Those revivals not only have been widespread and awakened the religious fervor of a significant proportion of the population, but also they have inspired collateral organizational developments and social reform movements.

The first Great Awakening took place in the American colonies from the 1730s to the 1760s. It came in reaction to the stern ethos of Puritanism and involved previously unknown emotionalism. Spearheaded by Protestant clergy such as Jonathan Edwards and George Whitefield, the preaching involved emotional pleas for repentance and personal spiritual commitment. Large numbers were converted to a vibrant Christian faith. The individual emotionalism of the spirituality it inspired set them apart from the dominance of Calvinist-inspired Puritanism. Many existing churches were transformed, and new churches came into being. Eventually social and political reforms ensued. Some historians claim that one of the reforms fueled by the First Great Awakening was political, the passion for personal independence, including independence from the English monarchy. Minimally, it may be argued that "Awakening" ministers added what religious inspiration there might have been for the Revolutionary War by encouraging an independent spirit within many converts.

A second Great Awakening took place in the 1820s and 1830s. Like the first, significant numbers were converted to a new ardor of personal faith. Upstate New York was the epicenter of those revivals. So frequent and passionate were the revivals there that it became known as the "burned-over district" at the time. The movement generated considerable religious passion, which later spawned several new denominations, including denominations such as the Disciples of Christ, Seventh-Day Adventists, and the Church of Jesus Christ of Latter Day Saints.

But some of that passion instilled a fervent sense of need for social and political reform. The abolition of slavery and temperance became two of its most persistent spinoff causes. Some historians claim that the second Great Awakening gave religious grounds for abolitionism and the Civil War. Certainly the words of the "Battle Hymn of the Republic" closely link Christian images, abolitionist sentiments, and military triumphalism. And that linkage between Christian imagery, religiously inspired social reform, and military triumphalism continues to exist in the Grand Old Party of the republic to this day. It has been the culture of the Republican Party for more than 150 years.

Some consider that a third Great Awakening took place from the middle of the nineteenth century into the early part of the twentieth century. It included the so-called prairie and sawdust trail revivals. It was largely confined to rural regions of the Midwest and the southern United States. Nevertheless, the fervor of it also gave rise to new denominations, including Christian Science, the Salvation Army, and the Jehovah's Witnesses. It also generated pressure for social reforms. One of the reasons that Christian revivalism adopted a certain moral code, including personal prohibitions against smoking, drinking, dancing, gambling, swearing, and public displays of affection, was that those were the core elements of saloon culture on the American frontier.

Frustrated by the limited success of personal appeals for abstinence, revivalist efforts became more political. The focus was not independence from the evils of British rule or abolition of the evils of slavery, but prohibition of the evils of alcohol abuse and its consequences, poverty and domestic violence. That inspired and gave political incentive to the passage of the Volstead Act in 1919, the Eighteenth Amendment to the Constitution, which prohibited the manufacture, transportation, and sale of alcoholic beverages.

All of those Awakenings in American history have five things in common. They involved great Christian religious fervor. They were widespread, with a significant segment of the population converted or indirectly inspired. They generated the creation of churches or denominations and social institutions, including colleges and hospitals. They instigated or lent credence to movements for social reform. Those reform movements became political, resulting in major conflicts.

Even the twentieth-century version eventually expressed itself in violent conflict. The passage of the Volstead Act resulted in the emergence of organized crime and the government's fight against it. Some might even connect the postmillennial emphasis (that Christ will return after Christians reform the earth) of the twentieth-century revivals with US involvement in World War I, "The War to End All Wars."

History demonstrates that religious awakenings, especially ones that have fundamentalist dynamics at work within them, eventually tend to express themselves in social reforms and political movements.

Fundamentalist movements are accompanied by tremendous religious fervor and emotional passion. They possess force that, when directed against perceived social evils or harnessed by political leaders, can result in significant social shifts and political conflicts, or both.

Chapter 17

~

What's the Problem?

The Current Scope of Christian Fundamentalist Aspirations

I f America has experienced that pattern before, why should there be concern about a rise in the influence of religious fundamentalism at this point in time?

Clearly, there has been an historical pattern to growth in the influence of religious fervor on politics and social issues. During the past three centuries, there have been heroic and very effective efforts in Christian evangelism. Those efforts resulted in widespread revivals. Those revivals were epitomized by heightened spiritual emotions and religiously inspired social concerns. Those social concerns were very specific. They focused on particular issues. In chronological order, those issues were personal independence, abolition, and prohibition.

Religiously inspired leaders of social reform movements developed political strategies. Those strategies included defining the social problems, educating the public about their causes and the negative effects of the evils they sought to reform, articulating methods of reform, arguing the case for advancing those reforms, electing representatives to accomplish the desired outcomes, and introducing legislation to institute those outcomes. Conflicts ensued, taking the form as they did, of the Revolutionary War, the War between the States, and the rise of organized crime and the government's wars against it. Social changes occurred in the wake of those conflicts.

The current influence of Christian fundamentalism is different. It departs from that historical pattern. While it is true that Christian revivals during the past four decades have resulted in religiously inspired social concerns for reform, Christian fundamentalists have become far more comprehensive in the focus of their desires for reform. The social reforms have been specific. They have been focused on curtailing abortion and homosexual rights. But something else has developed in the process. Frustration among fundamentalists has intensified over time because of the perceived lack of progress in reforming those perceived evils. Their frustration has spawned more rigorous political efforts to change laws. But it has also engendered a desire to change what they perceive as faults in the system of government, which seems to them to have frustrated their efforts. That has created a new vision for America. And that vision involves more far-reaching governmental reforms, rather than simply social ones. The scope of the Christian fundamentalist mission for political transformation beyond social change has become more comprehensive than ever before. There has been an expansive quality to it. Fundamentalists seek to change the government itself.

A war is under way. At the outset, that war targeted abortion as its identified enemy. It was waged through various media, on the streets, in the courts, in legislatures, and by means of democratic elections. The limited success of those methods during the past forty years has engendered increasing levels of frustration among those galvanized around that issue. Meanwhile, the gay rights movement has made significant advances. That has added fuel to the passions of many of the same fundamentalist reformers and another target issue of concern.

Fundamentalist leaders have increasingly identified the government, the political system of the United States, as the impediment to reforming those perceived social evils. Hence, the focus of this social war has shifted to changing the government. In a sense, it has become a war against the government of the United States itself.

The current rendition of the social or cultural war in which American Christian fundamentalists are engaged has expanded in an unprecedented way. Fundamentalists want to reshape the way government in the United States functions in order to accomplish their identified social goals. In the process, additional goals have also been developed, including matters having to do with sex, education, and public displays of Christian faith, among others. From their perspective, the functions of government and the absence of (fundamentalist) faith or values in government need to be changed.

That has given rise to two otherwise contradictory goals. One is the extension of government involvement in personal conduct for moral reasons. The other goal is to shrink government in its public influences over education, business, and other organizations. That has created a situation in which the strategy of their elected representatives is to exacerbate government dysfunction, except for limiting resources for public education and limiting access to abortion and gay rights in a number of states. The goal of shrinking government may seem contradictory to extending government's control over personal access to abortion or gay rights by individuals, unless the real goal is to promote a fundamentalist agenda.

If fundamentalist goals are achieved, the question is how far that agenda should go. What personal preferences and individual behaviors will be identified as in need of control? How would an ascendancy of Christian fundamentalism affect the priorities of US engagement in international affairs within the global community? How would other nations, both secular and those of other fundamentalist faith or ideological persuasion, regard the United States? What effect will more increasingly fundamentalist nations have on international relations?

Chapter 18

～

More Than Ever

The Merger of Fundamentalist Theology and
Political Vision Currently at Work in America

As I have mentioned, one stream of Christian fundamentalism is charismatic. Within the past two decades or so, there has been a growing movement among charismatic Christian fundamentalists, which has influenced other Christian fundamentalists as well. It has been dubbed the New Apostolic Reformation. In its inception, that movement simply emphasized a renewed pattern of ecclesiology. You see, the New Testament writings offer a couple of different ecclesiological models.

Ecclesiology is the field of theology that has to do with church organization. It involves how Christian believers organize themselves and how church authority is structured. One pattern found in the New Testament writings describes four orders of Christian ministry. They are most familiarly known as the laity, deacons, priests or presbyters, and bishops. There is at least one other way of differentiating ministries. St. Paul described them in his first letter to the Corinthians. "And God has placed in the church first of all apostles, second prophets, third teachers, then miracles, then gifts of healing, of helping, of guidance, and of different kinds of tongues" (1 Corinthians 12:28). They are not so much orders of ministry as functions of ministry based upon gifts, which include apostles, prophets, teachers, and so forth. Most Christian churches adopted the official model based on offices of authority. But New Apostolic churches have adopted the latter, more functional, model. The reason for the shift is that most New Apostolic churches follow in the Pentecostal tradition and emphasize spiritual gifts inspired by the Holy Spirit.

Many evangelicals and other Protestants have had points of disagreement with Pentecostal and other charismatic Christians. One of those quarrels revolves around the latter's readiness to believe in spontaneous, direct revelations from God. Other Protestants, Catholics, and Eastern Orthodox Christians think that varieties of Pentecostalism seem to put personal revelation on a par with scriptural revelation or church tradition. They disagree with that emphasis.

Three concepts have transformed the New Apostolic Reformation into what some observers have called a religio-political movement rather than strictly a religious one. The first is the conviction that the world is approaching the end-times. The second is the belief in *spiritual warfare*. And the third is a concept that has been called *dominionism*. Let's take a brief look at each of these, in turn.

Mainstream Christianity has always believed that God will bring history, as it has been known, to an end. Unlike Eastern religious traditions, which have been more cyclical in their conceptualization of history, Christianity is linear. History had a beginning and will come to an end. God is the one who inaugurates both. One of the orthodox doctrines of the Christian faith is the inevitable return of Christ. His eventual return will usher in God's eternal kingdom. Christ will return to institute God's perfect reign, and that will bring an end to human history as we have known it.

Christians throughout history have been taught to behave as if Christ may come at any time. The main reason for that emphasis has been to incentivize individual Christians to remain spiritually vigilant. Throughout the Middle Ages it was popular for preachers and morality plays to emphasize that Christ frequently returns incognito in every generation. They explained that Christ comes in the guise of needy strangers. This was intended to inspire hospitality, charity, and faithfulness.

There have been certain times when significant numbers of Christians firmly believed that Christ's eschatological—his ultimate—return was imminent. During the Apostolic Era (at the time of the twelve apostles), Christians were absolutely convinced that Christ would return, and that the end would come during their lifetime. That conviction is evident throughout the New Testament writings. In fact, many scholars believe that the book of Revelation was written to deal with the crisis of faith that ensued among second generation Christians when all but one of the apostles had died without the materialization of Christ's return. The book of Revelation intimated that the Roman emperor was the Antichrist and that they had to endure his persecutions until Christ's return. God would make all things right, not them. Their role was to believe, endure, and spread God's love and the gospel of Jesus Christ, not remake government. They contented themselves in transforming lives by individual conversion.

Since then, there have been other times during which the widespread conviction existed that the end-times were at hand. Contemporary circumstances in the world at those times roused that belief. During the sixth and seventh centuries AD, the bubonic plague struck the Roman Empire. Simultaneously, the western half of the empire was besieged with unrelenting assaults by various northern tribes until Rome fell. It was not too long thereafter that the eastern half of the empire was swept by Islam. At the time, many Christians firmly believed that those were precursors to the end and to Christ's return. Then again, during the fourteenth century, severe economic depression and the Black Plague ravaged Europe. Destitution, disease, and death were everywhere. Almost half of the population of Europe had contracted the plague. One third of the population died of the disease. Death could strike anyone at any time, and there was no defense against it. The future seemed hopeless. The only refuge, the only hope, seemed to be God's miraculous intervention or anticipation of Christ's return.

The chaos of the Reformation, the Counter-Reformation, and the Thirty Years' War also gave rise to apocalyptic thinking. Social upheaval, religious confusion, and warfare seemed unrelenting. People took what comfort they could from rigid dogma and readily saw those of different persuasions as inspired by the Antichrist. Protestants firmly believed that the pope was the Antichrist, and Roman Catholics had the same opinion of reformers such as Luther. They saw their struggles in apocalyptic terms.

We are currently in the midst of just such an era of conviction that the end is at hand. The New Apostolic Reformation, among other Christian fundamentalist groups, is largely convinced that its members have received special revelation that the end is near. That conviction has been used as a clarion call for extraordinary vigilance in the implementation of urgently needed new strategies for social reform.

Belief in spiritual warfare has also been extant among many Christians throughout history. It has not been a core belief or always identified by that nomenclature. But the Gospels are replete with incidents in which Jesus confronted demons and delivered people from demonic possession. Since that special period, there have been times and places in which sensitivity to demonic activity has been heightened. The Dark Ages in Europe was one such era. Throughout that period, witch hunts in Europe were frequent and widespread. The sixteenth and seventeenth centuries were another period of heightened attentiveness to demonic activity, both in Europe and its colonies. Haiti has long been sensitive to demonic activity. In recent years, Africa has been rife with claims of demonic activity. With the rise of the Neo-Pentecostal movement, so has the United States. Traditionally, spiritual warfare has been the practice of identifying and expelling or exorcizing evil spirits that have possessed or oppressed individuals. It has been accomplished by prayer, by taking authority over the evil spirits or demonic forces in the name of Christ, and by binding and expelling them.

The New Apostolic Reformation has taken the understanding of spiritual warfare to an unparalleled extent. Those involved in the movement identify three levels of spiritual warfare. The first is what has already been described. It focuses its attention on identifying demonic possession and delivering individuals from the influence of evil spirits by exorcism.

The second level of spiritual warfare has focused on demonic influences in locations and various organizations. It devotes its attention to witchcraft, other religions, and particular organizations like Freemasonry. Participants seek to take authority over the evil spirits that they believe influence the people who are in certain locations or are involved in particular organizations. They do that by physically staking out locations where such groups have gathered or intend to gather. New Apostolic Reformation groups come together to pray at those places in order to break the power of evil in those locations. It may also take the form of trying to exercise political pressure against the building of mosques or worship sites for other religions and meeting places for groups that they believe to be under the influence of evil spirits.

The third level of spiritual warfare is *dominion*. It is the practice of confronting and exercising dominion over "principalities and powers" or structures of government and "molders" of society at large. That is accomplished by prayer and, increasingly, by strategies of power politics. The initial focus of those efforts may have been abortion or homosexuality, but it has become far broader in scope.

C. Peter Wagner is the chief chronicler and an advocate of the movement. He was the person who coined the name "New Apostolic Reformation." In his book *Dominion! How Kingdom Action Can Change the World,* Wagner set the broad scope of the mission in his introduction to the book. Wagner gives lip service to the follies of failed Christian efforts to create theocracies. And yet, he writes, "Jesus taught us to pray that God's Kingdom would come and His will done on earth as it is in heaven. To that end in these present times the urgent mandate of God to the Church is to actively engage in transforming society. This means placing Christian leaders into positions of leadership influential enough to shape our culture."[ix]

That is the current vision for a cross section of Christian fundamentalists in America as well as members of the New Apostolic Reformation. Their ultimate goal is to achieve social transformation for American society under God's direction. They seek to use the political procedures of democracy in service of that goal by attempting to institute what they understand to be biblical standards of conduct and to elect like-minded political leaders to implement them. Wagner writes the following:

> The question is, how can taking dominion of society and infusing the values of the Kingdom of God operate within democratic government? In a democracy, while there is no established religion, religious people can be elected to office ... and can also rise to the highest and most influential positions in the other six non-government molders of culture. The rules of the democratic game open the doors for Christians and others with Kingdom values, to move into positions of leadership influential enough to shape the whole nation from top to bottom.[x]

Dominionism is the belief that God's law as set forth in the Bible should govern society. It envisions that Christians should control civil government in accordance with biblical values. It argues that Christians have the power conferred by the Holy Spirit, the right conferred upon the Body of Christ, and the responsibility conferred by God to take dominion over America. That is to say, they believe that it is essential in these latter days for Christians to exercise authority over the most significant aspects of American society. To participants in the New Apostolic Reformation this is the third level of spiritual warfare.

The vision of dominion is fairly straightforward. It is the conviction that right-thinking and Spirit-filled Christians must take dominion over American society on God's behalf. That includes dominating the political structures of American government. For some fundamentalist leaders dominion also includes "reconstructing" the US Constitution so that it more explicitly reflects biblical laws. These aspirations, as I say, are not limited to members of the New Apostolic Reformation. Numerous, contemporary, Christian fundamentalist leaders embrace the vision of dominion whether they are affiliated with the New Apostolic Reformation or not. Wagner writes, "I personally associate with a large number of Christian leaders who, along with me, believe and teach dominion theology. As far as I know, none among us would advocate that America—or any other nation, for that matter—should strive to become a theocracy."[xi]

Wagner vehemently argues that this is not a venture in theocracy. "When this happens and the people of God begin to advocate, propagate, and implement their values, this is not theocracy."[xii] You may notice that Wagner takes pains to repeatedly assert that this vision of dominionism is not theocracy. He argues that it is not theocratic simply because the plan is to institute God's law and Christian dominion by means of democratic processes. Wagner indicates that in democracies the majority of the voting public gets to have its way. He says that fundamentalists of this persuasion simply aspire to utilize electoral processes and other permissible political procedures to institute the values and beliefs of a critical mass of voters by means of state and/or national elections. Hence, since democratic procedures would be used to achieve Christian dominion, by definition, the goal cannot be considered theocracy.

I disagree. If theocracy is government that derives its legal legitimacy and authority from God (à la Gutman) and in which the ultimate authority and power is ascribed to God's leadership and divine laws guide legislation (à la Josephus), then it is theocracy. The manner in which that system of government is achieved is irrelevant. If "God's people," Christian fundamentalists and those who share their ideals, simply seek to follow God's leadership and institute "Kingdom values" and biblical laws, it can be nothing less than theocracy. Electing right-minded leaders to accomplish that end is merely a way of employing democratic procedures to institute theocracy by means of an elected oligarchy. The current theocratic state of Iran was instituted by means of the same democratic processes and procedures. It has been mediated by an oligarchy of like-minded officials. History demonstrates that democracy has been used to institute theocracy in the past. Among other instances, it happened in Geneva and Massachusetts Bay Colony, as well as Iran. It borders on duplicity to claim otherwise.

It is not that I object, in principle, to the vision of God governing a nation. Who could govern better than God? As I have said previously, though, that has never happened apart from human instrumentation. Imperfect human instrumentation of a theocratic vision has always failed miserably. It is only natural, absent a current robust vision for democracy, that theocracy would be appealing to fundamentalists. But theocracy is even more corruptible than democracy. The power it confers has always been abused. The human conduits distort God's ways and oppress citizens. Moreover, revisionist arguments to the contrary, the founders of the American form of democracy never intended it to be used to institute a theocratic nation.

The extent of this modern fundamentalist vision for dominance over American government and society is far reaching. Its logical conclusion is nothing less than theocracy. And it targets many of the pillars of American society.

The term "principalities and powers" was used by St. Paul in his letter to the Ephesians. He wrote, "For we wrestle not against flesh and blood, but against principalities, against powers, against the rulers of the darkness of this world, against spiritual wickedness in high places" (Ephesians 6:12, King James Version). Customarily, that has been understood as Paul providing rationale for Christians to endure the persecutions that they experienced at the time. Paul explained that Christians were not only just up against people but were also up against powers in the spiritual dimension. It was his way of stressing the importance of endurance, because suffering had meaning on a spiritual level.

The New Apostolic Reformation movement has taken that idea and wedded it with the concepts of spiritual warfare and dominionism. The result is this: on behalf of Christ, Christians should take political control over any structure that is not the way they perceive God wants it to be. The purpose of dominion is to prepare for Christ's eventual return. They interpret principalities and powers as centers of political and cultural control in this world. They believe that those structures have come under the control of evil spirits. They believe that it is the Christian vocation to deliver them from evil, from demonic forces, and to take dominion over them.

What are the identified "molders" or principalities and powers or kingdoms or hills, as they are variously called? Seven of them have been identified in the United States, and in most other nations, for that matter. That number has been borrowed from the seven heads of the Antichrist described in the book of Revelation (Revelation 13:1). The seven principalities and powers in America include government, business, education, science, arts and entertainment (the media), family life, and religion. The core conviction is that these seven are the central components of American culture, and that all of them have come under the dominance of demonic forces, basically expressed in liberal practices. Each must be taken over for Christ, basically by instituting conservative values.

Government must be taken over by right-thinking Christians. The objective is to do away with the wrong kinds of laws, to legislate the right kinds of laws, and to enforce them in the right ways. What are right laws? They are laws congruent with biblical laws. Which biblical laws? That remains to be seen. There are clear hints, of course. They include laws about abortion, sexuality, marriage, education, and religion in public forums.

Government must be drastically reduced so as to decrease its secular (demonic) influences. One way to reduce government influence is to reduce the number of government agencies. Another is to reduce the number of government regulations that agencies oversee. Another is to reduce its funding by reducing taxes. Taxes should be drastically reduced so as to limit government influences. That will suffocate such government-provided services as public education, which has been regarded as a seedbed of secular thought.

Defunding major government programs is a key method of wrestling dominion away from the spiritual forces of evil that inspire the current problems with the nation and the world. **Public education** must be defunded so as to lessen its secular influences, or at the very least to gain greater control over it to limit those influences. They regard public education as the bastion of secularism. They understand it as the seedbed of the humanist mind-set, which is demonically inspired. Science must be defunded for the same reasons. **Arts** and "culture" must also be defunded because they enshrine the worst of the demonically inspired culture and its essential manifestation, sexual promiscuity.

Business could generate financial support for the campaign by increasing contributions to like-minded politicians. After all, it is believed that the government has made the American economy all but socialist. Fundamentalists think that socialism is linked to atheism and, therefore, that it has been inspired by evil. Significantly reducing government regulations and taxation has a potential triple advantage. It could provide more money for the church. It could persuade business leaders to support the cause. And it could win more votes from those wanting to keep more of their money.

Science must be wrested from the influence of evil forces. Many of the regulations with which businesses have to deal under the current government are environmental. Scientific methodology is strictly empirical. Empiricism tends to be agnostic. Agnosticism is inherently at odds with faith. And that is why so many scientists have been at odds with Christianity over the centuries. Environmentalism, therefore, is based on a belief system that is false, and so its conclusions must be false as well. Environmentalism is identified with science and naturalism. Deregulating business has the threefold benefit of greater short-term profits for businesses, gaining their political support, and disempowering science's agnostic influences.

Traditional **family life** must be supported at all costs. That will involve curtailing the advances of the gay rights movement and the feminist movement. It may involve making it more difficult to divorce. It will certainly also involve severely limiting access to legal abortion. It will definitely involve outlawing same-sex marriage. And it will involve strong emphasis on sexual abstinence instead of the use of other birth control methods.

Religion is crucial. The belief among most Christian fundamentalists, and certainly among members of the New Apostolic Reformation, is that America was always meant to be a Christian nation. The idea of the separation of church and state is considered to be a myth perpetrated by humanists and liberals. Religion must become the cornerstone of America once again. By religion is meant Christian religion, and by that is meant Christian fundamentalism. Fundamentalists believe that liberal, mainline Christian denominations are not really Christian and that they suffer under demonic influences. They believe that they are under God's judgment and that is the reason for their decline in numbers. God has simply removed his blessing from them, and so they will shrivel and die. Other religions are false and to be ignored. That does not include Judaism, because the Bible indicates that Jews are God's chosen people and that they will be critically involved in the end-times.

This may well sound like an exaggerated view of an obscure sect, like some version of the Branch Davidian cult, but it is not. One of the apostles of the New Apostolic Reformation movement anointed Sarah Palin for God's blessing of her political candidacy for the vice presidency in the last election cycle. Recent candidates for the presidency have espoused intimations of just such convictions. Rick Perry's "Day of Prayer, Repentance, and Fasting" was closely linked with the movement. Interestingly, the repentance portion of that event concentrated on Christians' repentance of tolerance for different perspectives rather than on repentance of the personal sins of the participants. Michele Bachmann's political thought and approach to international relations, especially in relation to Israel, have betrayed influence by its teachings. And Rick Santorum's statements about religion, social policies, and personal morality, while reflective of Roman Catholic fundamentalism, are congruent with the philosophy and strategies of dominionism.

One of the central goals of this movement is to make the United States more biblical in its laws, a more godly and righteous nation. But how can elected government officials make the American people more godly and righteous? Godliness and righteousness are matters of individual choice, matters of the heart.

The dominion movement falls into the same trap as its predecessors. The New Apostolic Reformation, along the lines of traditional Pentecostalism, has its roots in the nineteenth-century American Holiness Movement. That movement emphasized perfectionism. The Holiness Movement believed in the perfectibility of the individual Christian. The problem is that that notion has always been erroneous. Christians are all human beings, and all human beings are imperfect.

St. Augustine's formula has defined Christian orthodoxy for the better part of fifteen hundred years. He stated that the human condition has three states of being. Before the fall of mankind, humans were able not to sin (capable of perfection). After the fall, humans were not able not to sin (incapable of perfection). In heaven, humans will be unable to sin (perfect). In this world, imperfect people cannot create the perfect kingdom of God on earth because we are unable not to sin. Humans will always fall prey to their own imperfections and insecurities. Fundamentalists with aspirations for dominion or theocracy are subject to their own imperfections and insecurities until their unrelenting needs for control will create a backlash or counter-reformation in reaction against their principles.

Dominionism and the New Apostolic Reformation, in particular, constitute yet another fundamentalist Christian effort to create God's kingdom on earth. It ignores the failures of past efforts either because of unfamiliarity with the details of history or simple blind egoism. By blind egoism, I mean the driving conviction that God is doing something special, that this is a special time, and that they are special people. That makes all past failures at theocracy moot, simply because everything is special this time. But all of the previous efforts to build God's kingdom embraced the very same convictions.

Chapter 19

—

It's a Personal Thing

The Personal Dimension of Fundamentalist Splitting

Different streams of Christian fundamentalism are active in the United States. Christian fundamentalists need to be increasingly scrupulous and exceptional. They tend to need to differentiate themselves from others, even from other Christian fundamentalists. Those of somewhat different orientations may collaborate for certain goals or against common identified adversaries; but once those goals are achieved or those adversaries are vanquished, they will tend to turn away from each other. They are only human, after all.

I received my bachelor's degree from a prominent American evangelical Christian college. Since its founding in the nineteenth century, that school has had a clearly defined statement of faith. The doctrines incorporated within it included the core beliefs that Protestant fundamentalists subscribed to when they adopted that name in 1922. It was, therefore, quite technically a fundamentalist college. Every student was required to sign a document that agreed to those points of doctrine and promised to conform to them. There was also a code of conduct that guided student behavior. It prohibited the following activities: drinking alcoholic beverages, using mind-altering drugs, smoking tobacco products, gambling, dancing, swearing, and physical displays of affection.

Virtually every student enrolled at that college was an evangelical Christian. We shared a common faith. We cooperated for a common goal, higher education and graduation with a degree. And we were divided. We called each other names. The names identified the division. There were two names: "Fundies" and "Liberals." Students from those two general groupings did not often fraternize with each other socially. It had nothing to do with faith or doctrine. It had everything to do with perceived mind-set, attitude, and behavioral demeanor. Fundies were perceived as more straight-laced and rigid, given to more conservative political points of view in relation to the Vietnam War and women's rights. Liberals were perceived to be more cavalier in their social conduct and/or given to more liberal views on those issues. Christian fundamentalists are not content to integrate differences but need to distinguish themselves even from each other.

Christian fundamentalists also tend to compare themselves with each other spiritually. They have cultivated what might be called a keen sense of peripheral vision. They possess an eagerness to be—and this term was often used—"spiritual giants." They want to compare well with their peers or to surpass them. They need to be special. They are only human, after all.

Once, an unplanned revival broke out at another Christian college. Word of it spread like wildfire. And the first response by students was not joy for the students at that other school but concern that we experience the same spiritual emotions. I was student body chaplain at the time and so arranged for a group of students involved in that revival to come and share what happened. They came to one of our chapel services, shared, and prayed for us. Quite a number of students were disappointed that we didn't experience the same revival of faith and spiritual feelings. Their reaction was to wonder what might be wrong with us, since God had not seen fit to bless us with the same sort of emotional revival. They wanted to be special to God.

Somewhat related to that yearning for spiritual experience as well as to the need to be distinguished, there was another division among students. It was between charismatic and noncharismatic Christians. The two groups looked askance at each other.

In their eagerness to continue to enjoy spiritual experiences accompanied by emotional symptoms, some students would attend revival events off campus. I attended one that featured a woman speaker. It was a time when women were not usually permitted to act as spiritual leaders. She shared her struggle. She said, "I prayed for years. I prayed, 'Lord, why have you given me this passion to speak your Word, when I have no right to speak?' Then the Lord revealed it to me. Jesus said that we will be baptized with the Holy Spirit and with fire. The Lord said to me, 'You have been baptized with the Holy Spirit, but you need to be baptized with fire.' And that's what he's called me to prophesy: 'It's not enough to be born again. It's not enough to be baptized with the Spirit. You also need to be baptized with fire.'" For many Christian fundamentalists, there is never enough. There is a never-ending need to expand the sphere of one's zeal for God. Moreover, altogether too many fundamentalists unconditionally accept the teachings of acknowledged leaders who claim God's revelation.

One of the students with me at that conference experienced something. He left college to join that small group, and I never saw or heard of him again. Christian fundamentalists are often willing to go to any length to be in the place that they think God wants them to be or to experience God's greater approval, power, or purpose. It is a way of being distinguished by God. They simply want to be special.

Christian fundamentalists of different orientations may collaborate for certain goals or against common identified adversaries; but once those goals are achieved or those adversaries are vanquished, they will turn away from each other. Protestant fundamentalists, evangelicals, biblical literalists, Pentecostal fundamentalists, charismatic fundamentalists, Roman Catholic fundamentalists, charismatic Catholics, etc., may cooperate, for example, in the overturning of *Roe v. Wade* to outlaw abortion, but they will always tend to think less of each other's faith than their own.

It is integral to fundamentalism to firmly believe that one's own convictions are superior to those of others. Evangelical Christian fundamentalists will always tend to think that charismatic Christian fundamentalists are somewhat overly emotional and prone to unorthodoxy. Likewise, charismatic fundamentalists will always think of evangelical fundamentalists as dry and uninspired by the Spirit, spiritually incomplete. Both will always look with some distrust toward Roman Catholic fundamentalists and vice versa. Sooner or later they will part company from each other over what to emphasize and how far to go. They need to be special. They are only human, after all.

And that is my point. Christian fundamentalists are just as prone to the same weaknesses as anyone else. They will accept that fact as individuals. It is simply that they have an extremely difficult time accepting that in groups. They want to be special.

Chapter 20

⁓

The Roots of Contention

Some Conflicts between Fundamentalism and
Democracy Embedded within Western Civilization

Modern democracy is a product of modern Western civilization. It is not a product of the Christian faith or the Bible. Of course, the most important core component of Western civilization has been Christianity. And in this overlap lies the root of social contention.

Samuel P. Huntington, in his book *The Clash of Civilizations and the Remaking of World Order*, lists eight basic characteristics of Western civilization. I will attempt to summarize and distill those eight characteristics, as follows:

1. **Western Christianity**: The coexistence of Catholicism and Protestantism within a shared Christian faith is the single most important characteristic of Western Civilization.
2. **Classical Legacy**: As a third generation civilization (ancient, medieval, and modern) Western civilization inherited a great deal from its previous iterations. It has inherited Greek philosophy, rationalism, Roman law, and the Latin language.

3. **European Languages**: Language is second only to religion in differentiating people in one culture from another. The West differs from most other civilizations in the multiplicity of languages spoken in one civilization.

4. **Separation of Spiritual and Temporal Authority**: Throughout Western history, first the church and then many churches existed apart from the state, and vice versa. That dualism of spiritual and temporal authority has contributed to the development of freedom in the West.

5. **Rule of Law**: Inherited from the Romans the tradition of the rule of law laid the foundation for constitutionalism. It safeguarded human rights against the exercise of arbitrary power.

6. **Social Pluralism**: Western societies have been highly pluralistic, composed of diverse and autonomous groups. Most Western societies included a relatively strong and autonomous aristocracy, a substantial peasant class, and a small but significant class of merchants and traders. That limited the absolutism that emerged in other civilizations.

7. **Representative Bodies**: Social pluralism gave rise to parliaments, unions, and other institutions that represented the interests of their respective constituencies. That spawned modern democracy. No other civilization has any comparable heritage of representative bodies stretching back more than two thousand years.

8. **Individualism**: Several of the aforementioned traits of Western civilization have contributed to the emergence of a sense of individualism and a tradition of individual rights. This is unique among existing civilizations. Most other civilizations have been collectivist.[xiii]

Woven within this tapestry of core characteristics of Western civilization, several threads are in tension with each other. Those tensions have strained various nations and constituent groups within Western civilization from time to time during the past four hundred years or so. Those same stresses exist in the current generation to the point that they threaten to tear the very fabric of American democratic society. The combination of Western Christianity with a classical legacy of pre-Christian thinkers, the separation of spiritual and temporal authority, and social pluralism possess inherent tensions. There are ways in which Christian faith can be at odds with the others. Diversity within unity has always been challenging, but all the more when the form of Christian faith is fundamentalist.

Islamic civilization far surpassed European Christendom in science and medicine during the Middle Ages. One of the reasons for that was the influence of the Greek philosopher Aristotle on physicians and other early scientists in Islamic civilization. By and large, Christian faith in Western civilization was resistant to pre-Christian classical legacy. The church served as the censor of acceptable thought in medieval Western civilization. The church rejected most pre-Christian classical thought, with the exception of Plato.

Plato and Aristotle, between them, created something of a philosophical watershed, which has persisted throughout the history of Western thought.

Plato taught that things in this world existed and found definition by virtue of their relatedness to heavenly or spiritual archetypes (ideals in the mind of God). Christian theologians adopted some of Plato's philosophical notions. His ontology, his understanding of the nature of things, connected temporal types with spiritual archetypes. He thought that each and every thing in the material world had its own spiritual essence. He was persuaded that that essence was connected to a spiritual reality in heaven. He observed that things of the same type have different properties. Some chairs were made of wood and others of stone and some people are short while others are tall, for example. That led him to differentiate between external form (accidence) and internal essence (substance). Christian thinkers found Plato's approach to be congruent with the biblical axiom that God is the Creator and Sustainer of all things.

Platonism became the foundation of medieval realism. Platonism was the basis of medieval Christian sacramental theology, for example. That is where the concept of transubstantiation originated. Bread and wine could retain their physical properties (their accidence) but their spiritual essence (their substance) could change into Christ's body and blood. Platonic thought dominated the Western approach to science and retarded its progress relative to Islamic and Asian science. In effect, Platonism sought truth only through faith, and that is also the basis of Christian fundamentalism.

Aristotle was a student of Plato. Contrary to Plato, Aristotle argued that things have their definition by virtue of their particular material properties and not by some spiritual essence or connection with God's thoughts. Aristotle sought truth through empirical investigation and analysis. Aristotelian thought is the philosophical basis of empiricism, naturalism, and modern science. There has been a long-standing tension between non-Platonic classical thought and Christian faith.

Let's take a look at a very real and current example of that tension in practice. At various times during the past several hundred years, certain individuals have symbolized the conflict between these two philosophical approaches. Simply mentioning their names evokes the tension. Galileo was one. The conflict was about which orb was at the center, the sun or the earth. Isaac Newton was another. The conflict surrounded what kept things on earth. But no one better illustrated the point than the naturalist Charles Darwin. His theory of evolution has consistently generated controversy. This conflict revolves around whether life-forms were each created as they are or developed over time. The Scopes "Monkey Trial" brought that conflict into full relief.

Darwin's theory of evolution continues to evoke strong, negative reactions among Christian fundamentalists to this day. Many Christian fundamentalists continue to object to exposing children to it in public education. Their objection is based not on safety issues, ethics, or morality but purely on religious grounds, and purely theological ones at that. One point of many theological differences among Christians is whether the creation story in the first chapter of the book of Genesis is to be understood literally or figuratively. Some Christians believe that the story describes precisely how God created life on earth, and others do not. There are devout Christians who believe in what has been called "theistic evolution." That is the idea that God created everything, and that he has used what we call evolution in the ongoing process of creation. Those who wish to eliminate exposure to evolution from public school curricula want to impose their particular hermeneutic, their own personal approach to the interpretation of that specific story in the book of Genesis, on everyone else. They want to protect their children from exposure to a point of intellectual dissonance with their own personal faith. This is a prime example of the tension between classical legacy and Christian fundamentalism.

A basic question separates Christian fundamentalism and classical legacy. Why do humans possess the capacity to reason and to make choices? In Umberto Ecco's novel *The Name of the Rose,* the Venerable Jorge states that reason was conferred upon humans for "sublime recapitulation." Is the purpose of the human capacity to reason simply and solely to understand what God has revealed and continually to repeat only what has been revealed, or is it also to make new discoveries of reality? Is the purpose of the human capacity to make choices simply to choose to obey God, or is it also to take greater responsibility in collaborating for the good of humanity and the earth as a whole? How different people answer that question indicates the tension between classical legacy and Christian fundamentalism.

There is another basic tension within Western civilization. It is somewhat related to the previous one, but more far-reaching. A strain exists in Western civilization between Christian faith and social pluralism. By definition, a pluralistic society is one in which there is mutually tolerated, if not respected, diversity. That diversity may be socioeconomic in nature with mutual respect among people of different occupations and levels of wealth. It also includes tolerance for diverse groups and organizations, even those that work at odds with each other, such as unions and corporations. It involves respect for peoples of different racial, ethnic, linguistic, and cultural backgrounds. It includes tolerance for differences of political thought. But it also includes respect, or at the very least tolerance, for people of diverse religious and philosophical persuasions. Christian faith, that is Christian fundamentalism, has often been at odds with pluralism, especially in the form of diverse thoughts, beliefs, and practices.

Several modern European democracies are essentially secular. Church has virtually no official role in those nations. Some would say that this is most notable in France. Other modern European democracies have an official state church but tolerate other religions and are largely secular in their ethos. Great Britain and Scandinavian countries are examples of that rendition.

It has become increasingly popular for Christian fundamentalists to differentiate America from European nations without explicitly explaining the rationale. The implication may seem to be an allusion to economic differences—that America is more purely capitalist and that some European nations are more socialist. But there is something else far more basic in the comparison. It has to do with the role of religion in American society versus the role of religion in many European societies.

That was one of the reasons that President George W. Bush emphasized the "new Europe," referring to Eastern European nations such as Poland. He was accentuating the prominence of states that are more traditionally Christian in ethos over against more secularized Western European nations. The primary issue is not whether Western European nations share democracy with the United States. They do. It is not whether Western European nations share capitalism with the United States. They do, even though some of them have more mixed economies than America does. The underlying issue is whether those nations share the same Christian faith with America or are secular humanistic states.

The United States has no official national church, and yet many would argue that it is anything but a secular state. In fact, as I say, the long-cherished idea of the separation of church and state has been called into question of late by Christian fundamentalists. Fundamentalists would argue that the term "church" in the phrase "separation of church and state" refers to particular denominations and not religion in general, that is, Christianity.

In the United States, the essential tension that exists is between social pluralism and Christian fundamentalism. How can people in community deal with it when the core values of some deeply disagree with the core values of others? How can people in community resolve the conflict between the core values of some and the defining behaviors of others? These questions continue to be pressed nearly to the breaking point in American democratic society. They coalesce around issues such as the teaching of evolution in public schools, birth control, the legality of abortion, and homosexual civil rights, among others. How can such apparently irreconcilable differences be resolved among the citizens of a democratic society when the citizenry is philosophically pluralistic?

Chapter 21

⁓

Strange Bedfellows

Historic Tensions between Christianity and Humanism

This conflict between Christianity and other ways of thinking within the same culture is nothing new, and that may be part of the problem. It has never fully been resolved. Almost five hundred years ago, when the Renaissance and Reformation were emerging, those two movements had a common enemy. That enemy was the inflexibility of medieval Roman Catholicism. As I have said, the hierarchy of the Roman Catholic Church functioned as the ultimate censor of Western civilization. Its censorship extended far beyond defining theological orthodoxy and liturgical or moral practice. The church determined what was acceptable or objectionable in other spheres as well. It had the power, especially where church and state collaborated, to prohibit free expression in the arts, sciences, philosophy, literature, and more.

At the outset, fledgling humanists and Protestant reformers found each other to be allies against a common foe. That foe was oppression by the hierarchy of the church. It is an Arabic adage, but the logic is universal: "The enemy of my enemy is my friend." Humanists like Erasmus, who were affiliated with the Renaissance, united with reformers such as Luther in their opposition to the inflexible controls imposed by the late medieval church's hierarchy.

Humanists, as the term implied, put man at the center of their attention. They placed man at the center of the universe, for that matter. They emphasized that human attention should focus on humanity. Simply consider the sudden shift that took place in the fine arts. Paintings of historical figures and contemporary individuals replaced biblical scenes. Statues of nudes replaced saints. The goal of the Renaissance was individual expression in an empirical world.

Protestant reformers, on the other hand, focused on the Bible. They placed Jesus as the center of their attention and put God at the center of the universe. Their goal was a more accurate, biblical Christian faith and the freedom to practice that faith unmolested. They wanted to clear away the erroneous accretions that had developed in official Christianity. They were determined to remove any barriers between people and God.

At best, humanists and Protestant reformers made strange bedfellows. Faith in man and reason is a far cry from faith in God and the Bible. One might argue that they were in conflict. Nevertheless, freedom of expression for their respective thoughts sufficed to unite them against what stood in their way. That alliance of convenience created an atmosphere of mutual tolerance. And that mutual tolerance helped to give birth to modern democracy. One of the most subtle and yet most significant aspects of that fledgling post medieval atmosphere was tolerance for intellectual pluralism. It was tolerance for diversity of thought.

Once the monopoly of Roman Catholic authority was broken and the European religious wars of the sixteenth and seventeenth centuries ended, expression of free thought became possible. Hence, pluralistic thought exploded in the eighteenth century. It created an entirely new atmosphere, called the Age of Reason. That, in turn, is what gave rise to such foundational values as the freedom of speech, which is really the right of free thought and expression. It was enshrined in the Constitution of the United States. Freedom of thought and expression provides the basis for freedom of religion, including fundamentalism.

Modern humanism and Christian fundamentalism continue to be completely distinct from one another. The International Humanist and Ethical Union developed what it called the "Minimum Statement on Humanism." This is how it defines humanism:

> Humanism is a democratic and ethical life stance, which affirms that human beings have the right and responsibility to give meaning and shape to their own lives. It stands for building a more humane society through an ethic based on human and natural values in the spirit of reason and free inquiry through human capabilities. It is not theistic, and it does not accept supernatural views of reality.[xiv]

You could say that the principles of humanism and Christian fundamentalism are at opposite ends of a philosophical spectrum. They hold different positions when it comes to ethics as well. Yet, both claim paternity to American democracy. It has been commonplace for Christian fundamentalists to label Christians of more liberal and moderate persuasion as humanists in Christian garb or with belief in God tacked on. One wonders if many of the Founding Fathers would not have fit that label. Nevertheless, the founders were willing and able to embrace citizens of both perspectives and sanctioned their diverse belief systems within American democracy. They may have made bedfellows as strange as their Renaissance and Reformation ancestors.

The very foundation of liberal democratic values is the inviolable right of free thought and expression. Differences of cherished thought will always exist. Mutual tolerance is essential. Sometimes disagreements become profound. Sometimes tolerance is stretched nearly to the breaking point. The strength of democratic values is tested by the ability to tolerate perspectives that different segments of society mutually abhor and to defend their right to exist. But what are societies to do when liberal democratic processes can be used to limit those same liberal democratic values?

Europe is grappling with this in relation to Islamic fundamentalism. European nations have experienced a surge in the influx of Muslims from Islamic nations. Though unaccustomed to liberal democracy, some of those immigrants have eventually become citizens. Many retain their absolute allegiance to Islam, including Islamic law and customs. Where a critical mass of the population is Islamic, fundamentalist movements have been afoot to institute elements of Islamic law, in particular political jurisdictions. As the critical mass of Islamic fundamentalists increases in pluralistic democracies, it is conceivable that they will be able to use the democratic political process to institute nonpluralistic, restrictive Islamic laws and customs in non-Islamic nations.

This exposes the Achilles heel of democracy. How can pluralistic democracy survive in the face of the expanding influences of fundamentalism? How can a pluralistic democracy retain its core principles in the face of growing numbers of increasingly avid fundamentalist voters, intent on changing the very nature of society itself? Fundamentalists are apt to use the very privileges of democracy, the right to voice and vote their convictions, to limit pluralism and even those democratic processes.

Frankly, I raise this issue in connection with the impact of Islamic fundamentalists on liberal democracies in Europe because it is less threatening for Americans. The same political dynamic has been playing itself out in America, but with Christian fundamentalists.

Fundamentalists of whatever denomination seem very happy to benefit from the principles of freedom of thought, speech, religion, and vote in democratic nations until they achieve the political clout to limit them for those who are different from themselves. Fundamentalists firmly

believe that their faith, principles, practices, laws, and sensibilities are the
only ones inspired by the only God. Ergo, logically, it is best for everyone
to live under them. Beneath the surface, most fundamentalists believe
that obedience is the best course—obedience to God as they understand
God's will to be. That is the reason that many fundamentalists tend to
be predisposed to authoritarianism rather than liberal democracy within
a pluralistic society. And it is the reason that fundamentalists feel free to
use democratic processes to further their agenda without compromise.

One recent episode provides an example of the issue of religious
authoritarianism in practice. Supposedly concerned to support the rights
of economically underprivileged women, the Obama administration
violated the boundary between church and state. It determined that,
under the provisions of the Affordable Care Act, medical insurance
coverage must include reimbursement for contraceptives by employers
who offer health insurance to their employees. Churches were specifically
exempted from that regulation. However, some churches, including the
Roman Catholic Church, own other organizations and corporations.
Those subsidiary businesses were not exempted from the new policy.
The Roman Catholic hierarchy conscientiously and vehemently objects
to the use of contraceptives. And so the American Council of Catholic
Bishops immediately identified the new federal policy as a violation of
religious freedom. The bishops argued that the Obama administration
was forcing the church to violate its religious principles regarding the use
of contraceptives. They argued that it is a violation of religious liberty
to require the church to pay for insurance that provided contraceptive
coverage for the employees of organizations that it owns.

The Obama administration admitted its error and changed its
policy. It proposed to require insurance companies to provide coverage
for contraceptives, instead, without requiring conscientiously objecting
religious institutions to pay for it as a separate cost. The bishops
still objected. They maintained that their objection was not about
contraception, per se, but about the government's violation of religious

freedom. And yet, no church would be required to pay for the proposed coverage. As I understand it, their reaction to the compromise proposal seems to betray an authoritarian streak. The institutions that the church owns employ staff members who are not members of the Catholic Church. Beyond that, more than 95 percent of Catholic women in America use some form of contraception during their childbearing years. The Catholic bishops seem unable to control the use of contraceptives, even among Catholic women.

American Catholic bishops appear to be in danger of the same violation of the separation of church and state that they level at the current administration. Perhaps their position is understandable since the Roman Catholic Church has always been ambivalent about the very notion of the separation of church and state. In 1899, Pope Leo XIII issued an encyclical in which he described the separation of church and state in the United States as the "American heresy." The American bishops' current argument can be construed as disingenuous. In effect, they seem to want government to perpetuate an economic disincentive to individuals who might otherwise use contraceptives. Contraceptives are expensive. Economically challenged women find it more difficult to afford them than less economically constrained women. Cost provides a disincentive to the use of contraceptives especially among the poor. Individual payment for contraceptives is more likely to reduce their use than if it were covered by insurers. Insofar as that is any motive in the bishops' argument whatsoever, then they are also infringing upon the boundary between church and state. They are attempting to use the state to discourage women from using contraceptives for financial reasons. That constitutes a reversion to authoritarianism, which is characteristic of fundamentalism.

Subsequently, a female student at Georgetown Law School testified before US House of Representatives Democrats to advocate medical insurance coverage for contraceptives. Her testimony became notorious when radio commentator Rush Limbaugh referenced it and labeled the student as a prostitute and worse. Note his dehumanizing tactic of crass intimidation. During the three-day period following her testimony, Limbaugh referred to that young student approximately forty times on his radio program. Also notice the exaggerated and overly repetitive attacks that he made against a private citizen. Authoritarianism in service of ideology has been prone to bullying patterns of behavior. They are characteristic tactics of propaganda. Individuals inclined to authoritarianism all too often justify the means they employ by their end goals.

Authoritarianism is a tricky matter. Frequently, those who wish most to avoid the control of others will attempt to exercise control over others. This is also a defense mechanism. It may take the form of what is called reaction formation. But whatever term is used, people most afraid of control will tend to abuse its use in order to feel safe from other people's control. Fear of persecution inspires some fundamentalists to avoid control by seeking control through authoritarian tactics.

At one time I had a little saying discretely propped up on my office desk. It was a quote attributed to Lao Tzu. It read, "A leader is best when people barely know he exists; when his work is done, his aim fulfilled, they will say: 'We did it ourselves.'" I kept it as a reminder to me of the importance of humility and of my goal to strengthen community.

The church I led at the time was located in the Bible Belt. Many of the members had gravitated to the church in reaction against their fundamentalist upbringing. Many others had undergone revival of their faith through one or another fundamentalist organization or program in the wider community. Parishioners of each orientation wanted to express their particular way of worship exclusive of the other, because each felt emotionally constrained by the other in public worship. People inclined to fold their hands in reserved prayer became unnerved when the people beside them wanted to praise God standing and with their arms upheld. Likewise, people prone to pray more demonstratively felt constrained when those beside them were far more reserved and seemed to disapprove. Since I was the pastor, it was common for individuals to meet with me to try to persuade me to change or suppress the practices of parishioners different from themselves. They wanted me to tell different segments of the church to change or leave. They were a bit like puppies tugging against each other over a sock or kids appealing to their mother while they squabble over a toy that each one of them wants. Parishioners simply wanted to have the church for themselves.

A parishioner came into the office to talk with me one day. She was reputed to have been a British opera singer. She was also a Christian fundamentalist. She came that day to encourage me, to embolden me. She wanted me to become more directive. She wanted me to urge those of a less fundamentalist orientation to change their spirituality or leave the church. In the process of our conversation, she said, "And I hate that sign. You should get rid of it." She mistook my aspiration for humility as timidity. She wanted me to be more assertive in my leadership style. She also objected to any visible quotation by someone who was not Christian.

The stress of opposing points of view within community can inflate intolerance. Under stress, people with strong convictions become more motivated to extend their convictions to others. The stronger the convictions, the more stressful the differences, and the more inflated the intolerance, the more intense the urge will be to opt for authorities to take sides and impose direction. That is called triangulation. Triangulation is the attempt to get others to join your side against another so that you can get your way. To a certain extent, in practice, triangulation has been integral to representative democracy. But triangulation also causes the predicament of polarization and dysfunction, which currently grips democratic governments.

Chapter 22

⁓

The Heart of the Predicament

*Freedom Is the Heart of Democracy and
Conflicting Claims Fuel Tensions*

If democracy has a heart, the heart of democracy is freedom. That includes the freedom to think, express, and choose.

The citizens of a democracy have the freedom to think as they wish. They have the freedom to adopt whatever ideas and convictions they find convincing. They have the freedom to embrace whatever beliefs they find compelling. They have the unalienable right to maintain whatever thoughts they like.

Likewise, the citizens in a democracy have the freedom to express their thoughts. They have the freedom to speak about them. They have the freedom to write about them. They have the freedom to demonstrate them in any way they wish, as long as it does not hurt others. They have the freedom to act upon them as they see fit, as long as it does not constrain the rights of others to do the same. Moreover, they have the freedom to choose ways to institute the thoughts they express.

The citizens in a democracy have the freedom to choose the political avenues they prefer in order to extend their convictions to others and to see them implemented. They have the freedom to choose politicians who will represent their thoughts at various levels of government. They have the freedom to choose political leaders and public officials who will promote their interests and implement their convictions. They have the freedom to choose political means to institute laws and policies based upon their convictions.

Individual citizens of a democracy tend to have limited points of view, their own. Individual citizens also have their own vested interests. By and large, throughout the history of democracy, citizens have gravitated toward others who share similar points of view. Citizens bond with those who share their vested interests. As they express their perspectives and find common ground, they will also develop their shared views. That has often given rise to the urge to organize and work to advance shared interests or to institute shared convictions.

That has been the way political interest groups and political parties have formed. Groups with somewhat different vested interests and convictions will form political alliances in order to gain greater influence upon the political processes that drive government. Those political interest groups will either join others to form a political party or will join an existing political party that expresses the willingness to represent the interests of those groups. Political parties then vie with others to gain positions of influence within government. From that position of influence, the political representatives of those parties will work to institute laws and shape policies that further the causes of those who voted for them.

The originators of the democratic system of the United States predicted that process. They did not claim to be clairvoyant or peculiarly divinely inspired. They used their God-given capacities to read, study, observe, reason, discuss, and achieve common ground. They found little guidance in the Bible except for St. Paul's emphasis on freedom and the

Bible's insight into human tendencies toward self-interest. Mostly they found their political guidance from pre-Christian classics, historical documents, and then contemporary political thinkers.

They devised a representative system of democratic government that took into consideration the likelihood of vying vested interests and transitory public passions. They conceived a system that limited terms of office, staggered them, and balanced the powers of three branches of government. They spoke of the potential evils of political parties. It was all done in the effort to limit the potential dominance of any combination of interest groups or political ideology. They did not wish to exchange the tyranny of a monarch for the tyranny of majority of the electorate, let alone an energized and well organized minority of the electorate. And that was particularly true of religious interest groups, which is one reason that the separation of church and state was further defined in the Constitution. They wanted to protect each from the dominance or even the undue influence of the other.

Why would the originators of the American political system specifically identify the need to separate state and church? Why would they not also insist on the separation of state and organized business, fraternal organizations, guilds or unions, veterans' associations, and philosophical societies? It was that they were particularly aware, through their study of history, of the threats that religion had posed to freedom in a state and that states had posed to the freedom of religion. Thomas Jefferson was most avid on this point when he wrote about how savage had been the history of Christianity in its inspiration of the destruction of the lives of men, women, and children. Opposing vested interest groups can dehumanize each other's constituencies, but only religion has the power to demonize those of differing points of view. Dehumanizing others serves the objective of domination. Demonizing can seek not merely to dominate but actually to justify destroying opponents.

Nevertheless, there are citizens of this and other democracies whose most basic convictions and practical interests are primarily religious.

That has always been true. It violates the very heart of democracy to disenfranchise citizens merely because their views are religious or religiously motivated. That would violate their basic freedoms to think, express, and choose as they wish. In democratic societies, fundamentalists have the freedom, indeed the duty, to advocate heartfelt convictions and to use all legal avenues at their disposal in the political process to advance their convictions. It is their right and their obligation as citizens to do so, and it must not be circumscribed or limited any more than any other citizens'.

There is a conflict embedded in this complex situation. The leaven of the Pharisees makes Christian fundamentalists absolutist and exclusive in their claims to comprehensive truth. Currently, that seems to make fundamentalists unwilling or unable to compromise with those of differing perspectives. It also seems to have prompted them to discourage their political representatives from compromise. Since compromise is essential to effective government within a democracy, the religiously based unwillingness to do so has contributed to the dysfunction of democratic government in recent years.

With the exception of violence, there seem to be few limits in the extent to which Christian fundamentalists can feel justified to go in the extension of their convictions to others. Their mind-set of exclusivity and absolutism leaves little room for pluralism under a system of laws predominantly shaped by its ideals. It would limit the self-same freedoms of other citizens who do not share fundamentalist convictions, values, codes of conduct, or sensibilities.

This seems to present democracy with an irresolvable predicament. Any attempts to limit the rights of fundamentalist citizens who seek to implement their convictions would violate their basic freedoms. And yet fundamentalists are prone to be so comprehensive in the scope of their convictions that the full exercise of their freedoms includes extending moral regulations. That has the capacity to curtail personal freedoms of other citizens. Attempts to limit the rights of those who do not share fundamentalist convictions and standards of personal conduct would violate the basic freedoms of those citizens. One way or another, someone's basic freedoms seem destined to be violated, and that cuts to the very heart of democracy. Indeed, it violates the integrity of democratic principles and would threaten to corrupt the intent of the democratic process. Problems can be solved, but predicaments cannot. Is this actually an irreconcilable predicament or a solvable problem?

Chapter 23

—

The Wisdom of Solomon

Stewards of Democracy Promote Liberty

Perhaps the Bible can shed some light on this apparent predicament in democracy. A story might be in order at this point. The story describes an apparently irreconcilable predicament. The story comes from the third chapter of the first book of Kings.

Once upon a time there were two women. They lived together in the same house. Within a short time of each other, each woman gave birth to a son. One night one of those women tragically rolled over her baby in her sleep. She awakened to find the boy dead. Quietly, she took her dead baby's body and placed it by the other woman as she slept. She took that woman's baby for her own and returned to bed. When the other woman awoke the next morning and found the dead baby beside her, she grieved. But she soon noticed that it was not her baby after all. The two women argued over the living boy, each claiming that he was her baby.

They brought their conflict to King Solomon for his judgment. Solomon had an easy, if not disagreeable, solution. He would command a soldier to take his sword and cut the baby in half. Then one half of the baby would be given to each woman. The woman whose child the baby really was offered to give up custody to save the child's life. The other woman agreed to split the child, even though he would be killed in the process. Solomon gave the baby to the woman willing to give up her claims for the sake of the life of the baby. She had proven that she deserved the child.

Any citizen, interest group, or political party willing to harm democracy is unworthy of it. Any interest group, political party, or movement that strives to limit the freedoms of others in order to pursue its own convictions or to impose its own values is unworthy to serve as caregiver of it. None should put their own convictions, values, or codes of conduct, no matter how admirable or inspired they may seem, above the core principles of democracy itself.

Let's take a working example. It is the most desperately controversial issue of all, one which divides American society as much as slavery did in the nineteenth century. The legal right of abortion is more divisive than any other facing Americans in our time. It involves religious conviction; ethics; morality; judicial interpretation of the Constitution; legal application by the courts; health and medical practice; economics; politics; and the basic rights for life, liberty, and the pursuit of happiness enshrined within America's most cherished documents.

I must begin on a personal note, for the sake of full disclosure. According to family legend, I was conceived during a reconciliation attempt between my estranged parents. Something happened when the reconciliation failed, and my father became aware that my mother was pregnant with their only prospective child. During a dinner meeting between my parents to discuss the pregnancy, my father, a practicing physician, drugged my mother. He returned her to his office and attempted to perform an abortion. Obviously, the attempt failed, and I am grateful for that failure.

Since the Supreme Court made its landmark decision in the case of *Roe v. Wade*, abortions have been legal in the United States. Prior to that decision, many abortions were performed under unsafe conditions. After the *Roe v. Wade* decision, abortions have largely been conducted in medical contexts, which have been safer for women. Tens of millions of fetuses have been aborted since that decision was made.

The controversy over the legality of abortion revolves around two axial and competing rights. On the one hand, there is the right of a woman to determine what will happen to her own body. Closely connected to that is the freedom of a woman to decide for herself how her life will be spent. Since *Roe v. Wade*, every woman has had the legal right to exercise her freedom of choice relative to one of the most physically demanding and time-consuming matters that she will ever face—bearing and raising a child. On the other hand, there is the asserted right of the unborn to enjoy the same rights that the woman bearing it enjoys. It would appear that the rights of those two individuals are mutually exclusive when a conception is unwanted, and abortion is contemplated.

Avid segments of the American population have configured themselves around the rights of each individual over those of the other. One side identifies itself with the concept of the right to life and the other with the right to choose. Pro-life supporters emphasize the right of the unborn to live. They assert that human life begins at conception and consider abortion to be nothing less than murder. Pro-choice supporters argue that human life does not begin at conception and emphasize the right of a woman to choose what happens to her body and with her life. The issue seems to present an irreconcilable difference and a political predicament.

People of Christian faith align themselves on both sides of the abortion controversy. A far greater percentage, however, identify themselves with the pro-life position. Christian fundamentalists have overwhelmingly allied themselves with that position and have taken a significant role in its leadership.

Their efforts have largely been invested in the prevention of abortions. They offer education, education that has often involved highly emotional illustrations of aborted fetuses. They have organized court cases and appeals, demonstrations, protests, and political pressure groups, and they have promoted the election of politicians who promise to overturn or significantly restrict the legality of abortion.

Some extreme actions have been taken. Tangentially associated with the pro-life movement, extreme individuals have bombed abortion clinics, assaulted medical personnel providing abortions, publically shamed or threatened women seeking abortions, and demonized abortion providers, pro-choice politicians, and judges upholding the legality of abortion. Such actions have not been sanctioned by the pro-life movement, but they serve the same goals of blocking access to abortions, stopping them, and making abortion illegal.

What happens when personal choices are outlawed? There is historical evidence that demonstrates the consequences of the legal prohibition of personal choices. Alcohol production, distribution, and sales were outlawed earlier in the twentieth century. That legal prohibition did not end alcohol consumption. Instead, it drove the liquor industry underground. The market for alcohol continued to exist because the demand for it continued to exist. Many actually credit Prohibition with the creation of organized crime in America.

The sale, distribution, and use of illicit drugs are illegal in the United States. American law enforcement agencies have been engaged in a war on drugs for a generation. Illicit drug distribution and usage have continued, simply because there continues to be a demand for drugs. In fact, the United States remains the largest single market for illicit drugs anywhere in the world. That has created escalating criminal conditions in such neighboring states as Mexico and Colombia. Drug cartels have come into existence to supply illegal drugs to profit from the demand. Those drug cartels and gangs are at war with each other and with law enforcement agencies, and that has bred a level of violence that terrorizes the populations of those countries. Many innocent bystanders have been murdered. American penal institutions are overpopulated. State and federal budgets are overwhelmed. But drug usage has not declined.

There is no reason to suspect that the consequences would be much different if abortion were outlawed. A black market or underground industry for abortion would be re-created in America. If abortions were outlawed, unwanted pregnancies would continue to be aborted as they were prior to *Roe v. Wade*, but even more widely. If abortions were outlawed, prosperous women would travel to locations in which abortion is legal. Women without the monetary resources to travel elsewhere would obtain illicit abortions. Those unable to afford it would give birth. The number of unwanted children would increase. Unwanted children are more likely to be neglected and abused. Infant and childhood mortality rates would likely increase. The rates of poverty, malnutrition, under-education, and inadequate medical care of unwanted children would likely increase as well. Imprisonment of medical personnel or illicit abortion providers would increase the numbers of prisoners. Larger numbers of those found guilty of child abuse would also be imprisoned. Prisons would become even more overcrowded. More convicted prisoners would be released early to provide additional space. And the cost to government would increase.

Outlawing abortion would limit the number of abortions to some extent, but the aforementioned collateral damages would also be felt. Those consequences, while unintended, would hardly serve the purposes of the antiabortion movement. They would be impractical. And they would hardly demonstrate the fruit of Christlike love.

Insofar as Christian fundamentalists are conscious of or willingly accept such consequences, they demonstrate the way of the Pharisees more than the way of Jesus's teachings and example. In Jesus's time, the Pharisees emphasized law. They coerced people to conform to it. They sought to punish people who disobeyed moral law. They sought to align themselves with or to manipulate secular officials in order to enforce their beliefs. That was not Jesus's way. He never aligned himself with any political group. He dealt with people as individuals, and did so with compassion, forgiveness, and guidance. He sought to meet people's concrete needs rather than imposing directives to coerce conformity.

How might sincere followers of Christ who also happen to oppose abortion respond then? While they might voice their convictions and vote for those who represent these convictions, they would also most certainly emulate Jesus's approach. They would resist expediency and behave with loving compassion toward women with unwanted pregnancies. They would dedicate their time, their skills, and their financial resources to come alongside those whose pregnancies are unwanted. They would earn their trust. They would provide the necessary funds, housing, personal support, and medical care for pregnant women to be able to decide to give birth. They would provide the means for them to rear their unplanned children, or the means to offer their children for adoption, and the guidance to know which decision would be better under the circumstances of their real lives. They would pray for the dead and provide for the living.

In that sense, the legality of abortion is actually an opportunity for Christians to demonstrate the love of God and Christ's healing power. The tendency to harness people's compassion for the unborn and to make efforts to control pregnant women by making abortion illegal is a temptation. It feeds upon the leaven of the Pharisees rather than the spirit of Christ.

The role of Christians is not to make other people do what they believe God wants them to do. Their role is to do what Jesus did. He loved others in order to demonstrate God's love, and taught them how to receive and give God's love themselves. By his actions and his words, Jesus earned people's trust and offered an example. God utilized that to touch people's hearts. That, in turn, made it possible for them to make various changes in their lives. That was the strategy Jesus employed. It enabled people to want to follow God's leadership more fully as they understood God's will to be. Theirs was an individual choice, not imposed by political legislation or law enforcement but enacted through God's grace because of the genuine faith and love that Jesus demonstrated.

Chapter 24

⁓

Freedom or License?

St. Paul's Writings Support the Importance of Individual Conscience and Mutual Tolerance

St. Paul had something to say about individual freedom within community. Apparently some of the originators of American democracy thought so. That's why some of them seem to have had collections of Paul's letters separate from the Bible. While St. Paul had nothing to say about political freedom as a universal right or about democracy, he did argue for individual freedom within Christian community.

Most of St. Paul's letters to various churches dealt, in part, with one conflict or another. Some of them seemed to be irreconcilable differences. Most of the issues that incited the power struggles in the first-century churches would seem ludicrous to us. Some had to do with traditional values. Others had to do with longstanding beliefs or convictions. Still others had to do with who could do what, where, and when. Those issues included whether Gentile converts should be required to be circumcised, whether Christians should be forbidden to eat meat that had been offered to pagan idols, or whether women could speak in church. Those issues threatened to tear apart the fabric of the newborn church.

Let's look at three issues in some detail. Three of the many divisive issues back then included eating meat offered to idols, Sabbath regulations, and unequal marriage. They were just as divisive as the matters of moral conduct that cause conflict in America today and were just as strongly advocated. The only difference was that those profound disagreements existed in communities of shared Christian faith, not within a pluralistic society.

The first was whether certain kinds of meat should be prohibited to Christians. You see, back in those days animal sacrifices were made to various gods. The meat left over from those sacrifices was sold to butchers to make money for the temples. Those butchers sold the meat to the man in the street.

Some particularly scrupulous Christians believed that no one should buy or eat meat that had been sacrificed to pagan gods and idols. Their conviction was based on two points. First, buying the meat helped to financially support pagan temples and their false gods. It was nothing less than promotion of idolatry and supportive to the religious competition. It was very similar to those who do not want to pay taxes because they might be used to support war efforts, abortion providers, or now even contraceptives. Their second reason was that some thought the very rituals used to sacrifice animals to other gods could cause the meat to become spiritually tainted. Who knew what that might do to a person if he ingested it? They believed that the meat was spiritually unclean and could well make a Christian spiritually unclean too, perhaps even possessed by demons associated with those gods.

Another burning issue was whether to observe a particular Sabbath day or not. Some argued that there must be one specified Sabbath, and it must be observed by all Christians. They believed that it was a biblical principle. After all, it was enshrined in the Ten Commandments. Others maintained that all days are special before God and should be devoted to God as such.

Another applied to marriage. Marriage can be challenging in the best of circumstances. But suppose a Gentile became a disciple of Jesus. Suppose the spouse, especially the husband, did not support his partner's new faith. What was a Christian spouse to do? Should the Christian divorce the Gentile spouse so as not to be suppressed in Christian faith or held back in spiritual growth?

St. Paul's answer to all these questions was the same. Essentially, he said that the individual's conscience should be his guide. Each believer should look to God for personal guidance.

St. Paul apparently believed that none of those issues, albeit very important to some, were of any ultimate significance to God. He seemed to believe that each person should do what he believed God wanted him to do. He seemed to think that, while people are tempted to do so, followers of Christ should not try to impose their convictions on others, even if it is out of concern for their spiritual well-being. Paul's working principle was to leave it up to God to lead. Trust God to do his part. Do not try to play God in other people's lives. And if a person did voluntarily choose to go against his own conscience in order to conform to other people's convictions, it should be motivated only by love and humility. Paul dubbed that sacrifice of personal freedom for the sake of others and the unity of the church deference to "weaker brethren." It implies that he regarded more dogmatic believers as weaker and more fragile in their faith.

The only time St. Paul became more rigid in his own views was over a more encompassing issue. Initially, all of Jesus's followers were Jews. Christians were Jews. At first, the term "Christian" did not exist. The earliest followers of Jesus constituted something of an unacceptable sect of Judaism. When the Christian faith started to spread outside of Israel, Gentiles began to convert.

Gentile conversions presented the most contentious issue the church has ever grappled with. Was it necessary for Gentiles to become Jews before they could become Christians? Was it necessary for Gentiles to act like Jews before they could have full standing as members of the church and disciples of Jesus? Did a man have to be circumcised? Did Gentiles have to learn the Torah? Did Gentiles have to memorize Jewish law and live up to it? In essence, to this St. Paul said, "Absolutely not!" This is where all his freedom thinking came into play. Christ had come to set people free from Jewish law. He came to set his followers free from legalism.

Now, if that were true for a church in which everyone shared the same faith, if not precisely the same values, it would be even truer for citizens of different persuasions in a pluralistic democracy.

Christians, particularly those claiming the Bible as their source of authority, are obliged to take this seriously. To conduct themselves otherwise reflects badly on Christ. It unnecessarily alienates people who do not embrace any form of Christian faith. Christians are obligated to try to apply those principles of community to their manner of conduct as citizens in a pluralistic society and a democracy.

I infer the following guidelines from these biblical examples:

- It is essential to learn from Solomon that those who are willing to sacrifice the freedoms enshrined in democracy for the sake of their own interests deserve least to have custody of them.
- It is valuable to apply St. Paul's lessons on individual freedom of conscience, of diversity within unity.
- Citizens of strong faith within a democratic community ought to conduct themselves by their own standards without imposing them on others.
- They ought to follow the dictates of their own conscience and allow others the same courtesy.
- They ought to trust God to take care of his own responsibilities in guiding the consciences of others.

194

- They ought to resist the impulse to make others live the way they want them to live. It interferes with God's work and reflects badly on Christ.
- No one can make others believe what they want them to believe.
- No one can make others voluntarily conduct themselves the way they want them to act, and if they are forced to do so, freedom is lost in the process.
- Loving humility within community requires deference to the sensibilities of those who do not share one's values.
- The attempt to control others is not Christ's way.
- It is important to honor the God-given privilege of living within a democratic society.
- It is important to appreciate that gift by protecting the core freedoms that define it, not only just for those who share a common faith, but also for those who do not.

Some may argue that the implication of this level of freedom is absurd. Wherever there is any kind of community, there is need for the regulation of conduct. People must be kept from hurting each other. They must be prevented from murdering each other, stealing from each other, raping or abusing each other, and harming children and animals.

Beliefs and values inform and inspire the laws that govern such behaviors. These laws provide punishments. And those punishments create disincentives to act in such ways. That is what keeps society safe and secure. It is what preserves society from chaos. Why should they not be shaped by biblical principles and expanded to make society better? As times change, so do the dangers that threaten to do harm. Christians in a democratic society need to be all the more vigilant and comprehensive. Therefore, do they not have the responsibility to promote biblical values?

Indeed they do, but not in ways that violate democratic principles or restrict the rights of others to follow their own convictions.

Chapter 25

〜

The Means Justify the Ends

Contrasting Jesus's Strategies with Fundamentalist Tactics

In 1738, Benjamin Franklin wrote a letter to his father. In it, he said, "I think vital religion has always suffered when orthodoxy is more regarded than simple virtue."

One of Jesus's most distinguishing characteristics, both in his actions and in his words, was that he turned everything upside down. What I mean is that Jesus approached religion and personal conduct in the opposite way from the established religious leaders of his time. Religious teachers contemporary with Jesus demanded that people adhere to what they taught, either because it was right or because their position of authority demanded it. They enforced conformity with threats of punishment.

Jesus claimed no authority of position from which to gain credibility. He did not use coercive power. He did not turn to politics in any way. He did not judge the correctness of people's beliefs or conduct. He was not authorized to function as a rabbi, and yet people addressed him as such. He had no platform within any existing synagogue or the temple,

197

and yet people paid attention to what he taught. He rarely ever appealed to doctrinal orthodoxy to prove his points, and he never tried to coerce others to follow his teachings on the basis of their doctrinal correctness. He never employed threats of punishment to enforce conformity.

Jesus was notorious for acting with compassion. Jesus healed the sick. Jesus forgave people's sins. Jesus went to where people were and addressed their needs. The power, the divine power that resulted from those encounters, drew people to him. His gracious ways were infectious. That's why they listened to him. That's why people gave him authority. That's why people made changes in their personal conduct. That's why they followed him. That's the reason they were receptive to God and to his change of their ways. He acted, as the prophet Zechariah said, "'Not by might nor by power, but by my Spirit,' says the LORD Almighty" (Zechariah 4:6).

Jesus found justification for his ends, the redemption and transformation of people's lives, by the means he used. Actually, to Jesus, the means were the ends. What were Jesus's means? His means were personal faith in God and love. And that was very practical to him. He urged people to treat other people the way they wanted to be treated. These were Christ's means and his ends—to receive and give love, the love of God and love among people. The ultimate test of true faith is love, love in action.

I am not primarily talking about the kind of love that needs to say, "This is going to hurt me more than it does you." People say that just before they inflict disciplinary pain on others, presumably for their own good. It has been popular to call that "tough love." It is the sort of action that may need to be taken in intimate relationships on some occasions. But tough love is not meant to justify actions against categories of people within a larger community or a nation, simply because something about them seems objectionable.

The political tactics that Christian fundamentalists propose to take must be tested against love. Is revisionism, the distortion of facts and reality to fit ideology, born of love? Is impatience or frustration born of love? Is anger (indignation) born of love? Is the intent to deny freedom to others born of love? Is blaming others for catastrophic events born of love? Does love scapegoat others? Is splitting people, turning people against each other, born of love? Is the dehumanization of others born of love? Is the demonization of others born of love? Is the judgment of others born of love? Is the attempt to control others born of love?

In his epistle St. James wrote, "What good is it, my brothers and sisters, if someone claims to have faith but has no deeds? In the same way, faith by itself, if it is not accompanied by action, is dead" (James 2:14ff). When James referred to deeds, he linked them to pure or true religion, and he described just what he meant. James believed that pure religion, as opposed to false religion, expresses itself in charitable deeds. He cited an example. To James faith meant providing for widows and orphans.

That is another concern that comes to mind about the contemporary Christian fundamentalist movement to reform the United States. It seems to be interested in controlling those who are perceived to be morally or spiritually wayward. It proposes to take control over government systems or programs with which it disagrees, simply to manipulate people to conform to its sensibilities. In that sense, fundamentalist efforts seem far more pietistic and moralistic than charitable. The word charity is derived from the Latin "caritas," which meant love.

While Christian fundamentalists are often generous givers, they are scrupulous to give almost exclusively to causes operated by fundamentalists. They are not known for their active concern for the chronically ill, those afflicted with chronic cognitive or psychological conditions, the aged, or others in chronic conditions of need. Christian fundamentalists want tangible results from their charitable efforts. They want to see houses built and the unemployed get jobs. They want to see moral changes and to see people fend for themselves. Mostly they want their efforts to convert others and will ordinarily contribute time, money, and efforts to causes that seek to do just that. They want gratification for their contributions and efforts. Who doesn't? But charitable deeds are not always immediately transformative. They are not always able to make people self-sufficient. They do not always make converts to one's own faith.

Mother Theresa was asked how she was able, day after day, to pour out her life's efforts to serve the destitute of Calcutta, when she knew how unlikely it was that any radical or enduring change would take place. Malcolm Muggeridge, one time editor of *Punch* magazine, was reputed to put that question to her. Her answer was simple, and it is reputed to have changed his life. She replied, "Each of them is Jesus in disguise." She looked into each face and tried to see the face of Jesus.

Jesus said, "Truly I tell you, whatever you did for one of the least of these brothers and sisters of mine, you did for me" (Matthew 25:40). That is Christ's love in action, treating others as you would treat him. Medieval Christians understood that as Christ's return. They believed that Christ returns whenever people cross paths with someone in need. The ways in which people treat those in need are the ways they greet Christ when he returns through the needy.

Chapter 26

⁓

What's Love Got to Do with It?

*Jesus's Approach to Love Applied to Abortion and
Homosexual Rights in Democratic Society*

What might Christ's love in action look like relative to the issues about which Christian fundamentalists are most zealously concerned? I would like to look at the two most controversial issues of current concern in the United States. They include abortion rights and gay rights.

First, at the risk of repetition, let's return to the abortion issue. Abortion has been the central galvanizing social issue for Christian fundamentalists for a generation. It has drawn their greatest response. Fundamentalists want to do whatever they can to make things right for the unborn.

As I have already mentioned, fundamentalists have responded to abortion in a number of ways. Fundamentalist leaders and pastors have made significant efforts to raise the consciousness of their constituencies. Churches have sponsored emotionally and visually provocative educational presentations about "the murder of unborn babies." The aim has been to engage the membership in the issue and to mobilize them to take action. There have been mass rallies. There have been innumerable pro-life demonstrations and marches in Washington, DC, at state houses, and outside abortion clinics. They have displayed posters of dead fetuses to women and girls as they enter clinics to dissuade them from obtaining abortions. They have made great efforts to elect political candidates who are pro-life or who make assurances that they will work to limit or illegalize abortion. They have opened pregnancy counseling centers with the express purpose of dissuading those considering abortion. They will pressure school districts to teach abstinence, to "just say no." They will work and pray that *Roe v. Wade* will be overturned as the law of the land. Many of those strategic responses to the abortion issue are power-based.

Fundamentalists respond in those ways because they see abortion as a social and moral issue, a terrible sin to be reformed, rather than as a human condition. Their responses are generated by compassion for the unborn, but also by intense frustration with their inability to prevent abortions. Their compassion for women with unwanted pregnancies has been far less obvious. If unwanted pregnancies were seen as a human condition to be treated with Christ's love rather than a social evil to be prohibited, their responses might be different.

Compassion for pregnant women would express itself very differently. There are several other strategies that might be employed instead. Support groups might be sponsored for newly pregnant women, especially single women. Those groups would offer loving acceptance and mutual support. Support groups for women who had recently had an abortion would be sponsored. They could simply provide emotional support and a context for women to share their burdens. Funds could be raised to enable single pregnant women to have the financial wherewithal to give birth if they choose to do so. Housing could be provided for pregnant women who need a home within a cooperative living situation. Affordable prenatal medical care and delivery services could be provided to uninsured pregnant women. Training in parenting could be offered. Continuing education and job training could be provided to improve the likelihood of employment with a living wage to support single mothers and their children. Low-cost and high-quality childcare services could be provided so that single mothers could work. Cooperative housing could be provided for single mothers. Scrupulous adoption services could be offered to those who choose to entrust their babies to other families to rear as their own.

Such efforts require far more commitment than preventing abortion by legal or coercive means. They are far more expensive. They are far more time-intensive than a demonstration or a petition or a vote. They require ongoing personal commitment instead of incidental involvement. And they may appear to reward the sexual behaviors to which fundamentalists object so vehemently. Nonetheless, they are distinctly more loving Christian responses.

How can I say that? Well, I use Jesus's example as the litmus test for what is more or less loving behavior from a Christian point of view. Abortion was not apparently very widespread in Jesus's time. The New Testament writings never mention it. But prostitution was mentioned. The reason I refer to prostitution is not because women and girls who become pregnant and choose abortion are like prostitutes in any way. It is simply that the social circumstances were similar.

In biblical times, Jewish society was patriarchal. Women were defined by their relationship with a male—with a father, a brother, a husband, or an adult son. Normally, women enjoyed no economic independence. If a woman never married and her father died, she could not inherit his estate. She was destitute or dependent upon the generosity of relations.

Divorce was commonplace and easily accomplished. It was unilateral and could be executed only by the husband. He had two options. He could declare three times before witnesses, "I divorce you." He could also write a certificate of divorce. The divorced wife was sent from the husband's house. She left without the children. They belonged to the husband. She had to fend for herself. She was ordinarily left with no material means of self-support.

If women had no one to take them in, they had few options for gainful employment. If a woman's husband died, normally one of her husband's brothers would marry her. Absent that, or an adult son to provide for her, the widow had few alternatives for self-maintenance. If she had minor children, the economic hardship was even worse. Options for economic survival were very limited.

Women had few economic alternatives if they were unattached to a man, especially when they had children. Prostitution was a means of economic support that many unattached women relied upon. And yet, publicly, Jewish society treated prostitutes as unclean sinners, unworthy of acceptance. They were severely judged and ostracized.

How did Jesus respond to prostitutes? Did he try to mobilize his disciples to prohibit the moral evils of prostitution? No. Did he lead demonstrations through the streets of Jerusalem decrying prostitution? No. Did he gather his disciples outside brothels to shame prostitutes and turn away clients? No. Did he press for prostitution to be outlawed so that prostitutes would be punished? No. Did he spend his time trying to browbeat prostitutes into changing their profession? No. Did he lobby political leaders to outlaw prostitution? No. But he could have if he'd chosen to do so.

Upstanding Jews of the time criticized Jesus for how he did treat prostitutes. He spent time with prostitutes. He exercised the supportive ministry of personal presence for the purpose of demonstrating and talking about God's love for them. He accepted prostitutes and was personally supportive of them. Beyond that, he discouraged divorce and encouraged charity for widows and orphans. In other words, he addressed the circumstantial causes of prostitution.

Jesus had at least three public encounters with women whose circumstances were compromising. One was a woman whom he met at a well in Samaria. She'd had several husbands and was cohabiting with another man without the benefit of marriage. It is notable that he did not criticize her but encouraged her spiritual growth. Another was a woman who had been caught in the very act of having sexual relations with a man other than her husband. Jesus blocked the customary religious penalty for her conduct, which was execution by stoning. He forgave her and encouraged her to change her ways. The third was the woman who interrupted a dinner party by her show of grief over her past and gratitude for forgiveness. He made a positive example of her to the rest of the group and pointed out how well she knew love and forgiveness. Jesus was criticized by the fundamentalists of the time for being soft on sinners and for associating with them.

In that day and age "righteous" folks knew how to treat "sinners." They shunned them. They ostracized them and had nothing whatever to do with them. They went so far as to cross the street to avoid them. They certainly never touched them or interacted with them. In fact, the only acknowledgment they made to their existence was critical or punitive. They publicly criticized the behavior in general and cast people in the light of their lifestyles. They drove them out of the community or, in certain cases, stoned them to death. They used them as object lessons of unfaithfulness and divine judgment.

Gay, lesbian, bisexual, and transgender Americans are often treated by Christian fundamentalists in similar ways as the "righteous" treated prostitutes and sinners in Jesus's time. Fundamentalists largely rebuff and ostracize them. They certainly do not welcome them within fundamentalist churches unless they conceal their orientation or identify themselves as sinners in need of forgiveness or healing. Fundamentalist ministries to such persons are geared toward redemption from aberrant behaviors and transformation of disordered conditions, rather than loving acceptance of persons.

It is apparent to me that almost no attention was directed to homosexuality in the New Testament writings. And yet, for some reason,

Christian fundamentalists have focused their ire on homosexual rights. Some will respond that St. Paul decries homosexuality in his epistle to the Romans. "Because of this, God gave them over to shameful lusts. Even their women exchanged natural sexual relations for unnatural ones. In the same way the men also abandoned natural relations with women and were inflamed with lust for one another. Men committed shameful acts with other men, and received in themselves the due penalty for their error" (Romans 1:26–27). And yet, the meaning of the terms cited is debatable. Some argue that the meaning of the terms in those two verses is clear. They assert that those terms refer to homosexual relations of any kind. Others argue that the terms suggest people engaging in casual sexual activity with members of the same gender rather than physical expression of affection between same-sex partners in committed relationships. Be that as it may, my point is that Christian fundamentalists have focused considerable attention on a few words that appear once in the New Testament documents and the meaning of which is debatable. But they have chosen to overlook biblical themes that were far clearer and universal in scope. Their focus and tactics are the concern.

It is quite clear to me that Jesus would treat people of gay and lesbian orientation differently from the ways fundamentalists ordinarily do. In our time, there is every reason to believe that Jesus would spend time in gay/lesbian bars, as he did with those who were dubbed "sinners" in public houses at his time. He would do it to woo the otherwise ostracized clientele to God's loving grace. Moreover, he would let God do the rest, not prejudging desired outcome regarding their lifestyles. And it is clear to me, as well, that Jesus would be criticized for it by those who consider themselves to be righteous, by fundamentalists, as he was back in his time.

The way Jesus portrayed love is personally outgoing. It is directly involved with people, especially the ostracized. It does not emphasize the issues that "the righteous" would otherwise use to define these people.

He devoted his personal time and efforts to establishing relationships. That was what created the authoritative, personal platform from which he could offer input into other people's lives. He never sought either to legislate morality or to dictate personal conduct. He never employed coercion, public leverage, or tactics of political power to inhibit people's choices but left that between them and God. That's my understanding of love from Jesus's point of view. And that is my understanding of how those who seek to follow Christ would do best to conduct themselves within the public arena and political institutions within democratic societies when it come to their moral concerns.

An essential part of the college experience is participation in "bull sessions." Students have always sat in each other's dormitory rooms to talk things over. It creates opportunities for bonding and to discuss matters of shared concern. It is true for military personnel in barracks as well. It is the main reason that many people hearken back to those years and those relationships as the most significant ones in their lives.

That was no less true for me at the Christian schools that I attended. We discussed everything from personal concerns and great thoughts to solving world problems. As you might suspect, we also talked about sex. Guys did, at least. The conversations might have had somewhat different twists though.

We discussed issues of masturbation, lust, fornication, and premarital sex. We frequently bemoaned that it was unfair of God to give us sexual drives that conflicted with our ability to cope with them as singles. Some of us blamed the evolution of social custom. Those students complained that we couldn't mate until married, and couldn't marry until educated and employed. They bemoaned the fact that we had to exercise heroic levels of self-control during the peak years of our God-given sexual drives. Others simply chalked it all up to temptation and sin. Yet God still gave us the drives. It all seemed like a double bind or a cruel trick. And we struggled to determine just how to cope, acknowledging that we often failed.

During those years, I was acquainted with a number of fellow students who were homosexuals. They dealt with their sexual drives in different ways. Two instances come to mind.

Two male students lived down the hall from me in my dorm. They were roommates. And both happened to have been gay. One of them had a deep desire to live "righteously." He was friendly with a female student, and they got along well. He asked her to marry him. They married within a week after his graduation. They separated a few months later and eventually divorced. It simply didn't work out. He had sublimated his sexual orientation and tried to act as if he were heterosexual. He hoped and prayed that God would change him. His strategy failed.

One of my friends at seminary in England was a forty-year-old gay man. He often confided his personal distress. You see, he tried to maintain a celibate lifestyle. Nevertheless, his natural urges and passions recurrently rose to the boiling point, at times. He prayed. He fasted. He asked for support. He tried to control himself. And he gave in to the drives from time to time. He engaged in "one-night stands" or casual encounters. His episodes of self-recrimination and loathing were frequent. He was often depressed.

Many gay and lesbian people no longer live in that psychological cul-de-sac. Some claim that the change is due to the wider social acceptance of homosexuality and stronger support from their communities. A far smaller number claim that they have been healed of their condition by ministries that are geared to that approach. Fundamentalists disdain acceptance of homosexual orientation and try to promote the latter approach.

How is it better to live? Is it preferable for people of homosexual orientation to try to quash their inclinations? Is it preferable to continually deny, suppress, act out, and live in a perpetual cycle of renewed resolve, failure, self-recrimination, and profoundly conflicted mind-set? Or might it be possible that God would rather homosexual persons commit themselves to monogamous relationships with same-sex partners? And if people disagree over the legitimacy of that possibility, is it necessary for them to impose their own standards on others? Is it necessary to pass laws or constitutional amendments to prohibit it? I wonder how Jesus would respond. Traditionally, God's grace has been defined as unmerited favor and unconditional love. Tough love is conditional and controlling. It withholds favor until it is earned. It offers love on condition of conformity. Which is the love with which God loves?

Chapter 27

Values, Values, and More Values

Another Cause of Conflict Exists in the Difference between Morality and Ethics

About fifteen years ago, I had a jarring experience. It was an experience of culture shock, and it was striking to me. I had just made a job change from one church to another. I relocated from the San Francisco Bay area, where I had served in ministry for ten years, to a church in the South. Within a month of my arrival, I attended my first meeting of the local community clergy association. It was composed of seven pastors of some of the largest churches in the community. They were an impressive group, intelligent and articulate. They were clergy at the very top of their field. I discovered that each meeting included a discussion of some issue of shared concern.

That day, the issue under discussion was premarital preparation. In the course of the conversation, one pastor mentioned that he required engaged couples to live separately until the wedding. He added that he refused to perform a marriage ceremony if an engaged couple cohabitated. To my complete surprise all of the other ministers in the group confirmed that they shared the same policy. I was astounded. It wasn't that way in the bay area.

I had been accustomed to treating engaged couples differently. I knew that more than 90 percent of engaged couples in the bay area cohabitated. I was also aware that the ordinary pattern of American religious affiliation was such that the vast majority of young adults stop attending church from adolescence until they have children old enough to attend Sunday school. I figured that the nostalgic ideal of a church wedding would bring young adults back into the gravitational pull of churches. And so I did not want their experience of church to be alienating. I wanted to use the teachable moment of premarital preparation to involve a positive experience of God, faith, and church. I did not want to put engaged couples in the position of misrepresenting their living situation. I did not want to coerce them. I did not want to cause them to incur additional expenses before marriage. I did not want to add any issues for potential conflict between the partners. I wanted, instead, to offer them a new opportunity to experience a Christian faith community in a positive light. I thought that some might benefit from it spiritually. I imagined that they could use the positive spiritual support. They might actually choose to affiliate with a church. And they might benefit from Christian input, which they might draw upon when they began to bear children of their own. And so I never seriously considered instituting a separation policy as a condition for marriage.

The motives of my clergy colleagues varied somewhat, but their conclusion was identical. Some predicated their policy upon upholding the standards of the community. Others talked about their own personal sensibilities and those of the majority of the members of their congregations. Still others appealed to conformity to biblical standards. Ultimately, though, their concerns reflected conformity to conventional norms that they found authoritative. They were primarily concerned with upholding particular values and imposing them on others.

The term "value" has been popular in recent years. It is one of those words that can have all sorts of different meanings, depending upon its usage. Value can mean low cost. It can refer to a deal or a bargain. It can refer to a personal preference. It can indicate the esteem that a person invests in someone or something. And more recently, it has been used to refer to principles of conduct.

Traditionally, two other words were used for principles of conduct. Those terms were "morals" and "ethics." Most people of religious faith, especially fundamentalists, tend to emphasize morals.

It is clear that humans develop in the course of life. Humans undergo all sorts of changes. They include physical, cognitive, and psychological development. For some time now, it has been generally accepted that humans develop morally as well. Several theories have been proposed to describe different patterns of growth in moral reasoning and decision-making. Lawrence Kohlberg devised one of the most familiar models. From his research, Kohlberg developed his theory of the stages of moral development. He claimed that, like cognitive development, people advance along something of a continuum from simpler to more complex patterns of moral reasoning.

To summarize, Kohlberg identified six stages. One of the ways he described each stage is by the primary goal that people seek to serve by their decision making at that stage. The primary goal at the first stage of his model is to avoid punishment by obeying authorities. At the second stage the primary goal is self-interest, getting something to benefit one's self by the decision one makes. At the next stage, the primary motive is to achieve harmony by conforming to norms, going along to get along. At the next stage, it is obedience to authority in order to promote law and order. At stage five, the motive of moral reasoning is to honor and promote the social contract among people in community. And at the sixth stage, moral reasoning is motivated by universal ethical principles, such as justice. Other moral theorists offer somewhat different stages or descriptions of them, but they all agree that there are stages. They also agree that the stages are sequential but that all people do not continue to develop to the later stages of moral development. They concur that relatively few advance to the final stage of development in moral reasoning.[xv]

Since people of religious faith are normally taught to obey specific rules of personal conduct, they tend to be predisposed to follow a pattern of moral decision making that adheres to concrete moral regulations. There may be four motives for obeying the accepted rules of their faith community. They may originate from the fear of punishment, the personal benefit of approval by the community, commitment to the standards of their community and maintaining the order of the community, or obedience to the authority of God. Fundamentalists may obey and promote rules of conduct for any of these reasons. But their primary motivation is the conviction that God revealed rules of conduct, and, therefore, those rules are inherently right and must be obeyed.

Fundamentalists will normally appeal to obedience to God's law as the basis of their decision-making. They believe that it is right because God revealed it. The essence of fundamentalist moral reasoning and decision making has been summarized in a bumper sticker slogan: "The Bible says it. I believe it. That settles it!" That can impede their ability to engage in ethical reflection and discussion. In that sense, fundamentalists can be constrained in their ability to develop overarching and altruistic ethical principles. They tend to focus instead on people's individual adherence to faith-based rules of conduct for the sake of conformity to God's will and obedience.

I find it interesting that one of the issues that fueled the discord between the Pharisees and Jesus was that Pharisees emphasized law and order, whereas Jesus emphasized universal ethical principles. Pharisees taught that the biblical laws ought to be obeyed because God revealed them. Moreover, to do otherwise would result in God's punishment or social disorder. On the other hand, Jesus taught that since God created humans in his image, then the ways in which people treat each other reflect the ways in which they treat God. If, therefore, people claim or actually want to love God, they must also aspire to love their neighbors (1 John 4:20–21). Jesus explained that love meant treating other people as one would want to be treated. That is an example of ethical reflection, and it yielded a universal ethical principle to guide people's ethical reasoning and decision making in various situations. Jesus's most often identified universal ethical principle was love.

Love has automatic connotations for most people. The word conjures images, and many of them are deeply imbedded in people's memories. They evoke feelings. Some of those feelings are warm, tender, and comforting. Others are sad, hurtful, or angry. Some bemoan that love is an overused word. How can the same word be used in connection with foods, pastimes, possessions, locations, and behaviors, as well as people with whom our lives are closely linked?

The English language is bereft of many words for love. And so, English speakers use one word in a number of different ways. That has not been true of all languages. The Bible was originally written in three languages. Much of it, the writings of the Old Testament, was written in Hebrew. A few verses here and there were written in Aramaic, which was a language closely related to Hebrew. The rest of the biblical literature was written in Greek. The Greeks had at least four words for love. One was "storga." It referred to instinctive love, the kind of love that parents of many species have for their offspring. Another word for love was "eros." It described, as the reader might suspect, everything having to do with sexual affinity and romantic love. "Philos" was another word for love. It had to do with the affection and bonding shared among friends, comrades, and people of common interest. Then there was the word "agapa." It was most often used for God's disposition toward humans and for human behavior toward God and other people. Love of this last sort was not necessarily accompanied by feelings. It was chosen behavior. It referred to any active, need-meeting service toward others.

Love is a universal ethical principle rather than a rule or law. That is easily proved by its applicability to most moral questions and its complexity. At first, you might think that this last expression of love, agapa, would be easy to determine. It has all sorts of practical applications. For example, it means stopping to help a person with a flat tire, although you might dread the inconvenience of it. It means inviting a person to share Thanksgiving dinner when they have no one else with whom to spend the holidays. It means providing or helping people to find the food, clothing, medical care, lodging, or any other material resources that they need. Those are easy applications of love. I say that it is easy not because it is convenient or painless but because it is uncomplicated. But it is also often difficult to discern how to express that kind of love in complicated situations with conflicting criteria.

Morality and ethics are different from each other. Morality generally focuses upon personal conduct. It emphasizes obeying rules, without necessarily reflecting on the rationale for them or understanding them within wider contexts. On the other hand, ethics focuses its concern on collective behavior and community standards. Ethics emphasizes overarching principles of conduct and motives for conduct. Ethics often includes collective standards of behavior that guide individual conduct. Ethics is more general, principled, and abstract. Morality is more individual, practical, and concrete. Often the most contentious debates over "values" actually reflect differences in the participants' level of moral reflection. They reveal the different levels at which people are operating morally. Different people speak on different wavelengths of moral discourse or from different starting points and with various ethical standards. Sometimes people seem unable to connect with each other. Instead of seeking common ground on the basis of which to discuss issues of concern, they become entrenched in their positions and frustrated with each other.

Those engaged in the public debate over social values tend to dismiss each other in derogatory ways. They seem to accentuate their respective final moral positions, rather than trying to grasp one another's motives for them or the reasoning behind them. Fundamentalists dismiss those who disagree with them by implying that they are valueless, immoral, or somehow under evil influences. Those with different points of view tend to label fundamentalists as people without compassion or concern for justice. In fact, fundamentalists are consistent in their concern for personal moral righteousness. That reveals their moral concern. Their opponents are often consistent in their concern for justice. That reveals their ethical concern. They simply have different points of view.

Various people have made significant contributions to ethics in public discourse, whether they have been affiliated with a particular religious faith or not. Mahatma Gandhi, while he had exposed himself to several religious traditions, did not exclusively affiliate with any one of them. He regarded them as much a source of discord as illumination among the populations he sought to serve. Humanists have been prominent in their contributions to ethics in Western nations. Citizens need not be religious or even spiritual to be able to make important contributions to the ethical dimension of political discourse in a democratic society.

As it happened, I believe, the Founding Fathers and framers of the Constitution were far less interested in rules of personal moral conduct than they were in ethical principles. The overriding principle around which they configured their reasoning seems not so much to have been love, equity, or personal righteousness, as it was liberty and justice. Liberty, or freedom, and justice are ethical principles that are particularly well-suited to shaping a government guided by their ideals. I believe that emphasis on universal principles so applicable to government is what made their efforts ingenious and effective.

Differences will always exist in moral development. Differences in moral development add to the diversity of perspectives in ethical reasoning within a democratic society. That diversity has the potential to enrich the mix and broaden the scope of ethical decision making for human behavior in community. That can be beneficial when citizens respect one another and seek to understand each other's ethical point of view in order to achieve common ground.

When democracy exists within a pluralistic society, it is almost inevitably futile to debate about which moral rules or codes of conduct should prevail. That tends to create a win/lose conflict, in which one segment of society may temporarily prevail, but other sides, either passively or actively, resist in some form of civil disobedience. When intense strife over moral issues exists in a pluralistic society, it means that a new social contract needs to be fashioned to address those concerns. It is preferable to raise the level of ethical discussion to focus on universal ethical principles, such as the ones that have been mentioned: love, justice, equity, and liberty or freedom. When agreement is reached at the level of universal principles, it can result in the formation of new social contracts. Then citizens who otherwise disagree on moral rules have a greater potential to achieve common ground.

Chapter 28

Justice and Equity

Absence of Concern for Poverty and Justice among Modern American Fundamentalists

Contemporary Christian fundamentalists in America almost seem to major in moral concerns and to minor or completely neglect universal ethical principles, even those of their own faith tradition. That is to say, many fundamentalists seem to focus maximum attention on issues that are either never addressed in the Bible or are limited to relatively few and debatable verses. Meanwhile, they have completely neglected far more pervasive, major biblical principles such as equity and justice.

It is an extremely interesting phenomenon indeed that American Christian fundamentalists have targeted needs for reform that are hardly ever actually mentioned in the Bible. They have focused their concerns upon such matters as abortion rights, homosexual rights, the contents of public educational curricula, and creeping secular humanism. Only one of those matters is even mentioned in the Bible, and that is sexual behavior between members of the same gender.

Sexual behavior between members of the same gender appears in not more than a handful of biblical verses. They are almost exclusively found in the books of Leviticus and Deuteronomy, nestled among hundreds of Jewish laws related to other sexual practices, ritual purification, laws related to physical illness, dietary laws, agricultural laws, regulations pertaining to the Jewish sacrificial system, and worship protocols, among many others. Those few verses appear to focus on casual sexual behavior outside a committed relationship. Indiscriminant sexual behavior among people otherwise uncommitted to each other is a focus of recurrent biblical concern.

Other than the six hundred various rules, regulations, and laws, the biblical writings emphasize several universal ethical principles. As I have already mentioned one of them was love, love for God and loving action toward other people. That was Jesus's core ethical principle, and so it appears most often in the documents of the New Testament. There were three others that were of far greater overarching concern than particular Jewish laws, including ones having to do with the sexual practices of individuals. Like love, they are universal ethical principles, not rules. They appear most often in the Hebrew scriptures. And they are not limited to the books of Leviticus and Deuteronomy, but are found in virtually every genre of biblical literature. Those principles are economic equity, justice, and faithfulness. Two of these three are hardly ever mentioned by American Christian fundamentalists, and I have often been baffled by that omission

Jesus departed from the Hebrew prophetic tradition in one way. Those who value that tradition may feel that Jesus's approach to love in action was faulty in this one respect. He did not seem to emphasize the social structures and circumstances that caused various oppressive conditions. Some might rhetorically ask if it is not preferable to remedy systemic or structural ills that affect people negatively than simply to urge people to act with loving charity toward individuals.

Let's take economic equity, or wealth and poverty, as an example. Jesus addressed many of his parables to the subject. He did so in ways that uncovered the underlying spiritual or psychological causes and outcomes of economic inequity. In the so-called Beatitudes, he pronounced blessings to the poor and curses to the wealthy (Luke 6:20–26). He challenged the "rich young ruler" to divest himself of his wealth and give it to the poor, if he wanted to be a disciple (Mark 10:17–25). He challenged the rich and comforted the poor. He taught that wealth competed with God for preeminence in people's lives (Luke 16:13). And yet, Jesus never seems to have spoken out against the prevailing social/economic/political systems of his time, which promoted economic inequity and injustice.

Before I continue, I need to underscore the difference between regulating by legislation the moral choices people make, and the social structures or political/economic systems that create harmful conditions. Legislating personal moral conduct mainly affects the individuals involved in those behaviors. Directing legislation to social conditions affects far wider segments of a population and the circumstances under which citizens live in community.

Consider the condition of chronic poverty. Ordinarily, poverty is not a personal or moral choice that individuals make. Except for those who voluntarily choose a lifestyle of poverty on the basis of individual conscience or vocation, poverty is a condition of life that is largely thrust upon individuals by economic conditions. It is true that individual choices, including education, career, investment, and recreational choices, may exacerbate poverty. But social, economic, and political systems are responsible for chronic intergenerational poverty. Those economic conditions are created and perpetuated by inequitable social structures and/or political and economic systems. The economic downturn that has prevailed for the past several years perfectly illustrates that reality. Millions of American families and tens of millions around the world have been thrust into poverty by systemic forces beyond their control. This has been caused by systemic conditions and not by the choices of those who have been impoverished.

Matters having to do with economic equity, with wealth and poverty, are far more pervasive in sacred scripture than virtually any other. The Bible directly relates them to God's justice. The biblical view of wealth or prosperity is that they are conferred upon individuals by God for a specific purpose. That purpose is to serve God by using wealth to provide for the needs of the poor. The wealthy were intended to be conduits, not reservoirs, of material resources.

The Bible teaches that God shows complete partiality toward the poor. God favors the poor. Conversely, God severely judges the wealthy. The Bible says that God despises economic inequity and disparities in access to justice, which economic inequity often promotes. The Bible states, "For the love of money is a root of all kinds of evil" (I Timothy 6:10). The Bible indicates that the basis of injustice is inequitable distribution of wealth and social/legal partiality to the wealthy. The prophets cried out against economically based injustice. More than half of Jesus's parables involved money and expressed disfavor toward those who possess or seek wealth. Jesus said, "No one can serve two masters. Either you will hate the one and love the other, or you will be devoted to the one and despise the other. You cannot serve both God and money" (Luke 16:13).

Most Christian fundamentalists in America have completely overlooked all those biblical teachings. They ignore the corruptions of wealth, God's concern for the poor, and the essential need for equity. They seem to act as if the only human impulses affected by the fall and Original Sin are sexual, and that, somehow, business and economic enterprises are immune to its influences. Instead, as I say, they focus their concerns on matters unrelated to the Bible or on a few verses having to do with personal moral conduct. Once again, it calls to mind what Jesus said about the Pharisees. He perceived that they scrutinized miniscule portions of the law to use against others while ignoring weightier matters that applied to their own lives. He told religious leaders, "You have neglected the weightier and more important matters of the law: justice, mercy and faithfulness ... inside you are full of greed and self-indulgence ..." (Matthew 23:23). Current expressions of Christian fundamentalism in America seem nearly blind to matters having to do with economic equity and social justice.

That omission not only diverges from the biblical tradition, but from Christian awakenings in prior history. The first Christian awakening in the apostolic era in Jerusalem immediately expressed itself in equitable distribution of resources, not in moral outrage at those who did not share their worldview.

Medieval Christian awakenings manifested themselves in addressing poverty. One of the clearest instances of that connection between spiritual revival and active concern for the poor took place in the thirteenth century. St. Francis of Assisi was smitten by God. It dramatically changed his life. He became spiritually devout and deeply prayerful. But he also renounced personal material wealth and did everything he could to serve the poor.

That new way, which integrated spirituality, was infectious. Young men and women were drawn to its sincerity and its integrity. New religious orders cropped up, including *the Order of Poor Ladies, the Poor Clares*, and several orders that adopted their founder's name, *Franciscans*. Their spiritual awakening did not express itself in moral outrage or attempts to gain political power. It expressed itself in active, loving service of those in greatest tangible need.

Eighteenth-century England experienced widespread Christian revival, which began in the Church of England. It was spearheaded by John and Samuel Wesley and later with the help of other revived clergy. That awakening came to be known as the Wesleyan Revival, borrowing its name from its most influential leaders. The renewal spilled over to the British colonies in America and was dubbed the Great Awakening there.

In Britain, the Wesleyans believed that societies, small fellowship groups, should exist to support the spiritual growth of new converts. They adopted a "Method" of spiritual formation that involved Bible readings, personal sharing, mutual support, and prayer. Those "Methodist" societies soon discovered that many were impoverished or oppressed by working conditions. In response, the Methodists pressed social reforms for the poor and laborers. That fostered laws for improved working conditions in primitive factories and the rudimentary creation of labor unions. Some credit the social reforms generated by the Wesleyan revivals with ameliorating social injustices and, thereby, saving Britain from the kind of revolution that engulfed France a generation later.

Other Christian awakenings also gave rise to concern for the socially and economically oppressed. In America, the First Great Awakening inspired the creation of schools and universities to address the desperate need for education in the colonies. The evangelical movement in nineteenth-century England gave rise to the abolition of Britain's involvement in the slave trade. Likewise, the Second Great Awakening in America inspired the movement to abolish the system of slavery in America. Similarly, at the turn of the twentieth century in America, the Third Great Awakening morphed into the "Social Gospel" movement. That helped to promote national programs and international organizations to address injustice, poverty, and poor education. Actually, the Social Gospel movement, which was spawned by the Third Great Awakening, had far-reaching influences on society. Those influences included the inspiration of child labor laws, the creation of Christians against Poverty, elements of the New Deal, the ethical underpinnings of Social Security, Medicare, Medicaid, and the civil rights movement.

Christian spiritual awakenings have always generated tangible concerns and movements to reform the oppressive conditions that harmed the neediest segments of society. The biblical emphasis on love in action, economic equity, and social justice was the source of those Christian reform movements.

Concerns for economic equity and social justice are conspicuously absent from the contemporary Christian fundamentalist agenda in America. Of course, selectivity has always been one of the central problems with which Christians have had to contend. Various Christians and groups have always selected different biblical passages, theological concepts, and moral values to emphasize. And they have interpreted them differently. That is another reason to question fundamentalism. It is one thing to believe that everything in the Bible is the infallible Word of God, but quite another to discern God's priorities and God's perfect meaning for those priorities in equal balance all the time. It is humanly impossible. And so the belief among American fundamentalists that they know what God wants for America, even though their agenda is without clear biblical evidence, is highly questionable.

Justice for the oppressed and equity for the poor, arguably among the most prominent ethical principles and public concerns in the Bible, are almost completely overlooked by contemporary American fundamentalists. There must be some reason for that omission of concern to reform the social structures that give rise to poverty and injustice. Let's consider the variables. Perhaps God has changed his mind and no longer cares about the poor and the needy or about justice. That would be singularly uncharacteristic of God. It could be that there is no need of concern for the poor. Poverty may not exist in America. That is patently untrue. In fact, poverty has increased at the most rapid rate since the Great Depression, and more Americans live in poverty now than ever before. That includes the working poor. Many employed workers are not paid wages that enable them to afford the basic costs of living. It may be that poverty is the fault of the poor, and that the state has no need to help the poor systemically. It may be that the victims are to blame for their poverty. Many American fundamentalists seem to think so, and yet the Bible never hints that poverty, inequity, or injustice is caused by the poor. It may be that most Christian fundamentalists are not poor. If that is the case, then it is possible that they are more concerned to preserve the social structures and current economic systems than to examine them with an eye to reform. And that may simply be inspired by self-interest.

When all is said and done, I can discern only three reasons for Christian fundamentalists' reticence to examine the justice of an economic system that benefits very few and seems to extend poverty. I have already mentioned the first. Perhaps fundamentalists or those who guide their thinking personally benefit from the system as it exists. It may be that they simply don't want to jeopardize the security of their own economic position. If that were the case, it would be selfish and hypocritical.

A second possible reason is that Christian fundamentalists in America have uncritically adopted capitalism and the free-market rendition of it that currently prevails as part of their faith. In short, perhaps they believe that the only hope for the poor is for the free market to work as it has, but with fewer constraints. And yet, if the past ten years has demonstrated anything, it has dramatically shown that fewer constraints on the free market do not help any but the richest segment of society. During the past twenty years, including years of tremendous economic growth, a tiny percentage of the population has become much wealthier. During that same time frame, the vast majority has become poorer, even when multiple members of a household are employed. Marriages have been stressed, and relations between parents and children have been compromised. Yet the economic system has not been identified by Christian fundamentalists as an issue of concern. They choose to blame the immoral climate, rather than economically overstressed families.

In fact, insufficiently regulated free-market capitalism has given rise to three economic crises during the past two decades. Those crises, whether they are called market corrections, downturns, or bubble bursts, have significantly reduced the wealth of nations and worsened the plight of the poor and the middle class in America. The crisis among savings and loan institutions, the so-called "dot com" debacle, and the most recent "great recession" were all caused by the lack of effective government supervision, in large measure. And so any conviction in the infallibility of free market capitalism would be a matter of faith rather than fact. Now, why do you suppose fundamentalists would identify humanism as unbiblical, while they cling to faith in capitalism, which is no less unbiblical?

Faith in the prevailing economic system is closely related to the third possible reason for fundamentalists' neglect of economic equity and social justice. The third possible cause of the fundamentalist disregard for economic equity and social justice is idolatry.

Chapter 29

~

American Idols

*The Root of the Idiosyncrasies in Contemporary
American Fundamentalism Is Idolatry*

Faithfulness was another of the universal principles enshrined in the Bible. Idolatry was the opposite of faithfulness. Idolatry was a primary concern in virtually all of the Hebrew biblical writings. It was a theme as prominent as economic equity and justice. Some would claim that it was an even greater concern. The biblical writers linked idolatry with economic inequity and injustice. Idolatry usually involved self-interest. People in biblical times usually turned to other gods to gain additional aid to improve their circumstances. Naturally, idolatry frequently manifested itself in concern for personal prosperity. Since it was inspired by self-interest, it also manifested itself in callous attitudes toward others. That was especially true of a callous attitude toward those who were economically, socially, and/or politically oppressed.

Although a recurrent overarching biblical concern, idolatry is rarely mentioned by American fundamentalists. It appears that they do not consider it to be a contemporary issue. And that is distinctly suspicious.

Some say that idolatry is irrelevant in our time. They may believe that modern societies have evolved beyond it. Many people suppose that idolatry was a superstitious practice, limited to less sophisticated, primitive peoples. They understand idolatry as the practice of worshipping physical images of false gods in polytheistic cultures. While those false gods may have had names and may have had graven images to represent them, they were actually forces in which people invested their trust.

Idolatry was and is far more than primitive worship of physical images (statues and the like). Idolatry essentially involves faith. It involves active trust in the power of certain forces. These forces may replace or coexist alongside the Creator. These forces or "gods" may take any number of forms. A god may take the form of a person, place, or thing. A god may be a personality, whether a named spiritual entity, like Baal or Zeus, a hero, a star, a political leader, or an athlete, among others. A god may be a force of nature, whether the sun, rain, fertility, the sea, or any other natural force. A god may be a political entity, whether a nation, a system of government, or a place. It may take the form of a philosophy, whether an ideology, a political point of view, or an economic school of thought. It may also take the form of a thing, whether possessions, treasured objects, precious metals and minerals, or currency. Idolatry simply involves what people operationally trust and value. It involves the devotion of people's time and energy. It is the practice of serving and honoring a force. It is what people worship as ultimately important to them, either as god or alongside God.

Worship is an interesting term. Most people think of it as involving prayer and adoration, but that is far too limited. People have images of bent knees, folded hands or bowed heads, and liturgy. The word itself comes from an old English term, "worth-ship." Worship is behavior that involves devoting active, ultimate value or worth to a force (whether persons, places, or things) by dedicating time and energy to that force.

Now, actively, operationally, and routinely, what might Americans trust and value as much as God, alongside God, or more than anything else? Three vie for that position, I believe. And the almost visceral reaction that people may have to mentioning them as idols will verify the extent to which contemporary Americans are idolatrous or not.

It is my considered opinion that three American idols transcend all others. The first is freedom. Another is America itself. And the third, underlying the others, is wealth or money. We are told that many people immigrated to America to find freedom, and that pursuit often primarily involved the opportunity to make their material fortunes. If freedom, America, and wealth motivated people to risk everything to achieve them, those people are likely to be susceptible to idealizing them. If people idealize them to the point of investing them with basic trust and ultimate value, then they are idols. If they are idols, then devotion to them is nothing less than idolatry. And, insofar as Americans, including American fundamentalists, ultimately value their own personal freedom, the nation that offers it, and the material wealth that undergirds both, they are involved in idolatry. That would explain fundamentalists' neglect of concern for economic equity and social justice.

If Christian fundamentalists in America worship these three idols alongside God, then any reconsideration of the current economic system would be unthinkable. It would be a violation of their basic faith. It would be heretical, even though it has absolutely no support in scripture. It would evoke an emotional response, usually defensive and angry. It would compel an uncritical fusion of their political/economic ideology with their Christian fundamentalist persuasion, even though scripture may contradict it.

Of course, if American Christian fundamentalists are involved in idolatry, they must defend themselves against their own cognitive dissonance, their own conflicted values. They will do what humans usually do to protect themselves from awareness that their behavior is incongruent with their beliefs. They will employ various psychological defense mechanisms. They will deny, rationalize, intellectualize, and suppress consciousness of it. One reaction is to employ a diversionary defense mechanism. Diversion involves concentrating on matters and behaviors that do not affect them or are not emphasized in the Bible. It involves emphasizing other people's behaviors rather than their own. That was the pattern of self-defense that the Pharisees employed.

This defensive strategy has a dual benefit. It serves to suppress consciousness of one's own divergent conduct by concentrating on the divergences of other people. But it also serves the purpose of causing one to feel righteous in the process. That would explain the energy fundamentalists devote to issues not emphasized in the Bible instead of ones that are.

I have come to think that the basic spiritual problem in America is idolatry. It is trust in and worship of a trinity of gods: freedom, America, and wealth. Currently, those three are indistinguishably interconnected. America has been reduced to individual freedom, and freedom has been reduced to wealth and the options it promises to provide. It not only predisposes fundamentalists to be disinterested in the biblical concerns over economic inequity and social injustice, but also it engenders disregard for other important matters that literalists would normally emphasize.

Those matters are enshrined in the Ten Commandments. They include keeping the Sabbath, honoring parents, avoiding false witness, and avoiding covetousness. A core requirement in observing Sabbath was to refrain from work and commerce one day each week. America no longer honors any Sabbath day. That omission has only one cause. And that cause is profit, which serves wealth.

The Commandments say, "Honor your father and your mother." That did not primarily mean obeying your parents, as we teach our children. It included that dimension for children, but it had even wider significance. Some ancient Near Eastern cultures cast aside those infirmed by age. This Commandment meant that adult children of aging or ailing parents should respect and provide for them when they could no longer provide for themselves. It involved providing support with dignity for elders in the community. How can we honor senior citizens without the dignified supports of Social Security and Medicare? The omission would have only one cause. And that cause would be protection of the value of the dollar. Detractors of Social Security and Medicare cite that they are the main contributors to the federal deficit. They point out that if deficits continue to increase, it will result in the devaluation of the dollar. They decry increased taxation to fund them because it would decrease short-term wealth and the added jobs that it might create. In the process, for the sake of the dollar and increased wealth, provision for the aged is jeopardized. That has only one cause. It serves wealth.

False witness was the practice of saying something in public to the advantage of oneself at the expense of others. Bearing false witness has become so commonplace in America that it is widely accepted in various contexts. It has become an art form, and clients pay a great deal for it. Bearing false witness has been institutionalized in business and politics. We have become inured to false claims publicly made and have come to expect and enjoy them. Whether they take the form of commercial promotions or political attack advertising, we expect false claims. That has one cause, and that cause is profit at the expense of others.

Covetousness is simply the desire to possess what others have. It is bedrock to commercial advertising. It drives consumerism and is essential to the stability of the American economy. It has one cause. That cause is profit, personal and corporate profit. It serves wealth.

The neglect of these basic biblical admonitions is solely driven by wealth, and points to the idolatry of it.

The idolatry of wealth may be the source of any divine judgment that fundamentalists claim God has visited upon America. That is, the idolatry of wealth is the likely cause of the adverse natural consequences that fundamentalists tend to describe as God's judgment. Those adverse consequences have had several expressions, and none of them have been directly related to personal choices about sex or reproduction. It may sound odd of me to say that, but that has been precisely what fundamentalist leaders have claimed.

One adverse consequence that has befallen America has been violent hostility toward America among people in other cultures. Customarily, Americans have attributed that to envy of our prosperity and as covetousness. Note the reference to desire for wealth as the motivation. That might just be a form of projection, displacing our own thoughts onto others. And yet, according to critics, their hostility has been caused by the inroads of American materialism into their cultures. Materialism and conspicuous consumption are outward and visible signs of the idolatry of wealth.

Another adverse consequence has been greed. Thomas Aquinas identified greed as one of the "seven deadly sins." Once again, people dismiss those who mention greed by accusing them of envy, as presidential candidate Mitt Romney has done. People are simply jealous of success and the fruit of hard work, he said. Nevertheless, greed has been the prime mover in the serial economic crashes that have taken place in this generation. Those crashes have involved the financial market, the stock market, and the housing market. The conditions that gave rise to those crashes have been unfounded bubbles in those sectors. The bubbles have been driven by greed. People have scrambled to various markets to profit from their inflated value. And greed is symptomatic of the idolatry of wealth.

Closely related to greed is debt. One consequence of worshipping wealth has been that Americans have financially overextended themselves. For example, many leveraged the theoretical value of their homes to sustain inflated lifestyles. Americans have spent more than they could afford to possess what they wanted. That has been true at every level. Individuals, families, businesses, and government, at every level, have all spent more than they could afford in order to live beyond their means. And that has brought America to the brink of disaster. It is another symptom of the idolatry of wealth.

Yet another adverse consequence of worshipping wealth has been to undermine the long-term viability of the environment. Most Americans, including American fundamentalists, have consistently chosen to support policies that promise short-term economic gain over long-term environmental viability. Defending the god of wealth has involved denial of real adverse consequences of pursuing wealth, unconcerned by collateral environmental damages.

Denial is a defense mechanism. Denial of the threat of climate change has involved unwillingness to hear the warnings of more than 95 percent of the scientific community involved in fields connected to climatology. Many have chosen to heed outliers in the field, instead. That is not unlike the Israelites choosing false prophets over the truth. It is more convenient that way. Difficult changes can be avoided that way. Idolatry of wealth and the individual freedom that it promises to confer vie with God for the position of preeminence among many Americans, including Christian fundamentalists.

People define themselves by their faith. Americans collectively define themselves by their faith. Their actions express their faith. When Moses asked God to identify himself, God said, "I am." God defined himself by being, not by what he had or by what he had done.

Increasingly, during the past generation or so, Americans have come to define themselves by what they have. I have a body. I have my health. Americans care very much about how their bodies look and function. I have an education. I have a job. I have a family. I have relationships. I have a house, a car, a retirement fund, and possessions. Who are you? I am because I have, and so I am free, and, therefore, I am an American. That portrays the nature of the idolatry.

Admittedly, the prevailing theological emphases and idiosyncratic interpretations of classical theology are influenced by the cultures in which they exist. Cultures are also influenced by the prevailing religious expressions of their populations as well. There is cross-pollination between religions and the cultures within which they exist.

The high priority that American culture places on wealth has shown itself in fundamentalist theology. It is noteworthy that Christian fundamentalists in America have embraced "Prosperity Theology" and its less sophisticated version, "King's Kids" theology, but have totally ignored virtually any theological reflections on justice or equity. Both of those theological paradigms have emphasized that God simply wants Christians to prosper materially, to attain wealth. I suppose that also explains the popularity that the tiny book *The Prayer of Jabez* enjoyed for several years. It is an illustration of American materialism cross-pollinating with Christian fundamentalism. Its message was elementary: pray the prayer that Jabez did and you will prosper materially as he did.

Why would Christian fundamentalists accept some ideologies or systems, even though they not inherently Christian, and reject others? Christian fundamentalists have identified humanism as inconsistent with Christian values, and so they actively reject it. They scrutinize government policies and programs to root out any semblance of humanist influences because they are ungodly, perhaps even demonic. And yet, they have not even questioned the precepts of the prevailing economic system as even remotely inconsistent with Christian values in any way. They resist any suggestion of it as un-American. And yet the particular evolution of that system has clearly enriched some and disenfranchised many more, creating increased poverty. Still, the Bible speaks at length and very critically of wealth. The unreserved acceptance of a currently popular economic ideology serves the god of wealth and betrays the idolatry of it among American fundamentalists.

Chapter 30

⌒

God's Way: Liberal or Conservative?

God Created Liberals and Conservatives
to Complement Each Other

C an it be that God inspires cognitive predisposition to conservatism or liberalism? Contemporary Christian fundamentalists in America seem to believe so. They have done something that Jesus never did. They have adopted a political ideology, almost exclusively conservative. They have aligned themselves with a political party, almost exclusively the Republican Party.

The Gospels reveal that Jesus frustrated his contemporaries. One of the reasons for their frustration with him was that he was not only unaligned with any party or ideology, but he was all over the map. Jesus was clearly conservative at times. But he was even more often liberal, even radical, in his words and actions. Sometimes he was neither and sometimes both. St. Paul was too. That indicates to me that God is not exclusively partial to any predisposition of thought, whether liberal, conservative, or anything in between.

Recent studies have demonstrated that there is a connection between brain structure and people's predispositions to liberalism or conservatism. *Nature Neuroscience* reported in its September 2007 edition that experiments conducted by scientists at New York University and the University of California in Los Angeles indicate that liberals and conservatives process information differently. Dr. Marco Iacoboni stated, "There are two different cognitive styles, a liberal style and a conservative style."[xvi]

Findings indicate that there is, in fact, a biological difference in brain structure between those with liberal and conservative tendencies. The April 7, 2011, issue of the *Journal of Current Biology* reported on a study of brain structure and cognitive styles. University College, London, studied ninety subjects. They completed thorough questionnaires with questions designed to uncover the cognitive styles, thought processes, and liberal or conservative predilections of the subjects. They were tallied on a five-point scale from very liberal to very conservative. The subjects also underwent CAT scans.[xvii]

In that experiment, Ryota Kanai's research group found a significant correlation. Liberals were found to have a larger anterior cingulate cortex around the corpus callosum, which is a brain structure that relays signals between the right and left hemispheres of the brain. It enables the brain to be better able to make sense of conflicting information. That assists a person to be more efficient at managing conflicting data to reach decisions. Such persons were more disposed to new ways of responding to presenting problems.

Conservatives were found to have a larger amygdala. That brain structure helps people to notice and to react to threats. It enables people to recognize potential danger and to be more alert to possible threats. Such persons seem more disposed to defense in circumstances of conflict, including cognitive conflict.

If the results of those studies are accurate, it would indicate that the differences between those of a more liberal predisposition or a more conservative predisposition are oriented in those ways by nature. One can choose to think that this biological difference is caused by accident of genetic composition, the crap shoot of genetics. One can also choose to think that God created people with those biological differences.

We accept that other biological differences exist among humans. Some of them result in different capacities of physical strength, speed, or intellect. Others result in differences of sensitivity in vision, hearing, smell, taste, or touch. Different ones of those capabilities are required in different circumstances.

If biological differences are God-given, it is likely that the capacities are God-given as well. It can be inferred that God might just have given those differences to different people so that they could complement each other's abilities within community under different circumstances. That might well mean that God, like Jesus, is neither merely liberal nor merely conservative, and that God is neither partial to liberals nor conservatives. God may well have given humans those differences as complementary strengths for use in different circumstances or roles. And, if that is the case, God has made liberals and conservatives to need each other, not to reject or demonize each other. It is logical to conclude that God intends liberals and conservatives to cooperate, not compete, and to compromise in the process.

That brings to mind a metaphor that St. Paul was fond of using. He employed the image of the human body as a metaphor for a Christian faith community. He wrote, "Now you are the body of Christ, and each one of you is a part of it" (1 Corinthians 12:27). There is that idea of complementary interconnectedness, or symbiosis, if you prefer. Paul amplified his thought, "The eye cannot say to the hand, 'I don't need you!' And the head cannot say to the feet, 'I don't need you!'" (1 Corinthians 12:21). More to the point, a larger amygdala cannot say to a larger anterior cingulate cortex, "I don't need you!" or vice versa.

The problem is that Christian fundamentalists in America have increasingly done just that. In fact, insofar as dominionism and the New

Apostolic Reformation are representative, it is even more extreme. They cast liberals, even moderates inclined to preserve government policies and programs, as collaborators with evil. They quite literally demonize fellow citizens of more liberal political, economic, and/or theological persuasions. They attribute ways of thinking different from their own as inspired by ungodliness. In fact, it is likely that they would reject the scientific studies that I have just mentioned on the same grounds.

In a nutshell, this crystallizes the critical problem of contemporary versions of Christian fundamentalism in American democratic society. Christian fundamentalists have become utterly intolerant of divergent perspectives that do not fit into their preestablished ideology and demonize those holding them. Fundamentalism has made it a virtue to be uncompromising. That seems to render conversation impossible, dialogue futile, and political compromise unattainable. Eventually that mind-set threatens to destroy democracy by rendering government incapable of achieving collective decisions relative to presenting problems. That has already begun to take place. Pragmatic problem solving is in danger of being sacrificed on the altar of ideological, even theological, purity. And that is a critical problem in the effect of fundamentalism on democracy. It is based in epistemological hubris, that there is only one exclusive way to know God and God's will, to perceive truth, and for government to respond to problems the right way. It denies the validity of other people's perspectives and the possibility that God made them different in order to achieve greater possibilities by collaboration rather than competition.

Chapter 31

⁓

The Civil and the Sacred

*Fundamentalists Fail to Differentiate between Civil
and Sacred Spheres and Blur Boundaries*

Another facet of the problem lies in a change of thought about the difference between civil and sacred jurisdictions. There seems to be some confusion between civil and sacred authority among many modern American fundamentalists. Perhaps it is not confusion at all but rather an intentional blurring of the line between the two.

Throughout history, except in the cases of theocratic states, there has always been an intentional boundary between civil authority and sacred authority. Civil authorities had responsibility for legislating, administering, and judging laws that governed the relationships and interactions among the citizens of a state. Sacred authorities had responsibility for interpreting, administering, and judging theological and moral laws that governed the conduct of people within religious community in relation to God and each other.

Even the Jewish kingdoms of Israel and Judah separated those authorities. Kings and their administrations monitored and executed temporal laws. The temple and its cultic leaders, the priests and, later, rabbis, administered sacred laws, moral conduct, and doctrinal orthodoxy. Theocracy exists when the cultic leaders achieve positions of authority in civil matters and/or when the civil authorities administer and execute cultic regulations.

Prior to the Reformation, whatever strife existed between civil authorities and the church arose over the precise boundaries between the two. It revolved around which province had sovereignty over which matters, and under what circumstances one had supremacy over the other. Those controversies never involved whether the state or the church had the right to exercise authority in its province. The issue was where the province of one ended and the other began. That debate ordinarily concentrated on such matters as taxation of the church by the state, and whether ecclesiastical courts had authority over civil institutions or civil court rulings had authority over church practices.

In that sense the American Constitution's clause concerning the separation of church and state was simply a hard and fast clarification of the traditional differentiation between the two. The state had no authority to decide upon requirements of church doctrine or the personal moral standards of a religious group. And churches had no authority to decide on the requirements of thought or conduct for citizens of the state.

There has always been some degree of disagreement between some citizens and certain religious practitioners. And there has also always been some consternation among various religious practitioners with regard to the laws of the state. Long-standing disagreement can lead to frustration. Intense frustration can lead to desperation. Desperation can lead to extreme efforts to change the identified source of those feelings. And those efforts can lead to one side or other overreaching its authority. They simply want to make people do the right thing from their point of view.

The problem it creates is really a question of boundaries. What are the limits? How far should it go? Is there no limit to the accommodation of religious sensibilities? Which ones take precedence? The current climate is rife with possibilities for overreach, with Christian fundamentalists making every effort to exert more control than ever over defining which matters in the civil arena are subject to sacred authority.

Chapter 32

―

Facing the End Makes Everything Different

The Role Apocalyptic Thinking Plays in the Political
Practices of Christian Fundamentalists

Many modern-day Christian fundamentalists take issue with honoring the traditional boundary between the secular and the sacred. They would argue that current circumstances demand a different strategy and different tactics. Some of these circumstances, these stressors, have already been described at length. They include immediate economic conditions, climate changes, international turmoil, the rise of Islam, the degree of departure from traditional values, the extent of government control, relativism, educational concerns, social dangers, moral decay, and the extent of the influence of humanism in government and society at large.

Not all of the circumstances that motivate political action by Christian fundamentalists are domestic. A most pressing concern for many fundamentalists is geopolitical. It specifically has to do with Israel.

I was serving a church in Charlotte, North Carolina. There are cities in the United States that are known as much for the prominence of the religious organizations located there than just about anything else. Obviously, Salt Lake City is that for Mormonism, but there are also cities known by the influence of Christian fundamentalist organizations as well. Charlotte is one of those cities.

It was not long after the 9/11 attacks, and I was standing outside the church. I was engaged in conversation with a young woman who was very active in the church as well as in other local Christian groups. She was bright, articulate, and respected in the community beyond the measure of her years. She was sharing some of her thoughts with me. She said, "I disagree with President Bush about why al-Qaeda attacked us. It wasn't because they hate our freedom. It is because America supports Israel." She continued, "I believe that God hasn't blessed America with wealth and military power because we deserve it. I believe that he has blessed us to defend Israel. Israel is still God's people. Israel is still at the center of God's plans for earth. Israel is where the final conflict will play out between God and Satan. Israel is God's Chosen People, and Christ will return there to rule. God created the United States to support and defend Israel in the end. If we support Israel, we are on God's side, and so God expects us to use all we have to back Israel. That's why we were attacked, because we're on Israel's side, because we're on God's side. It's just part of the price we have to pay."

To some Christian fundamentalists, the goal of restoring America as a Christian nation is less to make it more righteous for Christ's return than it is to make it more useful to God in the End. Some envision making America more Christian so that God can use the United States to stand with Israel against the forces of the Antichrist at the advent of Armageddon. The concept of Armageddon is another subcategory of Christian eschatology. It is the notion that the Apocalypse will climax in a cataclysmic conflict between the forces of God and evil on or near the Plain of Megiddo in Israel. In the minds of some fundamentalists, preparing America to be on God's side in that conflict trumps all of the ordinary reservations about honoring the boundaries between church and state. It justifies removing traditional boundaries precisely because they believe that the Apocalypse is near. Their desired outcome would include America's absolute support of Israel in international affairs in order to make a stand with Israel against Satan and his henchman, Antichrist.

Many Christians, especially Christian fundamentalists, have been aware of the dramatic increase of persecution of Christians in Africa, the Near East, and Asia. The February 13, 2012, issue of *Newsweek* reported that within the past decade, the number of incidents of Muslim persecution of Christians has increased by more than 300 percent. That fact raises concerns about the potential consequences of increasing numbers of fundamentalist-dominated nations of different persuasions in the world community. How could that lead to anything but intensified intolerance for religious diversity within those nations and conflict between nations for religious reasons? Christian fundamentalists, however, are inclined to connect the cause of the Muslim persecution of Christians with spiritual forces of evil. They are prone to interpret such persecution as another sign of the impending apocalypse. To them, it is yet another clarion call to greater political vigilance in anticipation of the rise of the Antichrist.

A considerable proportion of Christian fundamentalists are persuaded to see current events as signs of the times. That is, they discern them to be signs of the end-times. In light of the belief that the Apocalypse and Christ's return are at hand, a growing number of Christian fundamentalists believe that it is their God-given vocation to act more assertively. The likes of the New Apostolic Reformation are convinced that thoroughgoing reformation of American society is urgently demanded. They believe that reform must begin with the government, and then extend through its influences to the wider society and to the world beyond.

Yet, once again, that was not what Jesus said to do. He said, "A new command I give you: Love one another. As I have loved you, so you must love one another. By this everyone will know that you are my disciples, if you love one another" (John 13:34–35). His meaning was clear. Faith and God's love are caught, not imposed. God's kingdom is a communicable condition. It is transmitted by faith communicated through love, and that is infectious. It is not imposed, coerced, or legislated, and that is because those means never capture people's hearts, only their fear, their resistance, and their resentment.

Even though his times were just as chaotic and alarming as ours, Jesus never resorted to political means to make others join God's kingdom. The Jewish people in Jesus's time were in greater chaos than you can imagine. As today, apocalyptic thinking was rampant. It led to following self-proclaimed messiahs, who led extreme attempts to reform their nation by revolution. And all those efforts had disastrous results. They were a defeated nation, occupied by foreign troops. They were dominated by aliens, who were hostile to their religion and their culture. And yet Jesus never envisioned forcible political or cultural revolution.

To Jewish fundamentalists, Hellenism, which was the prevailing Greco-Roman culture of the time, was even more dangerous than humanism is to modern American fundamentalists. Back then, about half of all Jews were steeped in it and strongly influenced by it. Strict Jews of the time saw it as evil, polytheistic, idolatrous, morally corrupt, and very seductive. They wanted to protect their people from it. Threats and dangers were everywhere, and they were afraid to the point of defensive rage.

Profound frustration is not divine inspiration, but over time it can mask for it. Those Jews were desperately frustrated, and different ones employed different defensive strategies. Jews reacted in diverse ways and adopted various tactics. The Essenes ran away into the wilderness to escape the tribulations to come and to prepare themselves for God's arrival. Withdrawal was their way. The Herodians embraced Hellenism and colluded with the Romans to try to ensure peace. Collaboration was their way. The Zealots took the opposite approach. They took up armed resistance to fight the Romans, like freedom fighters against the British in the American colonies, or modern insurgents in Islamic countries.

Active violent resistance, terrorism, was their way. The Pharisees took a fundamentalist approach. They emphasized a rigid preservation of the faith and morality of the Jewish people. They clung to biblical tradition and scrupulous morality in order to reclaim the purity of the Jewish religion and culture. Uncompromising tradition was their way. The Sadducees tried to straddle the fence to ensure stability. They served the position of overseeing the only established institution that the Romans permitted, the temple cult. Political manipulation was their way. Many of those segments of the Jewish population despised each other. They tried to find common ground on the Sanhedrin, the Jewish ruling council, but they were often rendered dysfunctional by their differences.

Jesus was raised in that religious, cultural, and political maelstrom. From the time he came into the public spotlight and gained popular enthusiasm, those different groups targeted him. They targeted him for recruitment. Absent that, they made every attempt to use him to advance their own goals. When they could not, they tried to discredit him in the public eye. When that failed, they came to believe that it was necessary to eliminate him altogether.

You see, Jesus was surrounded by politics. He had every human reason to join forces with any of a number of viable groups to secure his position and to advance his cause. But he never allied himself with any political or religious movement. He never allowed himself to be used by any political group. He never tried to use any political groups or political means to accomplish his goals. He never was politicized whatsoever, nor did he ever employ political or other manipulative tactics to achieve the good objectives that he firmly believed God wanted him to accomplish.

Jesus thought that politics was a red herring. More than that, he regarded it as a temptation. Recall the story of Jesus's temptation in the wilderness. One temptation stands out. Referring to all the nations of the world, the devil proposed, "I will give you all their authority and splendor; it has been given to me, and I can give it to anyone I want to. If you worship me, it will all be yours" (Luke 4:6–7). That was a stupid temptation, if you emphasize the idea that Christ would actually entertain the notion of worshipping the devil. But that was not the temptation. The actual temptation was having control of the kingdoms of the world. The temptation was to fulfill his sense of God-given mission by using political power to impose God's ways on people. It would be quicker. It would be more efficient. And it would miss God's goal—people's voluntary devotion and their adherence to God's intention for their lives.

No matter how urgent and dire the situation may be God has never imposed his will or coerced people to conform to it. I suppose that would be God's major temptation. If God were tempted by anything, I can't think of a more compelling divine temptation than to take the shortcut by suspending free will and making people do what he wants. But no, God has always allowed people to make their own decisions and to experience the natural consequences of their choices. Why would God resist the temptation to control people only to have other people do it for him? His Spirit hints at new directions that people might take to reform their ways. He utilizes the loving acts and honest words of faith-filled people to prompt them to pay attention to God's guidance. He allows people the dignity of choice to decide whether to follow that guidance or not. That's how God operates. Why should those who claim to follow God's ways behave differently? Whenever people attempt to do God's part, they just mess it up, often causing an adverse reaction instead.

There is another question. If the end really is near and Christ will return soon, what point would there be in restructuring the United States government or dismantling its policies and programs? It would have no lasting effect. It would serve no enduring purpose. If the apocalypse is upon us, circumstances will eradicate governments. If Christ returns soon, he will establish whatever governmental systems and structures that he sees fit, if any.

Chapter 33

—

Prophecy

The Concept of Prophecy and Modern Fundamentalism

C urrently, there is widespread interest in prophecy. That fascination
is not limited to those who are particularly religious. I suspect
that much of the interest has to do with the conditions in the world
that have already been mentioned. A new year has just begun. It is now
2012, and many people throughout the world are intrigued by the date.
Secular folks, pagans, new age spiritualists, and others are engrossed by
the end of the Mayan calendar or the predictions of Nostradamus. They
wonder if the end of ordinary time is at hand. Christian fundamentalists
share that apocalyptic fascination but based in biblical prophecy rather
than other sources.

As I have mentioned in passing, God has a track record according
to the biblical writings. In the Bible, God has had a consistent pattern
in the manner in which he deals with humans. God's nearly constant
way of dealing with people is to let them experience the natural
consequences of their choices. God does not judge people by hitting
them with lightning bolts, unless they choose to stand on the fairway

of a golf course with an iron raised to the sky in the middle of a severe thunderstorm. And even that is a natural consequence.

The essence of the Hebrew prophetic tradition is that the prophets spoke about two matters. They articulated God's messages. Then they foretold what would happen if people didn't heed those messages. Biblical scholars usually call that twofold emphasis the forth-telling and fore-telling aspects of biblical prophecy.

God's message through the prophets was consistent. The prophets told people that God loved them and gave them everything they enjoyed. The prophets identified ways in which God was troubled about people's actions. They described ways in which people had been straying from God's intentions. They offered God's direction for alternative courses of action. They explained the negative outcomes that would ensue if people did not change their ways. They laid out the natural consequences of those choices. This is popularly known as God's judgment, but in a real sense the negative consequences were not God's punishment. Instead, they were God's warning that he would not protect people from the natural consequences of their choices. God's message was less, "I'm going to get you for that!" than it was "Watch out; you're headed for trouble! Change course!"

Let's take a prime example of biblical prophecy. During the sixth century BC, there were two superpowers in the Middle East. One was Egypt, and the other was Babylon (modern Iraq). Israel determined that it was in its own best interest to side with Egypt against the Babylonian Empire, instead of simply trusting God for its defense. They firmly believed that Egyptian chariots were irresistible. Through the prophets, God warned that there would be negative natural consequences. That was God's message, God's warning.

Then there was an action. An event took place. The conflict between the two superpowers reached a head. When the Babylonian army defeated the Egyptians in battle, the Babylonians saw Israelis as enemy conspirators and took them captive, en masse. It was God's judgment of Israel's failure to trust him, but it took the form of the natural consequence of Israel's political choices.

You see, God was always considerate enough to warn people first. God ordinarily sent individuals to warn of danger and to suggest alternate choices. The people were preserved from the negative natural consequences when they made corrective changes. That has been called repentance. But they suffered negative consequences when they did not. That has been called judgment. God warned people, but God also assured them that he would continue to love them even if they did not change. God promised to restore them even after they experienced the negative consequences.

As you might expect, the prophets were usually rejected for their messages. People don't like it when they hear inconvenient messages about potentially disastrous consequences to their choices. As you might also suspect, other messengers also cropped up to contradict the warnings of the prophets. They were called false prophets. Essentially, they distracted people from God's messages by calling their attention to other matters. God always allowed people to decide for themselves what to believe. The proof of which message was actually from God was retrospective, the natural outcome. The people experienced the outcome and realized which messages had actually been inspired by God. And then God sent messengers to explain what had happened. God's purpose was to enable people to learn from their mistakes in order to do better in the future.

That was God's pattern, God's ordinary way of doing things. Some scholars have called it the "word/deed/word" pattern of divine prophecy. God's warnings gave way to events, and those events gave way to God's explanation of the causes of those events. God always reiterated his love. God always called for the people to learn from their mistakes. God always reassured people of hope for new outcomes in the future. In that sense, God operated like a loving parent, intent on helping the kids learn important life lessons.

God has been doing it that way throughout recorded history. God followed this pattern: warning, consequence, explanation, and new beginning. Then, too, people have followed their usual patterns. Sometimes people pay attention and make changes to avoid the natural, negative consequences. And sometimes they do not, often employing the messages of false prophets as a defense mechanism to rationalize their decisions. But they suffer the consequences. God's consistent goal has been to teach, or perhaps better phrased, to help people learn how they need to live.

God did not divorce consequences from the behaviors with which they were connected. False prophecy tended to disconnect cause from effect, misrepresent God's message, and misinterpret God's meaning. Given the historic pattern of God's behavior and the nature of prophecy and false prophecy, how do current fundamentalist messages stack up? Do they follow a pattern of godly or false prophecy? Of course, outcome will tell the tale. But Jesus offered one other way of telling the difference in the meantime. He said, "By their fruit you will recognize them" (Matthew 7:20). What is the fruit, what are the telltale effects, of contemporary fundamentalist messages and efforts? According to Shakespeare in the words of Lancelot in *The Merchant of Venice*, "The truth will out."

Chapter 34

~

Another Possibility

Basic Changes in Human Behavior Patterns

Many American Christian fundamentalists may well reject the following ideas out of hand. Some may even regard them as potential fodder for the Antichrist. It is possible that they may lump these notions in a similar category with the United Nations or the European Union, as platforms for the Antichrist. As has been the case in the past, readers must decide for themselves which ideas are accurate and helpful or inaccurate and counterproductive, whether their source is godly or not.

Just suppose that all the previously mentioned signs and symptoms have different meaning altogether. Suppose they are not signs of the end-times, but of a desperate need for change in the usual ways we humans have been operating. Instead of the imminence of Christ's apocalyptic return, just suppose God is communicating far-reaching needs for change.

An alternate interpretation of the current conditions in the world is that they are God's warning that humans are headed in the wrong direction. Perhaps it is not a warning about impending apocalypse and God's intention to rescue the faithful from it. Instead, it might simply be God warning humanity that the ways in which we have been conducting ourselves need to change, or else there will be disastrous consequences. It may very well be that God's message is that the time has come for humans, including Christians, to change their ways, and that God will no longer protect us from the natural consequences of our collective choices and patterns of behavior.

History is a story. History is the recorded story of collective human behavior. Stories have themes. There are morals to stories. If there has been an underlying theme or overarching moral to the story of recorded human history, it has been this: humans compete in order to achieve their perceived self-interests. Humans have competed with nature. Individuals have competed with other individuals. Families have competed with other families. Clans have competed with other clans. Tribes have competed with other tribes, nations with other nations, ethnic groups with other ethnic groups, races with other races, and religions with other religions. These competitions have involved conflicts of various sorts. These conflicts have often resulted in winners and losers. Winners temporarily gain power, control, and material advantage over losers. That has been the normal pattern of human behavior throughout history.

Naturally, that pattern has been recorded in the Bible as much as it has in other historical documents. But that does not mean that the Bible endorses this pattern of behavior. In fact, I would go so far as to say that the first stories in the Bible all have morals that demonstrate the negative consequences of this pattern of behavior. The story of Adam and Eve, or the fall, describes the negative consequences of competition with nature and God (Genesis 3). The story of Cain and Abel describes the negative consequences of competition between individuals (Genesis 4). The story of Noah and the flood describes the negative consequences of competition among peoples (Genesis 6). The story of the Tower of

Babel describes the negative consequences of competition with God (Genesis 11). The Bible does not justify competition for self-interest. It simply describes it and its negative consequences.

One of the most poignant links between an instance of competition in the Bible and current events demonstrates the futility of competition. About four thousand years ago, give or take, there was a man from Ur named Abraham. God made a promise to Abraham. God said, "I will give the land to you and your descendants forever" (Genesis 12: 7). The land in question was around a place called Hebron, hence the term Hebrew. The extended region has been otherwise called Canaan or Palestine. Abraham's wife, Sarah, and his concubine, Hagar, were in competition (Genesis 16). Abraham had two sons. The first was Ishmael, born to Hagar. The second was Isaac, born to Sarah. Palestinians claim Ishmael as their connection to Abraham, and Israelis claim Isaac in the same way. Their competition for the same land continues to this very day. It has been an issue of sibling rivalry, or should I say spousal rivalry, that has drawn the whole world into the competition.

Competition in pursuit of self-interest is not only futile but has usually been destructive in its consequences. At this particular point in history, competition is absurd and can have nothing but disastrous consequences. I believe that God's message is that he will no longer protect humanity from the natural consequences of our collective competitive patterns of behavior in pursuit of perceived self-interest. It only serves the idol of wealth. Devotion to wealth has enslaved much of humanity, and it will bring unparalleled destruction if we humans do not change our ways.

There are simply too many humans on earth and too few natural resources to reasonably warrant competition for them. We are driven by our propensity to compete even more desperately than ever, of course. But that will only bring disaster closer. Recent economic events have proven that humanity has become a vast and complex web. Even though humans may be remotely located, we are intricately interconnected.

In fact, that intricate interconnectedness exists among all creatures. It always has, but the impact of humans has never been so determinative simply because of our sheer numbers and consumptive needs. God made us to be interconnected and interdependent. Any significant advance or decline in one part of this multidimensional global web negatively affects other parts and the integrity of the whole.

I believe that God may be letting us know that we humans need to make fundamental changes in our patterns of collective behavior.

- We need to recognize that in reality humans are **interdependent** with other humans and with all other creatures, instead of independent from them.
- Motivated by realistic concern for the well-being of the Creation, we humans need to **lessen our levels of reproduction** so that the level of population will not continue to grow beyond the point of viability.
- We need to **cooperate**, to **collaborate** with each other, instead of competing with those we imagine do not share our interests.
- We need to **share** resources with those who are deprived of them.
- We need to develop **effective ways to resolve conflicts and to achieve mutually acceptable compromise** among competing interest groups rather than settling them by conflict-based control. Multinational terrorism demonstrates that no matter how much power one side has, it cannot control others in any case.
- We need to **steward the natural environment and nurture God's creatures**, in full recognition that they belong to God and are not simply up for grabs for the most enterprising or aggressive humans.

These might just be the proper primary concerns for Christians in the present era, whether Christ's return is imminent or not. Since Jesus said that no one knows when that time will be, Christians are intended to act both as if Christ is returning now and as if he is not. Both demand that the citizens of democracies, including Christians, pay primary attention to such universal matters as these rather than devoting their attention to trying to control other citizens' personal decisions of moral conduct.

Some fundamentalists might well say, "Aha, this guy's just a liberal environmentalist in biblical clothing, and probably a communist too!"

Let's see what the Bible has to say, then.

Chapter 35

―

The Tree

An Example of Biblical Interpretation in Support of Change

I was in my first year of seminary and living in a New England college town. Since most seasoned clergy would ordinarily rather wrestle alligators than deal with youth, I was recruited by a local pastor to work with adolescents, as many young seminarians have been. The teens became energized by our meetings and carried their newfound spiritual enthusiasm with them to school.

As it happened, one of their teachers, a biology teacher, had fire in his belly about how the biblical religions had inspired the modern degradation of the natural environment. Citing the then recent thesis by Professor Lynn White, the biology teacher argued that the more primitive, pagan, nature religions were closer to the earth. He told the class that pagans had respected the earth more than Christians did. The young students defended their fledgling faith from his implied criticism.

To shorten the story behind it, I was invited to visit their biology class to make a presentation on the concept of Creation. That's not what my visit turned out to be. Instead, it unfolded into something of a debate.

I hadn't been told the particular scholarly extract that was the basis of the teacher's argument. When he referenced it in our dialogue, I realized that I had already studied "Lynn White's thesis" in *The Historical Roots of Our Ecological Crisis* (1967). As I recall, Professor White's central point was that since the biblical religions were foremost monotheistic, Christianity saw one of its primary directives as to fight all forms of polytheism and nature religion. In the process Christianity turned nature into an object of human dominance. Consequently, human industry developed as it did in the West because of Christianity's emphasis on natural resources as mere objects, devoid of spiritual significance. It regarded nature and its constituent parts as resources for human consumption and exploitation, to be used for survival and prosperity. Christianity removed any integrity, let alone sanctity, from other species and the environment as a whole. That cleared the way for the development of human industries, which used and abused other creatures and caused the depletion of natural resources. It began in medieval Europe and spread by way of colonialism to other parts of the world. In large measure Christianity was responsible for the current environmental crisis.

My argument began by contradicting the premise by pointing out that the Bible teaches that God made each and every creature. I pointed out that that bestowed inherent honor upon each and every creature. I argued that the Bible teaches a proper relationship between humans and other aspects of nature. The biblical writings, I pointed out, teach that the Creator made humans to tend and care for nature rather than use it up. I added that the biblical perspective was balanced. It taught humans neither to dominate the component parts of their natural habitat nor to be dominated by them. I concluded my comments by asserting that the Bible emphasizes the importance of stewardship, and that stewardship includes nurturing the integrity of natural habitats.

My argument, I then thought, was an accurate portrayal of the Bible. It was balanced. It was nicely nuanced. It was well reasoned. And, I now believe, it was absolutely naïve.

I had that little debate more than forty year ago. Since then, I've realized something. The Bible may say something, but how people of faith in it choose to understand and use it is an entirely different matter altogether. People who value the Bible are quite able to disregard any portion of it and to rationalize that in any way they see fit.

In effect, we people of faith in the Judeo-Christian scriptures are often very conveniently self-oriented in much of what we emphasize. We will deny it. We will rationalize it. We will intellectualize it. We deflect attention from our own incongruous behaviors and motives by focusing on the behaviors and motives of others. But we are susceptible to doing what we want to get what we want and then using our faith to gain heaven too.

Many Christians, especially Christian fundamentalists, primarily tend to focus on five matters. Each of the faithful will prioritize them differently, depending upon his or her particular personality, passions, and perspectives. One is to attain personal salvation, going to heaven after physical life ends. Another is to achieve peace, happiness, security, even prosperity, for himself and loved ones for the duration of physical life. Yet another is to save others from hell. Still another is to stop ourselves and other people from sinning and from theological error in the ways that are particularly disturbing to us. Last, and too often least, is to contribute to the well-being of other people and the world.

It may be crass to say so, but it all too often seems that personal survival and safety, in this life and in eternity, are the primary agenda for Christian fundamentalists. This stands to reason, I suppose, since humans are no different from other species when it comes to the instinct for survival. As far as we can tell, humans are the only creatures capable of conceptualizing life after death, and so it is only natural for us to extend our drive for survival and safety beyond the duration of physical life.

263

Since humans do possess the capability to conceptualize the future, we are able to apply that skill to the condition of the earth. We are capable of balancing our own present physical needs with our awareness of the ramifications of our overuse of natural resources. We are able to comprehend that our consumptive behavior will wear out the habitats within which we live. We are capable of making plans and taking actions to stem the tide of the environmental degradation that we cause.

At this point, the reader might justifiably ask what possible connection the Bible, theology, and environmentalism have with each other, let alone what relevance they have to politics and democracy. Quite recently, one of the Republican candidates for the presidency of the United States happened to have wedded all of them together. Former Pennsylvania Senator Rick Santorum accused President Barak Obama of what he called "phony theology." President Obama had claimed that his Christian faith inspired his conviction that government policies should respond to environmental problems. Santorum clarified his accusation. He explained that the president's theology was phony because it was not based on the Bible. He implied that the Bible has nothing to say about environmentalism. It is a new phenomenon, indeed, to make matters of Christian theological difference appropriate subject matter for political debate within American pluralistic society. But that is another indication of the influence of fundamentalism in contemporary American democracy. Since the door has been opened by presidential aspirants, let us consider whether the Bible actually has anything to say about the environment.

The Bible begins with a familiar story, perhaps the most familiar story there is. Some might call it *the first story*. It is the story of the first people in the Bible, the story of Adam and Eve. In the first chapter of the book of Genesis, it is written, "In the beginning God created the heavens and the earth" (Genesis 1:1). The description of that divine creation process is set within the context of a seven-day period.

The first chapter of Genesis describes God's creative process in poetic terms. The first chapter of the book of Genesis is a Hebrew poem. Ancient Hebrew poetry was not defined by rhyme or meter, but by thought parallelism, by the repetition of thoughts. Brilliantly, and worthy of God's inspiration, it used a seven-day workweek to present a framework for that thought repetition. The point of it was threefold. It reminded the hearer over and over again that God made everything. It presented it in a way to make the story easy to remember. And it used the days of a workweek to make it easy for the hearer to relate to as well as to learn how to do work themselves. Arguments about how long the process of creation took and to refute evolution are completely beside the point. Such arguments only serve to discredit the importance of the Bible in the minds of the skeptical.

As the Creation story unfolds, on the sixth day, God created land animals, including Homo sapiens. But the human creatures were distinguished with more description than other creatures. Indeed, the rest of the Bible could be said to be the ongoing saga of the human species and God's interactions and interventions on our behalf. That may be one of the reasons that humans are, excuse the expression, stuck on ourselves, because in the Bible God seems preoccupied with us above everything else. And so, perhaps, we humans may be forgiven for thinking that everything revolves around us. Remember that the Bible is about God's relationship with humans and our relationships with God and each other, not about God's involvement with other creatures.

Naturally, therefore, the Bible goes on to describe humans at length. "Then God said, 'Let us make mankind in our image, in our likeness, so that they may rule over the fish in the sea and the birds in the sky, over the livestock and all the wild animals, and over all the creatures that move along the ground.' So God created mankind in his own image, in the image of God he created them; male and female he created them. God blessed them and said to them, 'Be fruitful and multiply; fill the earth and subdue it'" (Genesis 1:26–28).

While the first point of the biblical story of Creation is that God made everything, there are at least two other points as well. One is that humans are special. The other is that humans were created to populate and subdue earth.

According to this story, Homo sapiens are special because they were created by God to be like God. It never says how, but biblical teachers, scholars, and theologians, probably from as far back as Moses, have not hesitated to speculate, and without any more information than anyone else. How are humans created in God's image, that is, like our Creator? Is it that God has opposable thumbs or walks upright or has larger frontal lobe development? No one has seriously suggested that God created Homo sapiens to look like God. And so, various theologians have emphasized different human qualities. God made us able to love, reason, choose, speak, make things, etc. In other words, some speculated that it was certain distinguishing human capacities that set Homo sapiens apart from other organisms and that make us special, like the Maker.

Some theologians thought that was insufficient. At least since the time of St. Augustine, emphasis was placed upon a specific biblical verse. That verse comes from the second chapter of Genesis. Incidentally, the second chapter of Genesis comprises a second, separate, and more Man-centered, Creation story. In Genesis 2:7, it is written, "Then the LORD God formed a man from the dust of the ground and breathed into his nostrils the breath of life, and the man became a living being." The word for breath, in that verse, was the Hebrew word, ruach. It meant breath, wind, or spirit. And so, classical Christian theology postulated that when God breathed the breath of life into Homo sapiens, God simultaneously breathed spirit, the soul, within humans. That became the distinguishing feature of Homo sapiens, according to Christian tradition. Humans were created in God's image, not merely because of their faculties or capacities, but because God created us with a soul. Humans are comprised of an eternal soul.

Another point of the first Creation story in the first chapter of the book of Genesis is that we have the capacity and the God-given right to dominate every other living organism on earth. It seems almost to be the raison d'être for humans. We exist to be fertile, reproduce, populate earth, and dominate every other creature. What an odd and rather self-serving raison d'être! That was not a reason for being, as much as it was a way of surviving in a very different epoch.

The reason for human beings is not found in the first story of Creation at all. But there is a reason provided in the second Creation story of Genesis, chapter 2. After God breathed (a soul?) into humans and made us different, something else was mentioned. Genesis 2:15 states, "The Lord God took the Man and put him in the Garden of Eden *to work it and take care of it*" (emphasis mine). According to that, God made humans to be resident caregivers of the natural environment within which he placed us. This might just constitute God's first covenant with Homo sapiens. God created humans to provide maintenance services for God's Creation on earth.

But the story continues. Stating that it was permissible for humans to eat the fruit of the plants they tended, God made one exception. God told humans not to eat the fruit of one of the trees in the Garden of Eden (Genesis 2:16–17). It was called "the tree of the knowledge of good and evil." That was most certainly the first commandment. Interestingly, that story has been sexualized, as often as not. All too frequently, the fruit of that tree has been interpreted as a euphemism for sexual involvement between Adam and Eve. Mind you, the way God made Homo sapiens, sexual activity has always been inextricably involved with human reproduction. Until very recently, humans have not been able to multiply without personal sexual involvement.

If one takes that story seriously, far more literally, the source of the so-called "fall" of mankind was something else altogether. The original sin was this: humans played God in relation to their environment. They competed with their Creator in a particular way. They thought that they knew better than their Creator what other creatures or aspects of their environment they could consume, and how they could use them. They misused the fruit of that tree. The humans in the story acted as they saw fit in relation to God's Creation, and suffered the negative consequences appertaining thereto. They felt exposed. They felt vulnerable. Animals were killed to provide cover for their sense of vulnerability. Paradise was lost. They lost the Garden.

They violated their God-given reason for being. Humanity's first God-given obligation was to use their special skills and abilities, not for their own consumption or for the exploitation of their environment, but to care for it instead. That is the biblical, the theological, justification for proper stewardship of the environment and its constituent creatures. Under current environmental circumstances it is the theological basis of environmentalism. It is based upon the Bible. And its guidance will urgently be needed in the forthcoming epoch more than ever before. Upcoming generations will be far more vulnerable than previous generations to losing the "Garden" altogether.

In this little illustration, I have attempted to offer the reader a brief exercise in biblical theological reflection. Most Christian fundamentalists may not agree with it, but that does not mean that it is illegitimate, faulty, or phony Christian theology. It does not conform to traditional interpretations of that story, but it is actually more true to the biblical story. It provides a legitimate example of the biblical justification for one of the aforementioned changes that humans must undertake as we face the realities of the present and their potential devastating impact on the future. For fundamentalists to neglect those realities and the changes they call for is bizarre. As I have just indicated, there is biblical justification for those changes. Why do Christian fundamentalists ignore them? It may be caused by the idolatry of wealth, but it certainly ignores God's contemporary signs and biblical guidelines.

Democracy must come to grips with reality. It must make necessary changes. Once again, these emphases include

- **interdependence** instead of independence;
- **cooperation and collaboration** instead of competition;

- **sharing** instead of monopolizing;
- **development of effective ways to resolve conflicts and to achieve mutually acceptable compromise** rather than dominance by conflict;
- **reduction of the rate of human reproduction; and**
- **stewardship of the natural environment by nurturing God's creatures and the natural resources upon which all life depends.**

Democracy is the cornerstone of any unified strategy for forward movement in these areas. Fundamentalist citizens must cooperate with other citizens in those efforts.

Chapter 36

—

Move Forward

Suggestions for Democracies in a Fundamentalist Era

Significant shifts have taken place in this era of fundamentalism. These shifts threaten to affect democracies deleteriously. They threaten to divide citizens to such an extent that it will disunite the nation to a dysfunctional degree. They threaten to reshape nations to an unprecedented extent. And democracies have shown themselves to be unprepared to deal with those challenges. I hope to offer a few recommendations in a spirit of helpfulness. They are practical suggestions for democracies, for elected public servants, for fundamentalists, and for the general citizenry of democracies. I offer these ideas to promote discussion within democratic society for everyone's well-being moving forward.

Democracies

I mentioned earlier that government came into being to address certain basic human needs. They are needs shared by many organisms. There seem to have been at least three primitive purposes for government. Those three needs were avoidance of internal conflict, resistance to

271

external aggression, and management of resources. And so the three basic reasons for government were order, security, and resource distribution— organization or regulation, protection, and provision.

A democracy is most effective when, without constraining the personal liberties of its citizens, it provides regulation in service of internal organization, protection from external aggression, and distribution of sufficient resources for its constituent members to survive. Government regulates internal relations among citizens so as to ensure that stronger, more aggressive citizens do not dominate other citizens, such that their survival and well-being are jeopardized. It applies to criminal aggression, which ordinarily calls for government to provide police protection. But it applies to the inordinate dominance of resources by the few at the expense of the many as well. It also necessitates that a democracy maintains a sufficiently effective system of defense against external aggression. And it calls for the establishment of systems of resource distribution that provides for the basic needs of the citizenry for life, liberty, and the pursuit of happiness. These basic needs include but are not limited to work, food, medical care, education, housing, and safety.

Naturally, over the course of time, needs change. Circumstances and developments create new realities and demand adjustments to a government's response. A most obvious example of this is when external aggressors threaten the security of a nation. Under these circumstances, a democratic nation may be justified in increasing its military forces and its financial support of them. That constitutes an adjustment in response to new realities. It may well involve the curtailment of individual liberties when it calls upon citizens to devote their lives to military service or their money to increased taxes, when they would ordinarily not choose to do so. Such changes in government response may also apply to other new realities as well. They may include compromising developments that threaten the material survival and well-being of citizens who do not have access to sufficient basic resources. They may also include compromising developments that threaten the environment or developments in organizations or institutions, including businesses, that threaten the well-being of the whole.

Different citizens will always have diverse perspectives and personal vested interests in connection with virtually any of these changed realities. They will disagree about whether compromising changes have taken place. They will disagree about whether particular changes demand specific government responses. They will disagree about which government responses are called for and the extent of response. In democracies, these different citizens will try to influence government to advance their desired outcomes. They will appeal to political representatives. They will organize and seek to influence political parties to champion their causes. Politicians have a vested interest in keeping their jobs. They will bond with the positions of their constituencies simply to advance the likelihood of their reelection. But that may not serve the best interests of the citizenry or the nation. That reality compromises the potential effectiveness of government to deal with new conditions.

The citizens of democracies seem convinced that democracy, while imperfect, is the best form of government. The proponents of democracy assert that it promotes freedom better than any other political system. They claim that the promotion of individual freedom is the most important purpose of government.

The most basic freedom and core obligation of citizens in a democracy is participation in electoral processes. Elected surrogates or representatives make political decisions and offer government leadership on behalf of the rest of the citizens. They are accountable to their constituencies. Voting is what makes a political system a democracy. And yet many citizens completely neglect the privilege and the responsibility of voting. A smaller percentage of Americans actually votes than in any other democracy. That provides the opportunity for the most highly motivated, including extremists of any persuasion, to enjoy more influence than they ordinarily would.

Admittedly, voting is somewhat inconvenient. People pay the price for the privilege of living in a democratic society by spending their time waiting in line to vote. It includes time citizens spend familiarizing themselves with issues and political candidates, and voting in primary elections and general elections. Time is a small enough price to pay for democracy. Some are cynical about the benefit of their votes, and yet they can be absolutely sure that there will be no benefit in neglecting to vote. Of course, one aspect of freedom in a democracy is the freedom not to vote.

The expenditure of time can be a disincentive for voting. It is important for as many citizens to vote as possible in order to ensure that the outcomes of elections are more widely representative and not inordinately influenced by extremists. Therefore, it is important to motivate citizens to exercise their franchise to vote. One way to motivate citizens to exercise that foundational responsibility is to make it equivalently inconvenient not to vote. Something like a reverse poll tax or fine would provide just such an incentive to vote. If people do not vote, they should be required to pay a fine to local and/or state governments for their negligence. It should be sufficiently expensive to motivate voting. Except in the case of verified medical conditions, every citizen should be required to pay a fine for not exercising their most basic democratic responsibility to vote.

It has been said that the greatest defense of democracy is an educated electorate. If democracy is as important as its citizens seem to think, they should be required to take and pass a course in citizenship and democracy. We require it of those who aspire to become naturalized citizens. And yet, many democracies act as if other citizens will learn about their system of government by osmosis. That leaves the door open for those with vested interests to educate segments of the electorate from their own ideological point of view.

The only way to counteract ignorance is education. Therefore, certified and supervised instructors should be provided to offer a required course. It should be a course in the principles and practicalities of citizenship within democracy. It should have a standardized curriculum with standardized testing. It should be required at every secondary school. The course should include history, the Constitution, systems of government, and the methodology of lawmaking and electoral laws. It should provide certification, and that certification should be prerequisite to voting at age eighteen. It should be required for adult citizens just as passing a driver's test is mandatory for driving. That will help to moderate the negative effects of ideologically biased educational efforts.

Education in citizenship within democracy must be impartial and objective. It must not be left up to those who have biased agendas and happen to be motivated by them. Indoctrination is not the same as education. Inciting citizens is not the same as educating them. The process of educating citizens in the exercise of the privileges of democracy is too important to surrender to osmosis or ideological zeal.

Moreover, official and intentional public forums should exist to promote reasoned discussions of public policies that concern citizens. They should be sponsored by local governments. Forums for political discourse should be sponsored by state or federal government, and should be broadcast on public media. They should probe matters of shared concern on deeper levels than political debates or campaigns ordinarily do.

In the spirit of the conclusions made by the authors of *God's Century*, these forums should include representatives of various religious perspectives as well as other points of view. The forums should not be biased, but monitored by impartial moderators. Their purpose should be to illuminate the underlying reasons for government policies and the objections to them. They should examine practical considerations of their implementation and potential ramifications. They should invite public questions and comments as well as presentations by panelists. Honest parallel presentations, instead of debate, have the dual benefit of promoting understanding and consensus-building. It has the potential benefit of informing citizens and bringing them together.

I would argue that the Constitution of the United States is not only the document that governs our collective life as citizens, but the Constitution is also the collection of those citizens as well. One of the main purposes of the former is the promotion of the unity of the latter. And so, the way we implement the Constitution, the way we function as citizens, and the way government operates must also promote a more perfect union and the common good of the whole.

Elected Public Servants

Elected officials have the privilege of representing the constituencies of the jurisdictions they serve. They are not hired merely to represent the interests of the people who vote for them but to promote the effective function of the government on behalf of all the people of their electoral jurisdictions. Their goal must not be to secure their position and power, but to serve the common good by promoting the unity and effective functioning of the state.

When I have prepared couples for marriage, I have customarily explained that they need to work together. I have mentioned that occasions arise when the two individuals will have different, even conflicting, interests and points of view, sometimes heartfelt. I have said that if marriage were a game, trying to win by getting one's way over the other is the wrong objective. I have explained that when one person tries to win at the expense of the other, that person will lose. Winning is losing because trust and goodwill are lost in the process. Winning erodes goodwill and mutual trust. The other person is turned into an object of competition, rather than a partner. Love is eroded in the process, and so is the covenant between them.

That is true in government as well. In a democracy, the citizens are the government. Citizenship within a democracy is a relationship with other citizens. It involves a mutually binding covenant. The covenant is that the citizens will work together to form a more perfect union, which will effectively solve problems that threaten functional organization, protection, and resource distribution. When elected servants compete with other elected servants for power or control and to get their way, the covenant is eroded. It violates trust, which is the reason that the approval rating of the US Congress is at its lowest point in history. The democratic system has been completely compromised by power-driven politicians and their most extreme constituents, particularly fundamentalists. Goodwill and trust have been eroded, and it threatens the covenant of democratic society.

Candidates for positions of public representation should be humbled by the privilege of that responsibility. They should offer their perspectives, proposed policies or programs, and convictions with dignity and mutual respect for other candidates. They are not competing for a prize. They are presenting themselves for the investment of a trust. Candidates campaign for elected office the way they will represent their electorates. Candidates who focus negatively on other candidates are the same as employees who focus on criticizing their coworkers. Who would hire or retain anyone known for criticizing or undermining his coworkers? Negativity, either by candidates, their staff members, PACs or Super-PACs, should factor against those candidates for public office.

If treating other people as you would like to be treated is a basis of community, then behaving otherwise destroys community. It creates dysfunction in government. The goal of elected public officials must be cooperation and collaboration, including compromise rather than competition. Otherwise, the democratic covenant is undermined, and effective government will be rendered dysfunctional. In the process, trust will be sacrificed, and society will be polarized. None of those outcomes serve the common good.

Politicians must resist the temptation to engage in demagoguery. Virtually everyone is frustrated, disappointed, or angry about something. It is relatively easy to discern those feelings and to deduce an emerging theme or shared sentiment. It is banal for those aspiring to public service to intentionally incite further anger, so as to harness it for their own purposes. There is a potential for those aspiring to elected public service to adopt a serpentine approach, to contort their own positions in order to gain personal support from various interest groups.

Getting elected is not the goal of elections. The goal of elections is to select representatives to serve as competent and effective participants in the leadership of democratic government on behalf of the citizenry. Candidates must prove themselves worthy by conducting themselves with dignity, integrity, competency, responsibility, and empathy for all citizens. They should treat other candidates with respect and courtesy.

In that spirit, elected public servants have a responsibility to promote consensus among their constituencies. They should not rely solely on input from like-minded political supporters or hired staff to craft arguments for ideological positions. They have the responsibility to cooperate with efforts to educate their constituents. That means that they should participate in public forums, listen to the spectrum of citizens in their jurisdictions, and promote consensus building.

Elected public servants would do well to sign contracts with America and with the people in their local districts on principles of professional conduct rather than policies. It has been popular for politicians to sign promissory agreements on policies, programs, political priorities, and taxes, of late. They do far better to make binding commitments to the practical application of the oaths of office they take. Those principles of professional conduct should include

- commitment to the well-being and effective operation of the levels of government for which they are responsible;
- the interests of all the citizens in their districts and not merely their supporters;
- responsiveness to all points of view without giving undue weight to financial contributors or lobbyists;
- mutually respectful treatment of other public servants;

- the avoidance of personal material benefit from the exercise of their responsibilities;
- personal rectitude in the conduct of their campaigns and the exercise of their duties; and
- accountability to the electorate.

Citizens of a democracy bear the primary responsibility for electing worthy candidates for public service. Self-interest and immaturity must be resisted. Would a voter encourage the promotion of a coworker who spent his time undermining the progress of work, gossiping about others, criticizing the work of others, or pandering to people's negative feelings? I certainly hope not. Neither should citizens vote for candidates who act that way in order to "get elected." Citizens must exercise discipline in the implementation of their obligations in a democracy and cultivate their capacity for discernment.

Candidates who demonstrate self-interest in the electoral process will serve themselves after they are elected. Negative or critical advertising about other candidates should not be rewarded with votes. Pithy sound bites should not be accepted over reasoned and well-explained positions. The electorate should see through self-serving attempts by candidates to fan the flames of their negative feelings. They should never give their votes to candidates who turn citizens of different perspectives into enemies. Candidates who appeal to our lesser nature will foster our lesser nature as leaders.

The quality of government in a democracy depends upon the collective expression of our higher nature, not our lesser nature, no matter how stressful conditions may be. During the time leading up to World War II, the people of Germany allowed their lesser nature to hold sway. During that same period the citizens of the United States largely followed their higher nature. Both were democracies. In the final analysis, the citizens of a democracy decide how their nation will conduct itself by virtue of the manner in which they engage in electoral processes.

Fundamentalist Citizens

God has blessed fundamentalists with citizenship in a democracy. Democracy is a blessing. It safeguards individual freedom. That freedom includes the right to believe what one is persuaded to believe. It includes the right to practice one's faith as one sees fit. It includes the right to pass one's faith on to others, or not. It includes the right to advocate one's faith-based convictions. It includes the right to cooperate with others to promote faith-based policies and programs. It includes the right to vote for candidates for public office who seem to share one's faith or one's values. All of these are part of the blessing of democracy. That blessing should not be squandered.

Jesus said, "From everyone who has been given much, much will be demanded; and from the one who has been entrusted with much, much more will be asked" (Luke 12:48). Much is demanded of the faith-based citizens of a democracy, and it is not simple or easy. Since citizens in a democracy get to decide how a state or its government will function, there is greater temptation for people of strong faith to play God. That is to say, it is tempting to think that one's own passions or frustrations are divinely inspired and must be accommodated.

Let God be God in the lives of other people. Resist the temptation to let frustration or anger over perceived unrighteousness in the conduct of others or their beliefs prompt you to try to control them. That is not how God has dealt with you. Treat others as you were treated by God. Give God the dignity of accomplishing his work in other people's lives, instead of trying to coerce or control them on God's behalf. God did not elect you to that role. It is important to exercise self-restraint over one's own impulses to control other people, especially in a democracy.

Closely related to that is the more ambitious temptation to try, in effect, to create a theocracy. Attempts at theocracy have always failed and, in fact, have always caused backlashes. By all means, serve the roles of salt and light, of preservation and illumination, but not by domination. History has consistently demonstrated that the more power people of faith accumulate the less loving and uglier it has been. At best, it has served only to create cultural Christianity. At worst, it has been terribly oppressive. God will establish his eternal kingdom in his own way and in his own time. It will not be established by might or by political power, but by God's Spirit in the end.

Remember that you represent Christ and that how you conduct yourself as a citizen in a democracy reflects upon him. If you are high-handed, mean-spirited, coercive, angry, controlling, judging, dogmatic, conniving, and demonizing, people take note. They are revolted by it and may attribute it to Christ. That repels people from Christ. It was not the way he operated and so misrepresents him to others. Instead, demonstrate the fruit of Christ's Spirit: love, joy, peace, patience, kindness, goodness, long-suffering (endurance), gentleness, and self-control. Add a little good humor as well. Try to operate as effective marketing representatives of Christ. How effective would a demanding and controlling sales representative be with potential clients?

There is something connected with misplaced efforts to establish theocracy. It is confusion between the sacred and the secular. People have every right, if they so choose, to try to enforce the beliefs, customs, practices, and moral conduct of others within a shared faith community. But a democratic state, no matter how large a role faith has had in its history, is not a shared faith community. A community of shared faith, by definition, is one in which virtually every member voluntarily shares most of the same principles of faith. Pluralistic democracies, by definition, are not faith communities. It is, therefore, very important for people of faith to differentiate between the sacred and the secular. Resist the temptation to impose sacred beliefs, practices, and rules or regulations of personal conduct upon society at large.

The role of the secular state is to develop and enforce laws to organize the common life of its constituent members. Which laws should be included will always be subjects of debate, and it always comes down to where personal and private conduct ends and the public good begins.

Ordinarily, personal moral conduct has been excluded from public regulation. The dividing line has usually been when personal conduct harms others. And that is the point of current debates, as it always has been. But attempts to control personal moral conduct have always failed. They drive the conduct underground, and that creates black markets. Let the state regulate public conduct, and let faith communities regulate the personal moral conduct of their voluntary members. It is more effective to deal with individuals by trying to convince them of the desirability of alternative choices to the behavior deemed harmful on a personal level.

Apply the values of your faith to the manner in which candidates for public office conduct their campaigns. Notice it when candidates try to manipulate you for your vote. Notice it when they try to stir the fires of your discontent. Notice it when they employ so-called attack ads, negatively focused on other candidates, rather than on their own positions and qualifications. Notice it when they try to pit citizens against other citizens, as if they were enemies. Notice it when they dehumanize or demonize others. Jesus said, "By their fruit you will recognize them" (Matthew 7:16). Pay attention to the fruit of political campaigns, and do not reward rotten fruit with your votes. Demand mutual respect and courtesy among candidates for public office. Pay attention when leaders, whether political or religious leaders, appeal to your lower nature to gain your support, and resist the temptation to give it to them. St. Paul called people's "lower nature" the "old man." All of us have a tug-of-war within us between our higher and lower nature. Notice when your lower nature is hooked and try to resist it.

I offer only two other things for your consideration. The first has to do with how you treat yourself before God. Ask God to reveal to you not so much how you need to change others as how God wants you to change. For example, might any form of idolatry exist in your life? Might the idolatry of wealth or ideology influence your passions? Might you be diverting yourself from attention to it by focusing on others and/

or embracing nonbiblical philosophies as if they were biblical? Might your lower nature inspire your political passions? I leave it up to God and you to discern the truth of that. I leave it up to you to deal with it, because it is a personal and private matter, not something for others to dictate.

The second has to do with how you treat others. The core of Jesus's teaching was this: treat other people the way you would like to be treated. He went further. He said, "Love your enemies. Do good to those who hurt you." That includes how we act toward those with whom we happen to disagree politically. It involves how we treat other citizens in a shared democracy, especially those with whom we disagree or of whom we disapprove.

If fundamentalist citizens wish their concerns to be taken seriously they must engage in respectful public dialogue with others. That should include the public exchange of ideas and the underlying reasons for them. They should treat those with different views in ways that demonstrate respect, recognizing that everyone is created in God's image and is worthy of the dignity appertaining thereto. Fundamentalists have an important role to play in public discourse, but they must earn the respect and trust of others in those efforts. People earn trust by the manner in which they treat each other in their common enterprise.

One of the most important contributions that fundamentalists can make to a pluralistic democratic society is to pray for the government. Citizens of strong faith can actively participate in good faith within a pluralistic democracy. They can do so without compromising their faith and values or fundamentally changing democracy and violating the pluralism of their society. They can let God be God and treat God as if he were in charge. They can mediate between God and the government with prayer. They can pray for God's guidance and inspiration of elected leaders, whether they happen to agree with them or not. Surrendering personal political preferences to God is part and parcel of faithfulness.

Citizens in General

Fundamentalists are not enemies or monsters. They only act that way sometimes. They are only human. Like all humans, fundamentalists can become frustrated, agitated, and almost driven to correct identified problems. Since they are only human and have a very strong desire to please God, they can interpret their own passionate convictions as if they were God's will for everyone. Naturally, they believe that God's will, as they understand it to be, will serve the good of the world. Like everyone else, fundamentalists sometimes overreach. It may help to see fundamentalists as just human after all.

At times they may seem to judge or to want to control others, the way others think or act, and the government under which we all live. That triggers a natural adverse reaction. It may cause resistance or rebellion against that control. In the process, it may be important to avoid the impulse to dehumanize fundamentalists. They are only human.

Fundamentalists may seem to be closed-minded. Some may well be. Nevertheless, it can be valuable to engage in conversations with them. It can be valuable to engage in public discourse. It can be frustrating. It can be intimidating to engage in dialogue with any ideologue, whether a communist or a fundamentalist of any stripe. They can seem like the embodiment of ideological infomercials. They may seem like robots, which monotonously repeat rote information. Sometimes they can seem better informed, but they have been trained in that from a particular point of view. But fundamentalists have as much to learn from others as others have to learn from them. Citizens must participate in public dialogues, whether they embrace particular ideologies or not. It is perhaps even more important for nonideological citizens to participate, since they constitute the majority of the population. They may be more interested in practicalities and effective decision making as well.

One of the unique provinces of religion is to ask and seek answers to universal questions, what some call "first order questions." They include such matters as who we are, where we come from, why we exist, what purpose life has, what ultimate destiny humans have, how we are meant to live, and what we are meant to accomplish in the meantime. Those questions can cause discomfort, but they make us all think more circumspectly. Engagement in dialogue with fundamentalists can enrich one's own perspectives on life.

Many nonfundamentalists are people of faith, nonetheless. It is extremely valuable for people of faith who are not fundamentalists to offer their considered convictions within the public forum. That includes Christians of many persuasions, but is most certainly not limited to them. People of faith in previous generations contributed their beliefs, ideas, ideals, and ethical convictions to the public discourse, whether they embraced traditional, moderate, or liberal persuasions. That has been eclipsed by louder fundamentalist voices in recent decades. Christians, Jews, and other religious practitioners would do well to reclaim the prominence of their position in public discourse.

Their muted voices may have two causes. One is a natural reticence to speak about matters of faith in public. Another is a disinclination to expose their personal faith to argumentation or criticism. Some religious practitioners feel insecure and undereducated in their faith positions. Some Christians are insecure about the reasons for their convictions. Some feel relatively unschooled in the Bible or other sacred literature and are hard-pressed to find authoritative justification for their political and ethical persuasions.

There are remedies to those conditions. Both are fairly simple. Familiarity with the Bible and with other religious/ethical traditions can only be helpful. Learn your faith. Read your sacred texts. Study the Bible. Think about what it says in connection with current events and issues. Then share thoughts with others privately and within the public arena. Personal shyness is no excuse for abrogating responsibility to participate in the public forums of the democratic process. And by all means, pray for God's guidance of government and also for his guidance of individual thinking.

Citizens of other nonreligious perspectives, spirituality, or philosophy have very important contributions to make. Many Americans consider themselves to be spiritual without being religious. Some would say that spirituality has more authenticity or integrity than religion. In any case, most people have their own values and ought to feel free to articulate them in public discourse. Some may feel hesitant to do so. They may have a high level of commitment to the privacy of cherished convictions. Not unjustifiably, they may also fear that they would be bullied, especially by fundamentalists, if they did share them in public. Citizens need not be religious or even spiritual to be ethical and to make important contributions to the ethical dimension of political discourse in a democratic society.

Be that as it may, it is important to be honest with fundamentalists, whether a citizen is a person of Christian faith, some other faith, spirituality or philosophy, or none at all. Ask fundamentalists the hard questions. Press them on the basis of their political beliefs. Jesus said, "Be like a child." So, like a child, keep asking, "Why?" "Why do you think the way you do? Why do you use the tactics you do? Why do you seem to see others as enemies? What do you hope to accomplish? What are your goals? Where do they come from? Where will they lead? What good will they do? What do you believe God wants you to accomplish?"

Point it out when you find that discussion seems to be fruitless. Simply use variations on such responses as these: "You seem to be so interested in your comeback to my thoughts that you don't seem to be listening to me. Is that the way God treats you? I am only human, and so are you. Try to treat me the way you would like me to treat you. The only difference between us is that you think you know exactly what God wants, and I'm not so sure." If the conversation still seems futile, and you cannot seem to find any common ground, there is only one thing left to say. It is simple, straightforward, and true. "We will simply have to agree to disagree then."

Such conversations may help you to develop your own convictions about ultimate meaning. They may help you to formulate your own foundational worldview. That can help to inform your political convictions, not merely short-term, self-interested ones. That can help to guide your participation in the democracy in which you are privileged to live. It can inform your voting and motivate your greater involvement in the democratic process.

Every generation of citizens in a democratic nation must renew the vision of democracy for its time and in the face of its challenges. The Bible states that a lack of vision causes the people to perish. Vision is essential to positive forward movement in any community. Without the personal ownership of a robust vision for democracy by its citizens, a nation can fall into one of two pitfalls. Without embracing a robust vision of democracy in each generation citizens can become complacent. That creates a potential for the pitfall of corruption. Without embracing a robust vision of democracy in the face of extreme challenge citizens can become desperate. That creates a potential for extremism. Corruption and extremism distort democracy. Democracy is not magic. It requires the dedication, discipline, and integrity of its citizens to safeguard democracy from distortion.

Following our higher nature and integrating it with our earnest, active, participation in democratic processes is the only thing that will ensure the survival and the strength of democracy in the future. The more widespread and diverse the participation of its citizens, the better the chance democracy has to thrive. In a democracy, a nation will be what the citizens make of it. Its survival is in our hands. With God's help we can make democracy thrive.

Epilogue

~

Toward a Theology of Government

Curiously, there has never been any category of Christian theology devoted to government. As far as I can tell, there has only been one official Christian doctrine related to government. It was called the "divine right of kings." That seems negligent to me and may well contribute to the efforts of fundamentalists to seize upon ideologies that seek to reshape democracy simply to promote their values. It is a remarkable omission, since government has been such an important aspect of human life. After all, most histories have been devoted to the record of how governments came into being, who ruled them, what they did, what conflicts they engaged in, and how they turned out. It seems to me that there should be some meaningful theological reflection about government.

The Bible is the sourcebook of Christian theology. It does not recommend any practical form of government. And so, if it is possible or even valid to explore a theology of government, it cannot be based upon any particular dictates on government in the Bible. The Bible merely offers general principles about human nature, which suggest hints for effective government. Any attempt to develop some elementary theology of government must be an exercise in what is called philosophical theology that draws upon the Bible for general insights into human nature.

Let's try and see what comes of it. In the Bible, it is written that the Creator made humans in his own image. "Let us make mankind in our image, in our likeness ... So God created mankind in his own image, in the image of God he created them; male and female he created them" (Genesis 1:26–27). If that means nothing else, it certainly means that humans possess unique dignity. That does not mean to suggest that other creatures do not possess integrity or honor. Other species were also created by God. It is written that God asserted the goodness, the inherent value, of all species. But some quality of particular dignity is integral to human nature. That is not because humans earn or deserve it. It is because the Creator made Homo sapiens that way. God made humans to reflect the nature of their Creator. Dignity is inherent to the ontology of humanity. It is core to human beings. Therefore, if government exists, it must be based upon respect for the unique dignity of each individual human within its jurisdiction. Government must actively respect and promote the dignity of each person. That is foundational.

Empirical observation and the Bible indicate that humans are clustering organisms. Humans seem always to have clustered in groups. Those groups have ranged from pairs to families, extended families, clans, tribes, confederations of tribes, geographically based groups, larger ethnic groups, nations, cultures, empires, and civilizations. Humans cluster.

Empirical observation suggests several reasons that have caused humans to cluster. One of the most basic reasons is that human offspring remain unable to survive on their own. Humans remain extremely vulnerable longer than any other species. That fact has required adult humans to protect and provide for their offspring longer than any other species do. That, in turn, has necessitated ongoing responsibilities for the well-being of offspring shared by adult humans. It has required divisions of labor among humans. That has served the survival of the species. It has provided protection from potential predators and the mechanisms for gathering the resources necessary to human survival. Humans cluster to improve their chances for survival through shared self-protection and procurement of resources.

As I have previously mentioned, there are basic realities of human existence. Like all organisms, each human needs a secure environment within which to survive. Each human needs defense from outside predators. Like all organisms, humans need sufficient basic resources to thrive. Humans need access to basic resources for life. And like all clustering organisms, there are those within the group who are stronger and could maliciously dominate the others. Humans need safety from those who would oppress them within their clusters.

Consequently, apart from protection of their offspring, humans have three other basic needs. They include effective resistance to predators and external aggression, provision of basic resources for survival, and avoidance of internal dominance and aggression. Those seem to have been the most basic motivations for primitive government. Government came into being and has had its basic role to ensure the security of its individual members from outside predators, the effective distribution of resources among them, and their safety from those within their society who would dominate them.

Empirical observation indicates that basic differences exist among the individual members of every species. Some of those differences are physical. Some are larger, and some are smaller. Some are stronger, and some are weaker. Some are faster, and some are slower. Some are healthier or fitter, and some are less so. Some of those differences are cognitive in nature. Some are more intelligent, and some are less intelligent. Some are more aggressive, and some are less aggressive. Some are more adaptable, and some are less adaptable. Ordinarily, those differences cause fitter members to thrive more than less fit members of the same species.

Empirical observation and the Bible indicate that those basic differences also exist among humans. Some humans are physically fitter than others. Some humans are more cognitively developed than others. That lends itself to the same outcome. Fitter humans are more apt to thrive than those who are less fit. In fact, the classic story of the competition between Esau and Jacob indicates that cognitive strength trumps physical strength.

The Bible and empirical observation demonstrate that humans are capable of using their strengths to get what they want. Often that has taken place at the expense of others. The better the hunter, the more meat and hides he collects. The more industrious the gatherer, the more firewood, nuts, and berries she collects. The stronger or smarter a human is, the more likely he will prosper. The weaker or less intelligent an individual is, the less likely he will prosper. Unrestrained, that inequality among humans tends to increase over time. Historically, governments were instituted either to institutionalize that inequality or to mitigate it. Whether in primitive tribes or in monarchies and dictatorships, the most advantaged frequently used their powers to consolidate and institutionalize their dominant position. Conversely, some governments were instituted to protect the weaker or less advantaged segments of a society from the more advantaged and powerful or to safeguard the well-being of everyone. The Bible's emphasis on justice and equity endorses the latter approach. It stresses the dignity of all humans.

The Bible and empirical observation demonstrate that whenever two or more people come together, other differences emerge as well. Individuals think, feel, perceive, conceptualize, and understand in ways that may differ from other individuals. Individuals have different personal preferences and perceived self-interests. Those differences have often inclined individuals to attempt to get their own way over others. Individuals will use different strategies to accomplish that goal. They will use superior physical strength, intelligence, psychological sophistication, and other mechanisms or combinations of tools to get their way. These strategies can become habitual. Individuals with more effective strategies may dominate others within their communities.

Dominance violates the dignity of the individual. The dignity of the divine image is violated by dominance both in those who are dominated and those who dominate others. One role of government is to safeguard its constituent members from dominance.

The Bible and empirical observation confirm that conflict has often ensued when dominant individuals or dominant clusters of humans come in contact with each other. These conflicts also violate the dignity of the individuals involved. They can be harmed in any of a number of ways, physically, emotionally, materially, circumstantially, or even mortally. Some individuals have been subordinated or enslaved in the process. Conflict violates the dignity of the individuals who are party to it, both those who are harmed and those who harm others. Another role of government is to decrease the threat of conflict and the harm it inflicts.

These peculiarities of the human condition and idiosyncrasies of human nature, including sin, have necessitated the establishment of government. The most rudimentary purposes for government are

- to safeguard and promote human dignity;
- to protect its citizens from external aggression;
- to promote the procurement and distribution of resources among its citizens;
- to lessen the negative impact of self-interest (a.k.a. sin) on others in community;
- to decrease the impact of dominance (a.k.a. sin) within community;
- to decrease the danger of conflict (a.k.a. sin) within community and between communities; and
- to protect its citizens from harm.

The Bible offers at least four universal principles that are able to guide the aforementioned functions of government and promote the dignity of individuals within a community. These four ethical principles are faithfulness, economic equity, social justice, and need-meeting love. The ways in which governments may safeguard individual dignity include promoting faithfulness, economic equity, social justice, and loving behavior among individuals and groups.

The principle of faithfulness has two meanings. First, it involves dependability and the encouragement of trust. A government should demonstrate reliability. It should be dependable in its consistency. It should not be capricious or variable. It must be able to be relied upon by its citizens. This implies the standard of a rule of laws that its citizens can understand and depend upon. A government's dependability engenders trust among its citizens. They will be able to have faith in the consistency and predictability of their government. Second, a government may also promote faith in a Higher Power beyond the government itself. That provides the government and its citizens with an external source for accountability. Whether called God, Supreme Being, Higher Power, Creator, Source, or Universal Force, the one in that position ensures the faithfulness of the government and the good faith of its citizens.

A government does well to encourage faith among its citizens. By encouraging faith, I mean that a government is wise to protect the right of its citizens to have faith and the freedom to practice it. It has been counterproductive for governments to adopt a state religion. This only serves to create a religious culture that eventually stagnates and atrophies in its positive effects. But governments must allow for the advancement of trust among its citizens, trust in God, and trust in the integrity of the government itself.

The principle of economic equity provides the basic guideline for how a government involves itself in the procurement and distribution of resources among its citizens. By equity I mean fairness. All the citizens of a state must have equal access to the basic resources required for safety and survival.

There are ways to promote economic equity. Whenever significant disequilibrium may arise from time to time, the government may be called upon to intervene to equalize conditions or level the economic playing field. The Hebrew scriptures addressed that by means of the policy of "jubilee." Every seven years times seven, twice each century, everyone's financial obligations were forgiven. Moreover, all property that had been forfeited during the prior forty-nine years was restored to the family that had owned it. This had four benefits. It helped to prevent chronic intergenerational poverty. It reduced the likelihood of social desperation. It staved off potentials for social unrest, government instability, and revolution. And it provided everyone with a new beginning. I am not suggesting that all governments should institute a jubilee policy. I merely mean to point out that the Bible makes allowances for governments to adopt effective policies to mitigate economic disequilibrium and to promote economic equity.

The principle of social justice guides governments in how they may lessen the negative impact of self-interest, decrease the impact of dominance, and reduce occasions of internal conflict. By social justice, I mean that every resident of a nation must enjoy equal footing under the laws of that government. A government must be impartial and even-handed in its treatment of its citizens. It must safeguard each individual's dignity and promote each citizen's rights. There are ways to promote social justice. One of the primary ways to do so is to institute forms of government in which the citizens have determinative input into the policies and practices of their government. That includes certain basic rights, including the freedom of independent thought, the freedom of expression, and the right of equal access to mechanisms for implementing their convictions within the government. This implies some form of democracy. But it also implies recourse to some form of impartial judiciary that applies the rule of law. It requires some system to which individuals may appeal for their personal claims and civil rights.

The biblical principle of love underlies the previous two in some respects. Need-meeting love guides governments in their efforts to lessen the negative impact of self-interest, dominance within community, and conflict among its citizens. It protects its citizens from harm. There are ways to promote loving conduct within community. Governments may implement and administer laws that apply the principle of need-meeting love in concrete terms. Loving action can be defined by the laws that seek to promote it. Unloving conduct can be defined by conduct that those laws prohibit.

The extent of a government's control over a society is a delicate balancing act. Individual dignity can be jeopardized by an underactive government as much as by an overbearing government. It depends upon discernment of the prevailing circumstances of the community it serves and how those circumstances affect the individuals within them. That discernment can be inferred from the levels of indignity, unfaithfulness, dominance, conflict, inequity, injustice, or unloving behavior that exist within the government's jurisdiction. It is the role of government to mitigate those conditions. Ultimately, the Bible offers the following guidelines for government:

- Government exists to safeguard the dignity of the individual.
- Government does so in three ways:
    - by providing effective security from external aggression,
    - by providing effective means of resource distribution, and
    - by providing effective means of group organization to reduce internal dominance and conflict.
- Government should be faithful, dependable in its consistency, and should promote the trust of its citizens in the government and in a Higher Power to which both the government and its citizens are accountable.
- Government should use the principle of economic equity to guide its facilitation of fair resource distribution among its citizens.

- Government should promote social justice among the inhabitants of its jurisdiction by evenhandedly protecting the rights of each individual.
- Governments should use the principle of need-meeting love to guide the conduct of its residents and to define its laws.

These principles provide a general framework for government. They are theologically grounded and draw upon universal principles found in the Bible.

This brief exercise in theological reflection on government is offered as food for thought for anyone interested in further reflection upon the purposes and functions of government.

Endnotes

i.   Monica Duffy Toft, Daniel Philpott, Timothy Samuel Shah, *God's Century: Resurgent Religion and Global Politics* (New York: W. W. Norton, 2011), 3.

ii.   Ibid., 17, 215–23.

iii.   Martin Marty and R. Scott Appleby, editors; *The Fundamentalism Project, Volume 1: Fundamentalism Observed* (Chicago: University of Chicago Press, 1991), 814–42.

iv.   Flavius Josephus, *Contra Apionem* (*Against Apion*), Book II, 17, trans. William Whiston (1773), http://www.sacred-texts.com/jud/josephus/index.htm.

v.   Emanuel Gutman, "A Religion in Israeli Politics," from *Man, State, and Society in the Contemporary Middle East*, edited by Jacob Landau (New York: Praeger Publishing, 1972), 123.

vi.   George Eman Vaillant, *Adaptation to Life* (Cambridge, MA: Harvard University Press, 1995), 75–90.

vii.   Vamik Volkan, *Blind Trust: Large Groups and Their Leaders in Times of Crisis and Terror* (Charlottesville: Pitchstone Publishing, 2004), 62–84.

viii.   S. R. M. Khomeini, *Islam and Revolution* (Berkeley, CA: Mizan Press, 1981), 29–30.

ix.   C. Peter Wagner, *Dominion! How Kingdom Action Can Change the World* (Grand Rapids, MI: Baker Books House, 2008), iv.

x.   Ibid., 15.

xi.   Ibid., 13.

xii. Ibid., 16.

xiii. Samuel P. Huntington, *The Clash of Civilizations and the Remaking of World Order* (New York: Simon and Schuster, 1998), 69–72.

xiv. http://www.iheu.org/minimum_statement.html.

xv. Lawrence Kohlberg, *Essays in Moral Development, 1: The Philosophy of Moral development: Moral Stages and the Idea of Justice* (San Francisco: Harper and Row, 1981), 147–168.

xvi. David M. Amodio, John T. Jost, Sarah L. Master, and Cindy M. Yee, "Neurocognitive correlates of Liberalism and Conservatism," *Nature Neuroscience* 10, (2007): 1246–47.

xvii. R. Kanai et al., "Political Orientations Are Correlated with Brain Structure," *Current Biology* 21, no. 8 (2011): 677–680.

Say What You Mean

~

A Brief Glossary of General Terms

Whenever you engage in a conversation like this, it is important to explain your terms. Permit me to define my meaning for the overarching terms I use.

democracy. A form of government. It is a system by which people in a geographical area organize themselves in order to make decisions and take actions relative to their common life. The defining methodology by which this takes place in a democracy is that each adult citizen has the right to participate in the decision-making processes. Citizens in a democracy have the right to communicate their perspectives directly and to vote to elect individuals to represent their points of view within the government of the jurisdiction within which they live.

economics. Involves the ways in which people procure, accumulate, distribute, and use resources. Those ways of dealing with resources also become organized and, over time, tend to become systematized. And those aspects of people's conduct relative to resources have ordinarily fallen under the jurisdiction of the systems of government(s) in the regions within which the people live.

fundamentalism. Defined by *Merriam-Webster* this way: "a movement or attitude stressing strict and literal adherence to a basic set of principles." Fundamentalism is a movement or mind-set of those who believe that the principles, writings, and/or traditions sacred to them are inspired and infallible and are to be literally interpreted, strictly followed, and purposely advanced. Increasingly in recent years, fundamentalists seem driven to seek to extend their principles to the wider societies in which they live.

government. Refers to the ways in which people are organized in order to make decisions and take actions relative to their common life, usually within the context of a defined geographical area. Those ways of organizing people tend to become systematized over time, and so governments are organizing systems that determine how people make decisions and take actions on their common life in specific geographical areas.

pluralism. Describes a condition in which a society or state is comprised of a diversity of citizens and other residents. Their diversity may include gender, age, race, ethnicity, language, sexual orientation, education, socioeconomic status, philosophical viewpoint, religious persuasion, theological conviction, political or economic ideology, moral values, and others.

theocracy. A form of government. It is a political system that organizes people around faith in a deity. Decisions are made and actions taken relative to their common life by seeking a deity's direction, by ascribing authority and power to a deity. Theocracy exists when the origins of government and state power derive their legal authority from a divine source and derive their legitimacy from a deity. The deity and laws attributed to divine source are definitive.

Bibliography

Armstrong, Karen. *Islam: A Short History*. New York: Random House, 2002.

Calvin, Jean. *The Institutes of the Christian Religion*. Edited by John T. McNeill. Philadelphia: Westminster Press, 1960.

Chasteen, John C. *Born in Blood and Fire: A Concise History of Latin America*. New York: W. W. Norton, 2001.

Current Biology. "Political Orientations Are Correlated with Brain Structure." 21, 2011.

Davis, Kenneth C. *Don't Know Much about History: Everything You Need to Know about American History but Never Learned*. New York: Harper Collins, 1991.

Diagnostic and Statistical Manual of Mental Disorders, Fourth Edition. Text Revision. Arlington, VA: American Psychiatric Association, 2000.

Eidsmoe, John. *Christianity and the Constitution: The Faith of Our Founding Fathers*. Grand Rapids, MI: Baker Book House, 1987.

Fisk, Robert. *The Great War for Civilization: The Conquest of the Middle East*. New York: Alfred Knopf, 2005.

Gutman, Emanuel. "A Religion in Israeli Politics." *Man, State, and Society in the Contemporary Middle East*. Edited by Jacob Landau. New York: Praeger Publishing, 1972.

Holmes, David L. *The Faiths of Our Founding Fathers*. New York: Oxford University Press, 2006.

Huntington, Samuel P. *The Clash of Civilizations and the Remaking of World Order*. New York: Simon and Schuster, 1998.

Josephus, Flavius. *The Works of Flavius Josephus*. Translated by William Whiston. Peabody, MA: Hendrickson Publishers, 1995.

Khomeini, S. R. M. *Islam and Revolution*. Berkeley, CA: Mizan Press, 1981.

Kohlberg, Lawrence. *Essays on Moral Development, I: The Philosophy of Moral Development: Moral Stages and the Idea of Justice*. San Francisco: Harper and Row, 1981.

Lambert, Frank. *The Founding Fathers and the Place of Religion in America*. Princeton, NJ: Princeton University Press, 2003.

Marty, Martin, and R. Scott Appleby, eds. *The Fundamentalism Project*. 5 vols. Chicago: University of Chicago Press, 1991.

Nature Neuroscience. "Neurocognitive correlates of Liberalism and Conservatism," 10, 2007.

Newsweek. "The Rise of Christophobia." February 13, 2012: 28–35.

Toft, Monica Duffy, Daniel Philpott, and Timothy Samuel Shah. *God's Century: Resurgent Religion and Global Politics*. New York: W. W. Norton, 2011.

Vaillant, George Eman. *Adaptation to Life*. Cambridge, MA: Harvard University Press, 1995.

_____. *Ego Mechanisms of Defense: A Guide for Clinicians and Researchers*. Washington, DC: American Psychiatric Press, 1992.

Volkan, V. *Blind Trust: Large Groups and Their Leaders in Times of Crisis and Terror*. Charlottesville, VA: Pitchstone Publishing, 2004.

_____. *Bloodlines: From Ethnic Pride to Ethnic Terrorism*. New York: Farrar, Straus and Giroux, 1997.

Waldman, Steven. *Founding Faith: How the Founding Fathers Forged a Radical New Approach to Religious Liberty*. New York: Random House, 2009.

Wagner, C. Peter. *Dominion! How Kingdom Action Can Change the World*. Grand Rapids, MI: Baker Book House, 2008.

Walker, Williston. *A History of the Christian Church*. New York: Scribner Publishers, 1918.

Wellhausen, Julius. *Prolegomena to the History of Israel*. English translation. New York: Meridian Books, 1957.

White, Lynn T. "Historical Roots of the Ecological Crisis." *Science* 155 (March 10, 1967): 1203–12.

Made in the USA
Middletown, DE
05 December 2016